FOR ALL PARTISANS FOR BETTER CITY THINGS

NEW YORK_GLOBAL.

Critical Writings and Proposals 1970-2020.

Richard Plunz

HOUSING
INFRASTRUCTURE
PEDAGOGY

ACKNOWLEDGMENTS

Of the trilogy, "HOUSING, INFRASTRUCTURE, PEDAGOGY," perhaps this collection is most engaged with the latter, as much of it reflects on my activities as a teacher. It puts in evidence my good fortune to have had decades of rich exchanges with students and colleagues, early on at the Rensselaer Polytechnic Institute, the Pennsylvania State University, followed by Columbia University and intermittently at the Katholieke Universiteit Leuven. My Directorship of the Columbia Urban Design Program over a period of 23 years has been of particular importance in furthering my discourse on urbanism. Also important to the evolution of my thoughts on ecology and urbanism has been my 15 years as Founding Director of the Urban Design Lab at Columbia University's Earth Institute.

This book project was initiated in 2016, with the encouragement of then Dean Amale Andraos. It was disrupted for two years by the pandemic. Over these six years I have been indebted to student assistants whose considerable skills were essential to retrieving, organizing and culling through more than 50 years of material. For the preparation of graphic materials I thank Isaac Warshauer (M.Arch 2019), Ashna Raman (M.Arch 2019), Maria Isabel Carrasco (MSAUD 2017), Nelson de Jesus Ubri (M.Arch, MRED 2021), Andres Julian Alvarez Davila (M.Arch, MSHP 2022), Audrey Dandenault (M.Arch 2022); and especially to Lucy Navarro (M.Arch 2020) who coordinated much of this effort. For selection and editing of texts, of particular importance has been the critical eye of Audrey Dandenault, whose advice was essential to making a final selection from the myriad options. I am also especially indebted to Paige Haskett (M.Arch 2023) who was engaged in all aspects of the final editing.

Much of the material in this volume is found in the Avery Architectural and Fine Arts Library, Department of Drawings & Archives. I am indebted to Janet Parks, former Curator of Drawings, who initiated the archive development in 2004. I also thank Chris Sala and Teri Harris for their recent assistance in completing the collection. I am also deeply appreciative of the support of Alessandro Cimini (MSAUD 2001) and Ignacio Lamar (MSAUD 1996) who have enabled my continuing archive work. Finally, my deep appreciation to Actar Publisher, Ramon Prat Homs, for his encouragement in seeing this project to completion; and to Maria Paola Sutto, who for many years has remained steadfast in her affirmation of the ideals embodied in this work.

Richard Plunz
15 March, 2023
Todi, Italy

NEW YORK_GLOBAL.
Critical Writings and Proposals 1970-2020.
Richard Plunz

10 **Introduction "ROUGH DRAFTS. Meander through the Great Acceleration."**

21 **1970 "VIETNAM"**

23 **1971 "DEVELOPMENTS"**

25 PLATE A "Utopia Ritrovata" Naples, Italy

29 PLATE B "Alternative Suburbia" Reading, Pennsylvania

32 **1976 "DISAGREEMENTS"**

36 **1979 "TOWERS-IN-THE-PARK"**

43 PLATES C + D "Towers-In-the-Park Densification" New York, New York

46 **1983 "NEW YORK RING"** (with Marta Gutman)

47 PLATE E "Ring Entropy" New York, New York

54 **1983 "PROGRESSIVE IDEALS"**

63 **1984 "RUMNINATIONS ON EDEN"**

65 PLATE F "Garden of Eden" Manhattan, New York

68 **1984 "ACADEMIC RESEARCH"**

71 PLATES G + H "Inner City Infill" New York, New York

80 **1985 "LET THERE BE BLIGHT?"**

85 PLATE I "Ring Prototypes" New York, New York

89 **1989 "DIAGONAL'S SEGMENTS"**

91 PLATE J + K "Segmentary Urbanism" Barcelona, Spain

97 **1990 "CRANE URBANISM"**

101 PLATE L "Crane Urbanism" Bab Ezzouar, Algiers

104 **1991 "BETWEEN EDGE AND FABRIC"**

110 **1993 "ARCHITECTURE AND COMMONPLACE"**

118 **1993 "BEYOND DYSTOPIA"**

119 PLATE M "Beyond Dystopia" Bronx, New York

123 **1994 "NEW DEAL DE-URBANIZATION"**

132 **1998 "REASSESSING '68"**

139 **1998 "SEVERAL CITIES"**

143 **1999 "DEADLOCK PLUS FIFTY"** (with Michael Sheridan)

147 PLATE N "Topography of Fear" New York, New York

154 **2001 "A GARDENERS LOGIC"** (with Iñaki Echeverría)

155 PLATE O "Water Urbanisms" Mexico City, Mexico

161 **2003 "SO SAYS . . ."**

166 **2007 "PEDAGOGY AND URBANISM"**

171 **2010 "LANDSCAPE IN A NEW KEY"**

179 **2013 "CITY OF HEALTH"**

184 **2018 "CROWDSOURCING INFRASTRUCTURE"**

185 PLATE P "Twitter Hotspots" Manhattan, New York

189 PLATE Q "Digital Sedimentation" Philadelphia, Pennsylvania

191 **2020 "REALIGNING PROPINQUITY"**

193 PLATE R "Beyond Archeology" Brussels, Belgium

197 PLATE S "Medieval Encystment" Leuven, Belgium

203 **INDEX**

NEW YORK_GLOBAL. Critical Writings and Proposals 1970-2020.

Introduction

ROUGH DRAFTS. Meander through the Great Acceleration.

When we get more houses than we can live in, more cars than we can ride in, more food than we can eat ourselves, the only one way of getting richer is by cutting off those who don't have enough. If everybody has more than enough, what good is my more-than-enough? What good is a wide meadow open to everyone? It isn't until others are fenced out that the open pasture begins to have real value.

—Do-Right Daddy in Nelson Algren, *A Walk on the Wild Side* (1956)

The writings and proposals collected in this book represent a meander through the "Great Acceleration," the present epoch defined by the spike in global anthropogenic symptoms.[1] Perhaps the most significant prognosis relates to CO_2 emissions, which have doubled within the last 50 years.[2] Almost 90 percent of historical carbon emissions have been produced within this period, the lifetime of my generation. This acceleration is directly related to our lifeworld transformations, within the context of the past half-century of global urbanization. There are many conceptions of the Anthropocene, engaging very different implications.[3] Here, I am concerned with the causal effects related to urbanism. For the urban question, my bias lies with density and propinquity.

These writings can be seen as urban traces; as analogs to the urban stratum of stratigraphers who research climate through the prediction of what might be understood of our culture in the next warming phase—millions of years from now.[4] These traces point to our crisis of knowledge laid bare by the Acceleration, entailing very different conceptions of what it really is, while simultaneously engaging the fundamental question of urban itself.

1) The use of the term "Great Acceleration" is relatively recent, referring to the spike in anthropogenic symptoms since the mid-20th century. For an overview see J.R. McNeill and Peter Engelke, *The Great Acceleration: An Environmental History of the Anthropocene Since 1945*, Cambridge: The Belknap Press of Harvard University Press (2014).

2) David Wallace-Wells calls attention to this generational reality in "Climate Reparations," *New York Magazine* (November 1, 2021). Historical carbon emissions data is found online at Carbon Brief, <https://www.carbonbrief.org/>.

3) Among numerous studies of the Anthropocene, particularly useful is Jeremy Davis, *The birth of the Anthropocene*, Oakland: University of California Press (2016). Davis makes the point of the large variation in interpretation of the implications; see p. 63.

4) Jan Zalasiewicz, *The Earth After Us: What Legacy Will Humans Leave in the Rocks?*, with contributions from Kim Freedman, New York: Oxford University Press (2008). The recent stratigraphic speculations have been of particular interest in understanding the immediacy through a long-term narrative on the consequences of our present-day condition.

They may be interpreted as "rough drafts" in the journalistic sense of a historical record, not to be completed, holistic, or even fully understood. In this sense, they align with Manfredo Tafuri's sensibility in understanding history as "the problem, not the object."[5]

So here within, the texts act as stratigraphic evidence to understand the potential reversal of the Acceleration—the possibility for a "Deceleration" phase. The critical lens for this moment engages sedimentary layers of HOUSING, INFRASTRUCTURE, and PEDAGOGY. The genesis of these texts and projects lies in teaching, such that over the years they are a measure of changes in the focus and substance of pedagogy, while concurrently pointing toward their limits in providing an effective understanding of our condition. Perhaps, they still hint at considerations for future actions, with the caveat that the circumstances of our prior moments cannot be retracted. They suggest the difficulties in addressing the Acceleration by using the same tools that created it. For urbanism, like all fields of knowledge, they reflect Jürgen Renn's observation that "we are not living in a stable environment that simply serves as a stage and resource for our actions; rather that we are all actors in a comprehensive drama in which humans and the non-human world take part equally."[6]

These tracings engage a formative period for the 21st-century city, both New York and globally, as the correlation between urbanization and climate exists beyond dispute within the context of globalization. The increase in urban population between 1950 and 2020 has been almost six-fold.[7] And during the same period, there has been a critical confluence between the United States culture and the planet in terms of influence on the Acceleration. Already by 1965, the United States accounted for one-third of the global economy. It squandered one-third of global energy on the justification of the "American Way of Life."

The society of consumption that originated in the United States became a global aspiration. Embedded was the "Dual City" downside: the enhanced gap between rich and poor in cities, a condition that evolved to much of the globe.

5) Manfredo Tafuri, "There Is No Criticism, Only History," *Design Book Review* (Spring 1986), pp. 8-11.

6) Jürgen Renn, *The Evolution of Knowledge. Rethinking Science for the Anthropocene*, Princeton: Princeton University Press (2020), p. 4. Renn provides convincing evidence regarding the changing nature of knowledge in this new era. Bruno Latour has also engaged with this issue, see "Agency at the Time of the Anthropocene," *New Literary History*, vol. 45 (2014), pp. 1-18.

7) A point well developed by J.R. McNeill and Peter Engelke, op. cit.

The extreme wealth differentials embedded new forms of oligarchic governance within political systems, complicating anthropogenic responses.[8] The U.S. model pioneered a symbiotic relationship, in which the society of consumption enabled the condition of global urbanization in its various forms, with a significant cause and effect on the scourge of environmental and societal consequences.[9] Such interconnections are perhaps the most coherent thread that knits together outcomes, and they have been useful in my hindsight.

During the formative years for these texts, I was interested in the prescient warnings from the "soft sciences." Already by 1956, the literary world of popular fiction was pondering the new societal order evolving before our eyes. The collateral damage from the affluence, expressed by Algren made the connection with enforced inequity contemporary in today's national political landscape.[10] By 1971, Kurt Vonnegut was describing escape from an earth where "everything had turned to shit and beer cans and old automobiles and Clorox bottles." Today, it is no longer the hyperbole it seemed to be back then.[11] The future of cities figured largely in a prognosis coming from the realm of social science. In 1958, the economist John Kenneth Galbraith pointed to the contradictions of "private affluence and public squalor."[12] And in 1961, the economist Kenneth Boulding was describing the "death of the city" in the context of a "frightened look at post-civilization."[13] Ezra Mishan had identified, so well, the modern automobile culture as the culprit.[14] Numerous such pioneering texts have since been amplified many times over.

From the realm of architecture and urbanism, Serge Chermayeff and Christopher Alexander offered in 1963 the pioneering critique of the urban

8) Thomas Piketty, *A Brief History of Equality*, translated by Steven Rendall, Cambridge: Belknap Press (2022).

9) J.R. McNeill and Peter Engelke, op. cit. For more specifics on United States' complicity, see Piketty, op. cit.

10) Nelson Algren, *A Walk on the Wild Side*, New York: Farrar, Straus and Cudahy (1956), pp. 109-110.

11) Kurt Vonnegut, "The Big Space Fuck," *Palm Sunday. An Autobiographical Collage*, New York: Delacorte Press (1981), pp. 226. For a useful literary survey related to the Anthropocene see Bryan L. Moore, *Ecological Literature and the Critique of Anthropocentrism*, Cham: Palgrave Macmillan (2017).

12) John Kenneth Galbraith, *The Affluent Society*, Boston: Houghton Mifflin (1958).

13) Kenneth E. Boulding, "The Death of The City: A Frightened Look at Post–Civilization," *Ekistics* 13, no. 75 (January 1962), pp.19-22.

14) Ezra Mishan, Appendix C, "A Note on the Interpretation of the Benefits of Private Transport," *The Costs of Economic Growth*, New York: F. A. Praeger (1967).

consequences of Boulding's de-urbanization, while demonstrating the potentials of new digital design technology that could address remediation.[15] 1965 yielded growing concerns about global urbanization and housing, including from the planner Charles Abrams, the Columbia Graduate School of Architecture, Planning and Preservation (GSAPP) urbanist whom we read as students.[16] And we read Percival Goodman, also from GSAPP, whose writing on the importance of communities was influential, even as the urban dystopia accelerated.[17] It was hard to ignore the Watts Riots of 1965 and the Detroit and Newark Riots of 1967 as harbingers of the growing crises related to race, equity, and housing—so closely monitored over the decades by another Columbia GSAPP colleague, Peter Marcuse.[18] The perspectives of European critics were useful in pondering the causes and effects embedded in the new urban order, with Henri Lefebvre's *The Explosion*, published in English in 1969, providing a vital link between dystopia and the "consumer society."[19] And for the question of praxis, the Italian Giancarlo De Carlo's aphorism that "architecture is too important to be left to architects" rang true.[20] Such was where this meander starts.

On the "hard science" side, in 1955 the technique was developed for making the first reliable measurements of CO_2 in the atmosphere. Stratigraphic evidence of the warming began with the first radiocarbon dating of the end of the last Ice Age.[21] Already by 1970, the Club of Rome had compiled its precise "world model" projections on the "nature of exponential growth" and

15) Serge Chermayeff and Christopher Alexander, *Community and Privacy: Toward a New Architecture of Humanism*, Garden City: Doubleday (1963).

16) Charles Abrams, *Man's Struggle for Shelter in an Urbanizing World*, Cambridge: MIT Press (1964); *The City is the Frontier*, New York: Harper & Row (1965).

17) Percival and Paul Goodman, *Communitas. Means of Livelihood and Ways of Life*, New York: Vintage Books (1960).

18) Peter Marcuse, "The Ideologies of Ownership and Property Rights," *Housing Form and Public Policy in the United States*, eds. Richard Plunz et al., New York: Praeger Scientific (1980), ch. 5; David Madden and Peter Marcuse, *In Defense of Housing: The Politics of Crisis*, London; New York: Verso (2016).

19) Henri Lefebvre, *The Explosion: Marxism and the French Upheaval*, translated by Alfred Ehrenfeld, New York: Monthly Review Press (1969).

20) Giancarlo De Carlo, "Legitimizing Architecture: Revolt and the Frustration of the School of Architecture," *Parametro*, 1/3–4 (1970).

21) Colleagues at the Columbia University Earth Institute were pioneering in the development of monitoring techniques as well as engaging the politics of denial. For a useful summary of climate politics in the United States between 1979-1989, see Nathaniel Rich, "Losing Earth: The Decade We Almost Stopped Climate Change," *The New York Times* (August 1, 2018).

the consequences to climate.[22] Memorable was the graph that showed a rapid doubling of atmospheric CO_2 concentration in the new world order of the next half-century. There were many other voices, including the evolving field of ecocriticism, and the development of a "critical ecology" for design, described by Tomás Maldonado in 1972.[23] Notable was the work of Helmut E. Landsberg on weather and health published in 1969, interrelating the next phase of "climate, human evolution, and civilization"[24] and prescient in relation to growing evidence of cross-species viral transmission related to climate, particularly in the current context of the COVID-19 pandemic global turmoil.[25] And during the pandemic, the growing health risks went hand-in-hand with growing economic inequities,[26] demonstrating the heightened confluence of causal negative environmental effects within the Acceleration.

By the end of 1979, hard science had fully processed the growing climate statistical data, collected since 1957, which remains indisputable today.[27] But at that moment there was the hubris, the mindset that science itself would overcome catastrophe; that somehow corrective actions would arrive in time, such that by some means there would be technological salvation. In retrospect, the hope that the same technology that created our dilemma could also be the solution was flawed. While climate Acceleration increased, the politics of addressing climate change was slow to accelerate. The intractability of climate response was driven by the global world economic order dominated by neoliberal ideologies. David Harvey has pointed to the enduring reality that "good business climate" has in fact accelerated the predicament of climate

22) *The Limits to Growth: A Report for the Club of Rome's Project on the Predicament of Mankind*, ed. Donella H. Meadows et al., New York: Universe Books (1972).

23) Tomás Maldonado, *Design, Nature, and Revolution: Toward A Critical Ecology*, New York: Harper & Row (1972).

24) Helmut E. Landsberg, *Weather and Health; an Introduction to Biometeorology*, Garden City: Doubleday (1969).

25) Colin J. Carlson, Gregory F. Albery, Cory Merow, Christopher H. Trisos, Casey M. Zipfel, Evan A. Eskew, Kevin J. Olival, Noam Ross, and Shweta Bansal, "Climate change increases cross-species viral transmission risk," *Nature* (2022), p. 1.

26) According to the World Inequality Database, "Between 2021 and 2019, the wealth of the top 0.001 percent grew by 14 percent, while average global wealth is estimated to have risen by just 1 percent. At the top of the top, global billionaire wealth increased by more than 50 percent between 2019 and 2021," *World Inequality Report 2022*, p. 46, <https://wir2022.wid.world/www-site/uploads/2022/03/0098-21_WIL_RIM_RAPPORT_A4.pdf>, accessed September 22, 2022.

27) Bill McKibben, "A Very Hot Year," *The New York Review of Books* LXVII, no. 4 (March 12, 2020), pp. 13-15. Among the more draconian accounts, see David Wallace-Wells, *The Uninhabitable Earth: Life After Warming*, New York: Tim Duggan Books (2019).

change, reflecting the limitations of our knowledge base: "understanding the spatial-temporal rhythms of capital accumulation requires a quite different framework [from] that required to understand global climate change."[28]

These writings and proposals begin in 1970, the year that launched a formative decade for climate research and action, including the first Earth Day, which advocated for fossil fuel reduction. Apart from all other evidence, for some of us in the United States, the interregnum of Vietnam and the advent of late 20th-century neoliberalism became a moment of truth ("VIETNAM" 1970). The war became the flash point for multiple pathologies and a clear indicator of where things were headed. First was the affliction of a decade of forced military conscription, in its threat and realities, and of witnessing the particular vulnerabilities of architecture and engineering peers—who typically ended up in Da Nang, some not to return alive, and others, including an early Columbia student of mine, who returned but could not survive.

The Vietnam War laid bare the deep pathologies that engaged the same technologies that promised to improve our domestic lives. Petrochemical innovation escalated to chemical warfare with the environmental desecration unfurled by Agent Orange. The escalation in cyber-technology, which evolved from the benign, post-radar cyber-philosophy of World War II to advanced surveillance via the early internet, was deployed at home and at war.[29] It all hung over our lives like an ether and, of course, in many ways, large and small, architecture and planning were affected. Vietnam was directly related to the U.S. urban condition, given the war's depletion of resources for the cities in general, combined with the continuing fallout from national de-urbanization strategies for the implementation of the "American Way of Life." In particular, there were the growing vulnerabilities of the remaining poor urban families relative to conscription. Such exposed the limitations of architectural and planning praxis, and in one way or another led to the following five decades of pedagogic commitments, put in evidence in these critical writings and proposals. But early on, the promise of institutional change and a new outlook for praxis was decimated by the Vietnam fallout in its many aspects ("DEVELOPMENTS" 1971).

28) David Harvey, *Spaces of Neoliberalization: Towards a Theory of Uneven Geographical Development*, Stuttgart: Franz Steiner Verlag (2019), pp. 95-96.

29) Vietnam became the test bed for merging both big data technology with advances in chemical warfare, Yasha Levine, *Surveillance Valley: The Secret Military History of the Internet*, New York: Public Affairs (2018). Also see J.R. McNeill and Peter Engelke, op. cit, pp. 177-181.

The destructive force of "urban renewal" in U.S. cities, combined with the incredible mediocrity of "reconstruction" led to a series of projects that engaged urban fabric morphogenesis. Already by 1980, these concerns had become the object of several Columbia design studio initiatives addressing fabric pathologies focused on the remediation of a compromised cityscape that was continuing to lose spatial and functional coherence. One such effort dealt with restitching high-rise public housing with the surrounding urban fabric, using sites in Harlem and the South Bronx ("TOWERS-IN-THE-PARK" 1979).

While New York remained a primary focus, learning had engaged parallel urban pathologies elsewhere, for example in Mantua, in Philadelphia.[30] Later on, with the Bosnian War and the destruction of Sarajevo and Mostar, a moment of clarity opened in understanding the earlier New York urban renewal aftermath. As Marshall Berman has described, "victims of urbicide [were] trying to start city life again, not only to make homes for themselves but to make new communities grow out of the stony rubble"[31] ("NEW YORK RING" 1983). There was also the psycho-ecological dimension of the destruction embodied in Adam Purple and his "garden," constructed from the urban detritus of the Lower East Side - perhaps a more effective commentary on the unfolding ecological disaster than anything to come out of the academic studio discourse ("RUMINATIONS ON EDEN" 1984).

Inevitably, within the neoliberal landscape of that moment in the United States, critical academic discourse would have its discontents. In architecture and urban design, the ideological dissonance appears early on, when the so-called "old left" Modernism of the 1960s confronted the shades of neoliberalism embodied in the Postmodern ("DISAGREEMENTS" 1976). For a period, Postmodernism would stick, and Columbia GSAPP was not immune, situated as it was in the fashion-world centroid of New York City. The debates would continue for more than a decade, making an understanding of the previous "Modern" period of historical interest ("PROGRESSIVE IDEALS" 1983).

30) From 1968-1970, the author originated and directed the Pennsylvania State University Mantua Workshop in Philadelphia. See: "Mini-School: Building with People," *Connection*, Graduate School of Design, Harvard University, VI, no. 3 (Spring 1969); *Mantua Primer: Toward a Program for Environmental Change*, United States Health Services Research Branch, Publication Planning 1, University Park: Department of Architecture, Pennsylvania State University (1970).

31) Marshall Berman, "Falling Towers: City Life After Urbicide," *Geography and Identity: Living Geopolitics of Identity*, ed. Dennis Crow, Washington, D.C.: Maisonneuve Press (1996), pp.192.

Of related interest was the question of academic research in architectural and urban design, especially in comparison to Europe, where such activity was much more robust ("ACADEMIC RESEARCH" 1984).

European urbanism, while more coherent in its praxis, was far from exempt from New York realities; although, especially for urban design, there were important distinctions to be understood. Of particular interest was the Barcelona model that became an exemplar of relevance for reconstruction in New York ("DIAGONAL'S SEGMENTS" 1989). And apart from Western Europe, there was the massive urban project of the Soviet Union, with exponential growth since 1957 to two million units per year. It provided an analog for understanding the limitations of reductivistic social housing and urbanism in New York[32] ("CRANE URBANISM" 1990).

There was the interregnum of the 1980s in New York, with the imperative to understand the dysfunction that engaged the fallout from the maturing neoliberal economy, especially on housing production ("LET THERE BE BLIGHT" 1985). And of particular consequence was the role of the Manhattan waterfront in the promotion of private investment in housing as a kind of alchemy in terms of inventing a new production economy ("BETWEEN EDGE AND FABRIC" 1991).

At the same time, there was the continuing cacophony from the pedagogical side of the discipline as it transitioned from Postmodernism to the critical abstraction of "history-theory," a perspective on reality that, in Richard Rhorty's words, nurtured "views on practically everything except what needs to be done."[33] In retrospect, perhaps that moment, in some small way, reflected the negative effects of the larger global anthropogenic Acceleration, as witnessed by the death of mediative knowledge for understanding the precepts of "formal" urbanizations of the Global North, in contrast to the overwhelming proliferation of the "informality" of the Global South.

In the United States, of particular note has been the lack of means within our "formal" models for addressing the continuing inability to provide affordable housing, and so on.

32) Henry W. Morton, "Housing in the Soviet Union," *Proceedings of the Academy of Political Science* 35, no. 3 (1984), pp. 69-80.

33) Richard Rorty, *Achieving Our Country. Leftist Thought in Twentieth-Century America*, Cambridge: Harvard University Press (1998), p. 78.

Knowledge deficiencies reflected gaps in contemporary design pedagogy: ("ARCHITECTURE AND COMMONPLACE" 1993) crucial historical amnesia conflated with the political realities of increasing national suburban domination reflected in the 1995 census, with origins in the New Deal ("NEW DEAL DE-URBANIZATION" 1994), and the lack of engagement with political realities on the ground. Included was the ultimate recognition of the failures of public housing in the U.S. and in New York in particular ("DEADLOCK PLUS FIFTY" 1999). These realities would merge, as well, with new digital tools, reflected with the first computer design studio at Columbia GSAPP ("BEYOND DYSTOPIA" 1993) and the context of Columbia itself a generation after 1968 ("REASSESSING 1968" 1998).

Distinctions between HOUSING, URBANISM, AND PEDAGOGY began to blur and merge in new ways as the rate of Acceleration increased. The global options for field study increased as well, opening new opportunities to measure like and difference between cities ("SEVERAL CITIES" 1998). The normative logics of urban design operations were challenged more and more by the realities of the "informal," for both the design of infrastructure and housing, with no better example in the Western Hemisphere than the ecological pathologies of Mexico City ("A GARDENER'S LOGIC" 2001). Heightened realities permeated urban design pedagogies, including concerns originating with China ("PEDAGOGY AND URBANISM" 2007). Of necessity, urbanism had to be penetrated by pedagogy ("SO SAYS . . ." 2003), reflecting the counsel of Henri Lefebvre four decades earlier that our conception of "[urbanism] masks a situation. It conceals operations. It blocks a view of the horizon, a path to urban knowledge and practice."[34] Suddenly urbanism becomes globally strategic, as the Acceleration builds. ("LANDSCAPE IN A NEW KEY" 2010)

The discursive field for architecture and urban design becomes more transdisciplinary in the latter period of these essays; as students' interests diversify and the challenges of the Acceleration acquire a more self-conscious and dedicated response. Of particular importance in this moment were the initiatives via the Urban Design Lab at Columbia University's Earth Institute, including those in Africa ("CITY OF HEALTH" 2013); and the return to the virtual urban world for a next generation of spatial infrastructure informed by the deployment of new social media unimaginable at the dawn of the

34) Henri Lefebvre, *The Urban Revolution*, Minneapolis: University of Minnesota Press (2003), p. 160.

internet ("CROWDSOURCING INFRASTRUCTURE" 2018). A final text reflects on the century that has unfolded since the first global conflagration, World War I, as a harbinger of priorities that will continue in varied forms including the importance of keeping urban spatial and social coherence in a world that must re-urbanize with increasing immediacy if deceleration is to gain agency. ("REALIGNING PROPINQUITY" 2018)

A challenge in this meander has been negotiating mainstream theory and praxis dominated by a self-reinforcing ecosystem of critics and academics—coteries that are largely self-referential within an endemic collective cognitive dissonance in design thinking generated by a lack of rigorous and analytical bases for integrating the problematics of HOUSING, INFRASTRUCTURE, and PEDAGOGY. Yet within our epoch of acceleration, global cities have come to share these challenges more than ever, and, in many ways, cities are on the front line in managing deceleration.[35] Cities also share concerns about entropy in one guise or another in spite of the accelerated global urbanization. Embedded within the period of this meander were Detroit, Hanoi, South Bronx, Sarajevo, Mosul, Beirut, and Kharkiv, among many other desecrated cities. Perhaps today, understanding urban destruction is as important as understanding urban creation. The entropy question engages the many forms of urbicide, biblical in its origins but now told many times over as a consequence of both natural and human-caused events. Still unresolved are the questions laid so bare by Vietnam that confront the design and planning professions in our own backyards. My urban odyssey begins in my own backyard where I have always found something of what I have witnessed in so many other places and contexts. New York figures prominently in these writings, but New York shares much with cities everywhere. New York lies at the origins of this material and of my outlook. I have never strayed for long.

35) Recent studies by the EcoDataLab at UC Berkeley confirm precisely how important urban density is to reduction of GHG emissions. See Nadja Popovich, Mira Rojanasakul, Brad Plumer, "The Climate Impact of Your Neighborhood, *The New York Times*, (December 13, 2022). <https://www.nytimes.com/interactive/2022/12/13/climate/climate-footprint-map-neighborhood.html?searchResultPosition=1>

1970 "VIETNAM"

Adapted from notes for a talk to striking students at Pennsylvania State University in the aftermath of the Kent State University killings of May 4, 1970. Richard Plunz Papers, Department of Drawings & Archives, Avery Architectural and Fine Arts Library.

We are the architects and planners who must now confront the reality that the Vietnam War has come home. The tragedy of Vietnam appears to know no bounds. In Southeast Asia, the United States military is now in Cambodia; and in the United States, the military is now at Kent State with four dead students and nine wounded, not so far from here. It is important that we do not view the tragedy of Vietnam simply as a freak aberration. The enormity of our situation instead points to Vietnam as an extension of larger dysfunction in our society. We must confront Vietnam as one of many transgressions made not by malfunctioning institutions but by institutions that are simply no longer functional. Yet we continue to depend on these institutions and perpetuate them. We have many Vietnams—less obvious but perhaps more agonizing and of greater potential magnitude.

This brings us to our own realm as architects and urbanists. Individuals aside, the architecture and planning professions have traditionally averted responsibility for institutional problems in the political and social spheres. Now it is time to question this portrait of self-immunity. As professionals, we must admit our own liabilities, especially related to the travesties that are occurring in our cities. We are players in these games, ironically under the guise of humanism yet with mainstream priorities misdirected.

Architects have a long history of engaging in trivial work with elite patronage and institutions. Within the 20th century, Modernist architects strove to alter this trajectory, to become "social architects." In reality, however, we have become social only in the sense that what we do now affects large numbers of people, such that our work is no longer trivial. Yet we remain dominated by the priorities of elite institutions, which are myopic catalysts for change in our cities as they are for everything else. Even with good intentions, we lack options to change wrong commitments and wrong investments.
Planning as an institution needs to engage a new phase of politicization.

The traditional practice of plan development and its implementation is evolving into two distinct and separable activities, such that the preconceiving of a plan of action and its democratic implementation become at odds. To do one implies that the other will not be done. As antidote, we can no longer consider a "plan" as an end but, instead, as a strategic vehicle through which political decisions may be made. In this scenario, a new definition of professional is required. We are coming to realize that the old Team 10 credo of the 1950s is overly optimistic: "We can do anything today; the problem is not how to do but what to do." Today it remains "how" as well.

Let us hope that when future generations discuss the canons of Modern architecture, they will not be limited to our present-day apparitions; to the aesthetics of Le Corbusier or Mies van der Rohe; or to the various others who maintain claim to a new architecture through a supposed response to technology and society. We must also look to what is really being built, including the study and documentation of the architecture of global poverty. We must include the crude transformations that are occurring in our cities in response to the emergence of a social technocracy: the appalling projects of our large urban planning efforts. We must question the most basic assumptions involved in "urban renewal" in the United States—the logic of taking private land, from the poor, through eminent domain, for the private use of others, while providing something inevitably worse.

We are in a neoliberal, post-Marxian moment that represents an attempt at change from above and middle—with a "revolution" that dares not to go into the streets, the factory, and increasingly the ghetto. It is opposed to the aspirations, grievances, and values of those most disadvantaged.

Our society is ruled, as no other has been, by the drive for production. As our production is powerfully oriented toward consumption, and as our consumption is limitless, so is production. To produce something means to destroy something else—whether Vietnam or increasingly our own cities. A dilemma of our production is that it must grow until there is nothing left to destroy. With "urban renewal," we posit change through destruction. Our universities are further geared to this production and no amount of well-meaning special courses or days of concern will solve such problems. Required will be a withdrawal of resources from the lucrative production market to the job of making workable alternatives. We must begin in the University.

1971 "DEVELOPMENTS"

Excerpted from the unpublished manuscript, "Developments: 1968-70," for *Le Carré Bleu* (1971). Richard Plunz Papers, Department of Drawings & Archives, Avery Architectural and Fine Arts Library.

The most important urban environmental legislation in recent years was probably the Omnibus Housing Act of 1960 (S-3497). The design professions were most widely affected by the portion under Urban Renewal (Title V), usually referred to as the Neighborhood Development Program (NDP).[1] NDP was intended to free Urban Renewal funds for the immediate implementation of urgently needed projects within Urban Renewal areas. In addition, it was intended to engage the affected communities in making decisions regarding design and construction. This provision for construction was accomplished through the mandatory formation of "Project Area Committees" (PAC Groups). They were composed of community residents who were to serve as participants in the expedition of the work, and they were granted limited resources with which to hire professional advisors.

PAC Groups were formed as "goodwill of Congress" forced by several circumstances following community resistance to the tactics of Urban Renewal by the urban residents affected by it, with no consultation. The magnitude of their anger was considerably amplified by urban rioting, dating from 1964.[1] In New York City, for example, frustration with the lack of participatory planning propelled initiatives such as Citizens for a Local Democracy, which advocated for the replacement of councilmanic districts with subdivisions of representation into a number of autonomous local governments, with proper checks and balances between governments at all scales. These units would be determined by strong social and geographic communities, each containing a "Town Center" housing commercial, recreational, and civic facilities, in addition to governmental offices.[2]

1) "Housing Action: S3497," in *Congressional Quarterly Almanac*, 90th Congress, 2nd Session (1968), p. 324; "Congress Studies Urban Policies, Extends HUD Act," in *Congressional Quarterly Almanac,* 91st Congress, 1st Session (1969), pp. 387-388.

2) In New York City, frustration with the lack of participatory planning propelled initiatives such as Citizens for a Local Democracy. See "What a Democratic New York Would Look Like (A Plan Without a Master)," centerfold advertisement in *The New York Review of Books* (October 22, 1970), pp. 27-29. See also New York City League of Women Voters, "Who Do You Elect," pamphlet, 1970.

Congressional action was a response to local community political leaders becoming disruptive, and needing to be kept occupied, as their methods became more and more guerilla-like. PAC Groups were seen as an effective means of occupying the crucial middle-ground community leadership. In their roles as community participants, they steered leaders through the bureaucratic channels of the Department of Housing and Urban Development (HUD) and local redevelopment authorities, which is to say, it placed them at the mercy of the HUD bureaucracy. On occasion the PAC Group was also very effective in turning community struggles inward, causing internal problems and preventing community interference with city and federal processes.

United States intervention in Southeast Asia was also an important factor. The cost of foreign commitments seriously hampered developmental programs in our own cities at a time when urban pressures were greatest. In response, NDP became one convenient means of extending our urban commitments without additional outlays of money. Urban Renewal funds, which amount to between four and five billion, were normally spent over a 15-to-20-year period under a grant reservation system. However, certain funds were released for immediate expenditure by NDP, saving the equivalent in new revenue money for Vietnam.

The effect of NDP on the design professions was probably most extensive in its influence on the implementation of the ideology of "advocacy planning." Advocacy had been variously practiced for several decades, usually as a reaction by communities and professionals against Urban Renewal or other governmental programs. Several such efforts have had considerable (although short-lived) success, such as the Syracuse Community Action Program or the Child Development Group of Mississippi. In spite of its comparatively long informal history as an idea, the term "advocacy" has existed only since 1965, with the definitive narrative made by the planner Paul Davidoff. It was programs such as NDP that caused it to flourish as an ideology officially sanctioned by both governmental and professional organizations. The professions were ripe for the exploration of Davidoff's ideal:

> *The advocate planner would be responsible to his client and would express his views. The advocate planner would devote much attention to assisting the client organization to clarify its ideals and to give expression to them ... In order to make his client more powerful politically, the advocate might also become engaged in expanding the size and scope of his client organization. But*

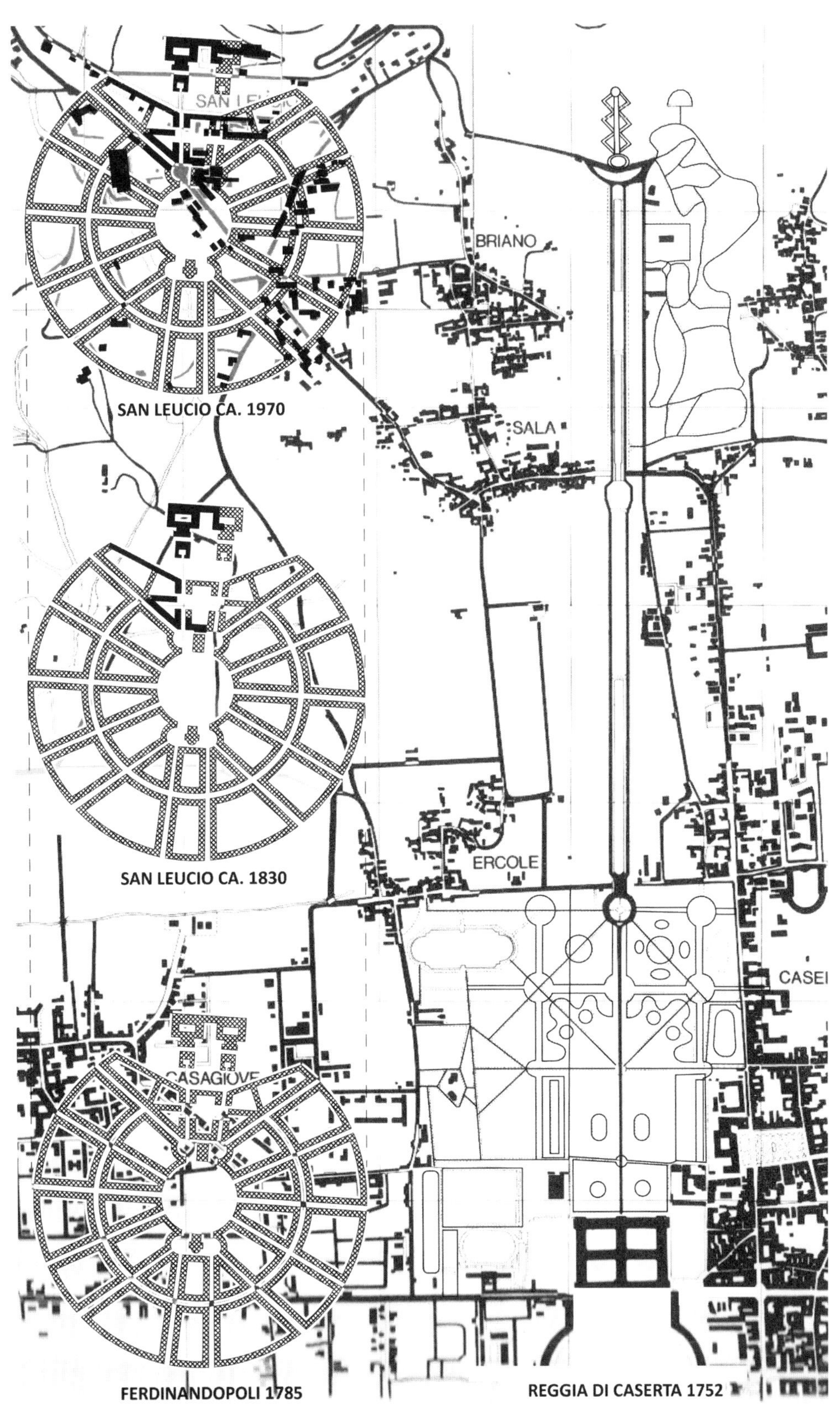
SAN LEUCIO
BRIANO
SAN LEUCIO CA. 1970
SALA
SAN LEUCIO CA. 1830
ERCOLE
CASE
CASAGIOVE
FERDINANDOPOLI 1785
REGGIA DI CASERTA 1752

PLATE A
"Utopia Ritrovata" Naples, Italy

1971-1973. Research into reconstruction and planning for Ferdinandopoli, Naples, Italy. Research teams from Pennsylvania State University and Politecnico di Milano.

Research into the plan of the utopian industrial colony of Ferdinandopoli, in present-day San Leucio, near Naples, Italy—according to the design of Francesco Collecini, as commissioned by Ferdinand IV, Bourbon King of Naples. The lack of graphic record of original plans required reconstruction from written descriptions of Ferdinando Patturelli and from field surveys. A larger, three-year project engaged extensive archival and anthropological field study, culminating in design proposals for future development within a unique historical and cultural environment.

1971-1973. San Leucio Project, Pennsylvania State University Department of Architecture, in consultation with the Facoltà di Architettura and Politecnico di Milano. Pennsylvania State University: Richard Plunz, Faculty and Principal Investigator; Student Team: Michael Graybrook, Timothy Hartung, James Kells, George Miller, David Beer, Andrew Cupples, Paul Flood, Mark Liebendorfer, James Stavoy, John Sysko. Politecnico di Milano: Eugenio Battisti, Faculty; Student Team: Giuseppe Bolzoni, Paolo Caputo, Rolando Ferioli, Patrizia Giudici. Graphic representation: Nelson de Jesus Ubri (M.Arch MRED 2021), Audrey Dandenault (M.Arch 2022).

PUBLICATION: *San Leucio: Vitalità d'una Tradizion. Traditions in Transition*, ed. Richard Plunz, New York: G. Wittenborn (1974); Also see Richard Plunz Papers, Department of Drawings & Archives, Avery Architectural and Fine Arts Library; Biblioteca R.A. Plunz, Archivio di Stato di Caserta, Italy.

the advocate's most important function would be to carry out the planning process for the organization, and to argue persuasively in favor of its planning proposals.[3]

Implied are circumstances in which the client organization is unable to look after their own planning needs, requiring some paternal second party to translate their desires to a third party, which is in turn oppressing him. Under earlier noninstitutionalized circumstances, this situation might have been legitimate. However, the logic is questionable in our present context; for the prime oppressor is Urban Renewal, which is in the position of providing funds to further its own oppression under the guise of containing it.[4]

Many designers' interests in the advocacy of NDP were generated by the kinds of things that always interested them, an important one being commissions. For the first time in an Urban Renewal program, neighborhood resident groups were given limited governmental funding with which to seek out professional advice. Considerable paranoia and competition were generated because clients' requirements opened up a field of concern that was generally alien to the experience of the average architect or planner, and the clients knew it.

There were other motivations, perhaps the most important being the idealism of young professionals and students. There is probably not one school of architecture in the United States which has not, in the past three years, participated in some kind of advocacy program; and many universities were directly, or indirectly, responsible for the 150 "community design centers" now in existence. In these efforts, several circumstances forced the goodwill of the schools. Architectural curricula appeared more and more absurd, attempting to train design technicians for an obsolete technology, making a phrenetic situation in which students were much wiser about priorities than many of their tenured faculty. Most schools were willing to place the noisy students (and faculty) in communities. In addition, most urban universities, due to the nature of their institutional development, are geographically in the middle of oppressed communities and have used advocacy efforts to alleviate both student and community pressure in their attempts to expand and control

3) Paul Davidoff, "Advocacy and Pluralism in Planning," *AIP Journal* (November 1965), pp. 331-337.

4) Such are the arguments of the critics of "advocacy." See Frances Fox Piven, "Advocacy as a Strategy of Political Management," *Perspecta* 12 (1969), pp. 37-38; Elliott A. Krause, "Functions of a Bureaucratic Ideology: 'Citizen Participation,'" *Social Problems* (Fall 1968), pp. 129-143.

without undue difficulty. It is probably safe to say that, within the university, the movement has died of natural causes (lack of students).

The community design centers have difficulties. It is impossible to physically improve a neighborhood without adequate funding, and it is frequently difficult to organize around social problems without the hope of solving their expensive physical counterparts. It is also not practical to think of adequate funding in any terms other than governmental. Yet adequate governmental funds have not been provided, and do not appear to be forthcoming in the immediate future. Only 35 programs out of 322 initial requests for NDP could be funded, and now that number has risen to only 80. In 1969, funding for the program was frozen for seven months, seriously disrupting efforts by communities to make it work. By 1970, Nixon threatened to discontinue the program, claiming among other things that it was "inflationary." He then limited the funding to $1 billion, rather than the $2.3 billion authorized into law by Congress, setting off an intense lobbying effort by mayors and city officials to maintain legal funding. Funding was drastically cut for the 1970-71 fiscal year. Moreover, a very popular notion all along has been that most of the money has gone to those cities that gave Nixon voting majorities.

Nixon also made it quite clear that "community participation" does not mean "community control." He took firm measures to insure that NDP as well as similar efforts are safely in the mayors', rather than communities', control; something that Mayor Daley assumed all along, at the cost of flagrant repression of democratic means in Chicago's programs. As early as 1969, in North Philadelphia, the North City Area-Wide Council had sued HUD for control of their programs.[5] The courts would not hear the case, and the nebulous 1966 Model Cities Act remains interpreted in favor of federal control, quite in line with Nixon's "New Federalism," which is designed to give more direct local controls to local governments in dealing with communities, while also extending indirect federal controls over that autonomy.

It would be difficult to find accounts that do not agree that NDP has accomplished little that is visible. This apparent lack of progress is not bad. No community planning programs have really worked in the United States simply because social sensitivities and processes are too fine-grained to adapt to the coarse methods of planners; and new political realities require methods that

5) The experience of the North City Area-Wide Council, Inc., Philadelphia, is documented in "Maximum Feasible Manipulation," *City* (October/November 1970), pp. 30-38.

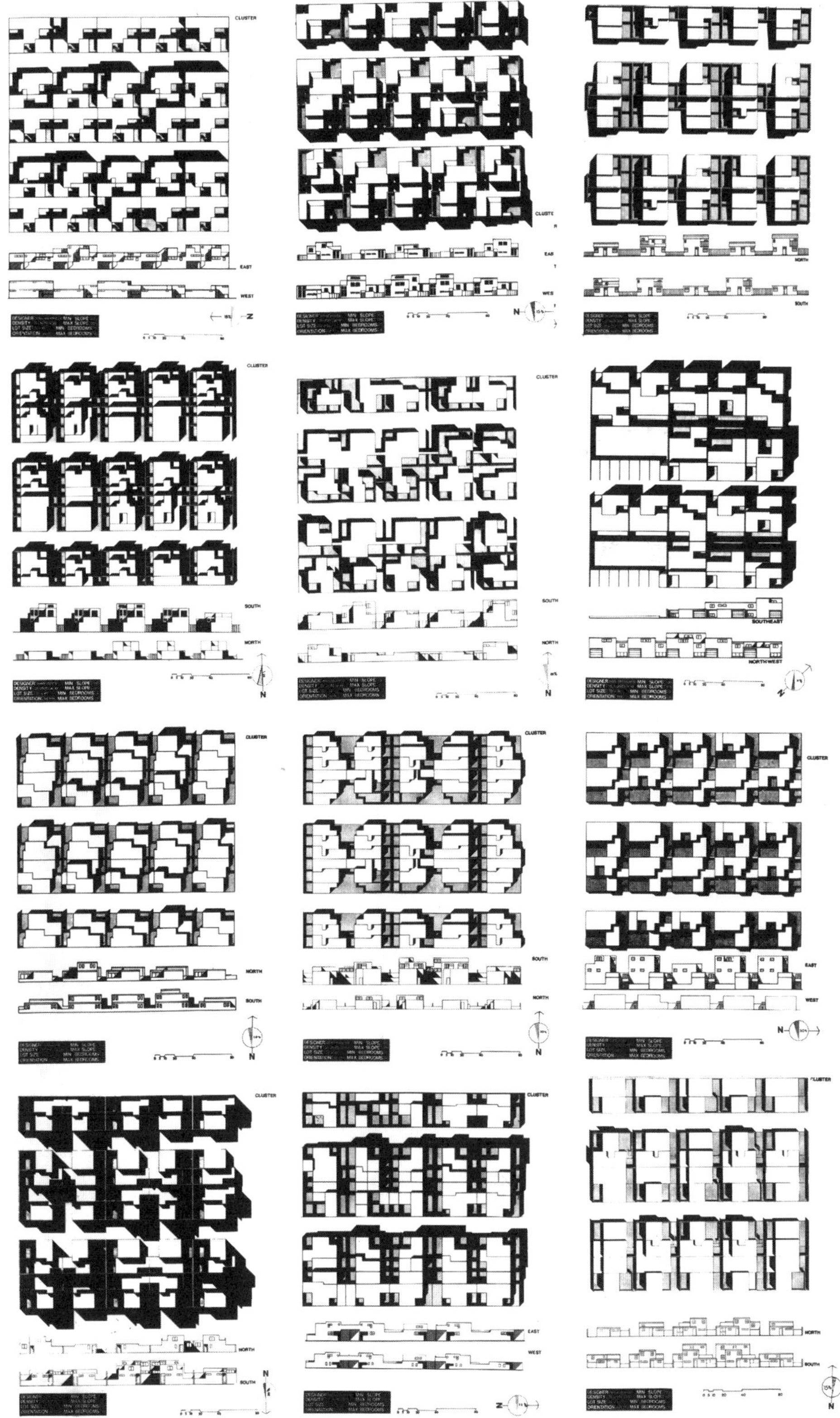

PLATE B
“Alternative Suburbia” Reading, Pennsylvania

1970. Suburban house design prototype research. Pennsylvania State University architecture studio, Fall Semester.

Proposals for alternatives to post-war suburban development in the United States, in response to growing negative anthropogenic evidence inherent to suburban culture and the “American way of life.” The hypothetical sites challenged continuing suburban sprawl, focusing on declining land availability and challenging the isolated house typologies. The first iteration engaged a test bed “rule system” for slope and solar orientation alternatives within clusters of a “neutral” square lot configuration. The housing clusters were required to support the integration of the automobile within the built mass, and to provide flexibility for modification and expansion over time. Outdoor space was limited to contiguous courtyards. Construction was assumed to be normative stick-built. The research protocol evaluated the first iteration to produce a revised “rule system” for the simulation of ideal pattern alternatives applicable to actual sites.

1970. “Alternative Suburbia,” Pennsylvania State University Architecture Studio, Fall Semester. Faculty: Richard Plunz, Lawrence Regan; Third-Year Students: James Bassett, Steven Carnahan, Robert Daley, Lewis Everline, John Floyd, Peter Folen, Lawrence Gilbert, Michael Graybraok, William Greene, Timothy Hartung, Earl Hoyland, John Kelleher, Gregory Lee, Mark Liebendorfer, Wesley Litzinger, Stephen McLaughlin, Mark Pierce, Daniel Poncavage, Paul Shaffer, David Stanley, Michael Zanin; Fifth-Year Students: David Cronrath, Earl Crossland, Jeffrey Gingerich, Richard Harn, William Nycum, William Reehl, Lawrence Schan, Richard Teodari. Graphic reconfiguration: Lucy Navarro (M.Arch 2020).

PUBLICATION: *Housing Manual for an Alternative Suburbia*, eds. Richard Plunz and Lawrence Regan, 1971 Berks County Planning Seminar report v. 3., University Park: Pennsylvania State University Department of Architecture (1971); Richard Plunz, “Alternative Suburbia. A Retrospective Rationalization,” *Lotus International* 10 (1975), pp. 18-23. Also see Richard Plunz Papers, Department of Drawings & Archives, Avery Architectural and Fine Arts Library.

do not yet exist. NDP, if nothing else, was a symptom of the beginnings of a new planning mentality that taught valuable lessons to all sides.

Probably the most immediately hopeful development is what communities have learned. It is now much more difficult for professionals or students to enter a community. Communities know better, based on their experiences. Left on their own, they can at least disrupt things, which at this point, is considerably more effective than plugging their leadership into HUD. "Advocacy" as it has occurred has been much more for HUD programs than for communities' desires. It is futile to advocate anything for people who have no position of power with which to reinforce their demands; and it is rather questionable for professionals to try to supplant community power with their own. If communities had legitimate power in the first place, such advocacy would be unnecessary. The real issue lies in the democratic allocation of power: a well-defined hierarchy from Nation to City-State to Community. A commitment to the redistribution of political power must accompany any commitment to environmental improvement, and things will remain at a standstill until this is accomplished.

The redistribution of political power will require some basic changes in the political system itself. In this respect, the short-run prospects for any extensive environmental action (other than the "clean air" palliatives) are limited. An optimistic appraisal is that it will probably take five or six years to lose the stench of Nixon, and another 10 years for a new political means. (More pessimistic appraisals are probably not worth the effort in this context.) This period of inactivity in large-scale environment building may be better than the alternative, which is to build more large-scale mistakes now. Everyone has found, of late, that we do not know very much. Our cities could not survive another 20 years of Urban Renewal, even at their present level of non-accomplishment. In our present situation, designers can probably benefit most from taking notes. Preparation for any large-scale environmental intervention should begin now, and will take over a decade, beginning with systematic evaluation of our mistakes of the past two decades.

1976 "DISAGREEMENTS"

Excerpted from unpublished transcript, "Disagreements," a lecture in the "Architecture As We See It" symposium with J. Max Bond Jr., Romaldo Giurgola, Michael Mostoller, Jon Michael Schwarting, Robert A.M. Stern, Graduate School of Architecture and Planning, Columbia University, September 15, 1976. Richard Plunz Papers, Department of Drawings & Archives, Avery Architectural and Fine Arts Library.

As you will perceive, I have disagreements with some of my colleagues here, but I want to make clear from the beginning that I am optimistic about the profession of architecture, although not necessarily the profession which we now know. I should admit at the outset little regard for the mainstream practitioner, and even less for the mainstream avant-garde (at least in New York).

I feel that in our lifetimes, the unfolding of new kinds of opportunities for architects will be enormous. Many opportunities will be outside of today's profession. I suspect that an "alternative profession" will develop, to do the tasks systematically excluded from today's mainstream activity. These entail the exclusions that now account for production of most of the built environment. It is an important irony that what is thought of as contemporary architectural practice comprises only a small fraction of total building. I am not advocating for more architects. I am only saying that those who do most of the building are bound to emerge from anonymity sooner or later, regardless of their professional titles. This "second profession" may cause a split even more disruptive than the old Beaux Arts / Ecole Polytechnique schism of the 19th century.

One of the things that always strikes me as odd about the profession is the apparent limitations on learning. This thought is a risky one, but I would like to mention it anyway by asking, why architects repeat so many mistakes? Why has the profession never instituted an effort to systematically evaluate its buildings? How can any profession be immune from such basic self-improvement? To be sure, there is some technological learning, although a Hancock Tower or a Philharmonic Hall can slip through. But for behavioral criteria, there is next to no learning of substance. Perhaps it is felt that the evaluation of building performance will interfere with artistic license. But, for example, do such arguments hold for the 100-year history of architect-designed mass housing in New York City, which has never been properly evaluated? I wonder why should not the evaluation of building design be as important as building design itself?

The profession's only organized (or quasi-organized) means of evaluation occurs in the media; of course, media coverage is good for business. In fact, one sure way to succeed in architecture is to coerce the press, which consists of a handful of glossies and even fewer newspaper columnists (who seem to write things that are closer to advertising copy than news). The glossies primarily show the latest in fashion and are passed from drafting board to drafting board in the constant search for the latest in stylistic nuances. Rarely is anything deeper involved.

There is also a spate of new "theory" and "criticism," which is interesting. Or at least the terms theory and criticism indicate some new attempts at built environment evaluation. Some of it is exciting work—for example, the research of Philippe Boudon in France.[1] But much of it I find to be the work of neophyte architectural historians who are ransacking history in efforts to find precedents for the idiosyncrasies of their own *au courant* "theories" while producing "criticism" which really is nothing more than self-justification. So little of this activity transcends aesthetic taste-making. The glamour of aesthetics wears thin quickly, which one needs only to pick up a 1956 glossy, or even a 1966, to ascertain. Underneath remain the social and technical issues, as always. As Ad Reinhardt put it, "The next revolution in art is always the same old revolution."[2]

The problem of balancing behavioral criteria with aesthetic criteria in building has been sublimated within architectural thought since the Renaissance, and has beset the so-called "Modern Movement," like all predecessor movements. The Modernist rubric "form follows function" did not provide the behavioral response in building as is implied, and "Modernist" imagery has been no more successful than any other imagery in dealing with the issue of relating buildings as artifacts to the patterns of human behavior they must accommodate. The Modern Movement did represent a momentous transition

1) Philippe Boudon, *Pessac de Le Corbusier. Préface de Henri Lefebvre.*, Paris: Dunod (1969); "Pessac de Le Corbusier," English edition, *Lived-in architecture: Le Corbusier's Pessac revisited*, translated by Gerald Onn with a preface by Henri Lefebvre, Cambridge: MIT Press (1972).

2) *Art as Art: The Selected Writings of Ad Reinhardt*, ed. and with an introduction by Barbara Rose, New York: Viking Press (1975), pp. 59-63.

in building technology, related to both structure and aesthetics, and caused by severe economic realities.

Current "Postmodern" challenges to the Modern Movement take the form of mannerist reinterpretations of both the early Modern functionalistic and earlier classical eclecticism. For the architect who understands the mechanics of aesthetic evolution, Postmodern mannerism, or whatever, must seem like the most opportune vehicle for stylistic revolution. But I see this as only a very temporary aberration. Such revolutions are too opportune to deal with deep social issues in architecture, which are also waiting in the wings. My own perception of the grand sweep of history is that our basis for "knowing" the social functioning of buildings is on the cusp of a momentous transition of far greater significance to architectural thought, even than the earlier Modernist technological adjustments.

Aesthetic and behavioral issues have evolved to such a level that they cannot be separated flippantly. Political and social problems are rather messy, and do not always appeal to architects' more anal tendencies. Nevertheless, political and social problems are becoming more and more interwoven with problems of form and imagery. Excursions into "pure" aesthetics may be immediately gratifying and have always been justified by the argument that great artistic achievement will ultimately benefit society as much as short-range social betterment. This is fine for architects to say, but it is said too often, especially at a time when our perceptions of aesthetic worth may be changing rapidly.

I prefer the messy problems, and I think that the real excitement in architecture in our lifetimes will come from those sources. But to paraphrase Aldo Van Eyck, messy problems are like contraband, which must be sneaked into the profession through the back door. Once in, they become monsters, which, as of yet, the architect's training cannot deal with. However, alternative forms of professional engagement that come close to these problems, are emerging, hidden away in government, or in universities, and even in a few small exploratory private practices. Of course, once the shouting is over, there is little glamour involved, and the evolution will be slow, as one might expect. The development of a behavioral basis for design must gravitate toward a meticulous concern for the smallest aspects of the use of environments, as well as the largest.

Nicolai Hartman wrote in the early part of the century on the formulation of ontologies.[3] He argued that after a certain point in the evolution of disciplines, the smallest categories begin to gain in importance, ultimately affecting the largest. Meyer Shapiro described a similar phenomenon for the evolution of stylistic analysis; that analytic refinements come about, in part, through a search for problems where small differences may be disengaged and described precisely.[4] I think there is no reason to believe that the behavioral analysis of building function can be achieved in any other way.

This implies, for those architects who are interested, that several decades of rather tedious and thankless work must ensue, with maintenance of commitments which are somewhat out of the mainstream of present-day ideologies about creativity in design. Good designers must be involved, as their contributions can be unique among the expertise of those who study the relationship of buildings and culture. Whether or not such activity is creative in the artistic sense is not an issue for me. I am always suspicious of architects whose artistic pretensions run high: a kind of wearing of their art on their sleeves.

3) Nicolai Hartmann, *New ways of Ontology*, translated by Reinhard C. Kuhn, Chicago: H. Regnery Co. (1953).

4) Meyer Schapiro, "Style," in A. L. Kroeber, *Anthropology Today; An Encyclopedic Inventory*, Chicago: University of Chicago Press (1953), pp. 287-311.

1979
"TOWERS-IN-THE-PARK"

Excerpted from "Transformation of the 'Tower-in-the-Park'," *Lotus International* 24 (1979), pp. 61-65; "A Prospectus for the Taft and Mitchel Houses, New York City" with Daniel Ocasio and Albert Smith, *Housing Form and Public Policy in the United States*, ed. Richard Plunz, New York: Praeger Publishers (1980), ch. 16.

Transformation of New York City Housing Authority (NYCHA) housing sites was first explored at Columbia during the spring semester, 1976.[1] Excerpts from the studio brief provide an overview of the scope of the research:

This studio will be concerned with urban redevelopment of areas surrounding public housing high-rise towers built during the two decades following World War II. Although specific case-study sites will be in New York City, many of the issues raised will have implications for other cities, since national ideology and a desire to establish uniform standards resulted in the unrestricted superimposition of this type of housing on U.S. cities. However, New York is somewhat idiosyncratic, if not for the greater "success" of its public housing over many other cities, at least for its higher site coverages and relative conditioning of its residents to high-rise living.

Currently, federal and local concern in many cities is focusing on public housing redevelopment, especially for projects of 1950s vintage, which are reaching a stage of deterioration that will soon require major corrective action. In some cities, disrepair has led to partial or total abandonment – the most dramatic example being the partial site razing of Pruitt-Igoe. To date, the more corrective action has emphasized renewal of mechanical, electrical, and

1) These studies were an extension of a series of housing studios, all involved with exploring issues in the design of low-rise housing, which were developed over several years by Richard Plunz; among the most important was a study of fine-grain, adaptive infill housing for the Mantua neighborhood in Philadelphia, with a representative design solution published in: *Mantua Primer: Toward a Program for Environmental Change,* Baltimore: U.S. Public Health Service (1970); a study of expandable, one- and two-family "carpet"-type housing published in *Housing Manual for an Alternative Suburbia*, University Park: Department of Architecture, Pennsylvania State University (1971); and a study of linear housing designed for growth and change within a specific cultural setting, with two representative design solutions published in *San Leucio: Vitalità d'Una Tradizione*, New York: Wittenborn and Co. (1973).

waste systems, with rather cosmetic site and building treatments that might be considered restoration rather than redevelopment. There have been no realistic and comprehensive studies of project redevelopment that have come to terms with the spatial pathology which has generated the basic problems of the high-rise form.

This studio will concentrate on dealing with spatial pathology through two related strategies. First will be the redesign of the existing high-rise towers at the lower floors. One of the possibilities that should be explored is the reorientation of ground-level apartments to achieve direct outdoor access, similar to low-rise housing. The second objective will be the development of all ground-level open space, through the design of new horizontally organized low-rise housing which extends the towers into surrounding areas.

Land is available for new construction within the boundaries of most public housing projects, where a high percentage of the site is open ground space, and in surrounding areas, where building abandonment is prevalent. New planning and design should involve a redevelopment of the horizontal network which was largely eradicated by the project towers. A fine-grained neighborhood should be re-established, with an emphasis on maximizing the benefits of a ground-related organization and a hierarchy of spatial scales, from stoop to baseball field. It will be considered desirable to introduce a maximum number of new low-rise apartments within the site, while maintaining adequate open space for recreation and parking.[2]

Students were required to select a site from the 235 projects operated by NYCHA; selection was based on each student's individual criteria, within the overall goals of the studio. Due to time and resource limitations, the scope of the study was restricted to consideration of the potential of each site for rehabilitation as a purely spatial exercise. The physical characteristics of each site differed widely.

2) The Columbia studio studies included Taft Houses by Daniel Ocasio, Mitchel Houses by Alfred Smith III, Baruch Houses by Frederick Bell, Franklin Houses by Lawrence Glogau, and Carver Houses by Padriac Steinschneider; the material represented here originated with the studio work of Daniel Ocasio with much of their design presentation modified and redrawn by Patrick O'Malley, and a part of their neighborhood analysis redrawn by Christine Hunter.

The problem was structured by the following sequence of investigation: (a) research into the historical circumstances surrounding the original site and the building of the project; (b) documentation of the present day physical and social characteristics of the site; (c) development of schematic site alternatives which increase density and coverage through the integration of low-rise housing with the existing towers; and (d) detailed design development of a single alternative, including the design of apartment types.

Realism in terms of scale, cost, and building technology was emphasized. Partly to facilitate these goals and for other conceptual reasons, the investigation was limited to the use of variants on linear row-type housing, which is the most familiar traditional house type in New York. Other desired objectives were continued occupancy by most residents during construction and the feasibility of incremental implementation of the project.

The greater difficulty of meshing new low-rise housing with the existing towers, compared to the extension of new housing to adjacent abandoned areas, became apparent during the design process. The integration of infill housing within the project site thus seemed a more challenging problem, and as a result, the students' actual design development tended to be limited to existing project boundaries.

Precedents for these studies exist in relation to the steady growth of criticism directed against the "tower-in-the-park" ideology, which had first appeared in the architectural polemics of the Modern Movement in the 1920s. As early as 1924, Lewis Mumford objected to the "'sanguine people'... who fancy that it is possible to have high residential buildings surrounded by open space and gardens; they even talk as if the problems of housing might be solved on a grand scale by erecting such buildings."[3] In 1957, Mumford fiercely attacked Le Corbusier's "Marseilles Folly," including various scaled-down versions that were being built in U.S. cities, especially for the urban poor.[4] Considerable skepticism of the credibility of Le Corbusier's ideas also came from the progressive literary circles of some of his own countrymen within post-war France.[5]

3) Lewis Mumford, "High Buildings: An American View," *The Architects Journal*, LX (October 1, 1924), p. 487.

4) Lewis Mumford, "The Marseilles 'Folly,'" *The New Yorker*, XXXIII (October 5, 1957), pp. 76-95.

5) Certainly, references to the "tower-in-the-park" by Jean-Paul Sartre and Simone de Beauvoir indicate that they viewed their intellectual counterparts in architecture from a somewhat caustic stance.

But during the post-war era, versions of the "tower-in-the-park" proliferated everywhere. The approach was strongly endorsed in New York City by the Mayor's Committee on Slum Clearance,[6] a powerful policy group headed by Robert Moses. Even at the end of his long career, Moses insisted that to "accommodate large numbers of people more comfortably, the answer is vertical construction on less land. Instead of a building four or five stories, covering 80 or 85% of the land, you go up four or five times as high on 20% coverage. This will leave plenty of open space, playgrounds for the kids, and better views."[7] The fact that high-density alternatives to the "tower-in-the-park" were slow to develop was undoubtedly due in great part to the tremendous initial economic advantages of the high-rise tower. By the 1960s, Mumford's arguments were being reinforced by those of Jane Jacobs, who claimed in *The Death and Life of Great American Cities,* published in 1961, that the construction of high-rise towers had destroyed traditional residential patterns necessary for community existence in urban areas.[8]

With the formation of the Housing and Development Administration (HDA), an innovative New York City agency created by Mayor John Lindsay during the mid-1960s, some attention began to be paid to architectural design issues involving the use of high-rise towers. These issues surfaced in the work of Lawrence Halprin and Associates, commissioned by HDA to study the redevelopment of open space in the city. Halprin's report, published in 1968, included schematic proposals for the redevelopment of several tower project sites.[9] Similar ideas were further developed by the Office of Planning, Design, and Research within HDA and by HDA-commissioned architects.[10] This work began to erode the "tower-in-the-park." HDA was not the only outlet for such exploration. Community groups, concerned about conditions in their neighborhoods and skeptical about the city's ability

6) In the 1956 report of the Mayor's Committee on Slum Clearance, there is not a single project illustrated that did not use high-rise slab blocks in a green, park-like setting: *Slum Clearance Progress: Title I, NYC* (New York, 1956).

7) Robert Moses, *Public Works: A Dangerous Trade,* New York: McGraw Hill (1970), p. 426.

8) Jane Jacobs, *The Death and Life of Great American Cities*, New York: Random House (1961).

9) Lawrence Halprin and Associates, *New York, New York*, New York: New York City Housing and Development Administration (1968).

10) A redevelopment of the area surrounding Independence Towers, a NYCHA project in Williamsburg, Brooklyn, that used a strategy similar to the one adapted by this studio, physically connecting low-rise infill housing to the existing high-rise towers, was published with other schemes in "Urban Housing: A Comprehensive Approach to Quality," *The Architectural Record*, CXLV (January 1969), pp. 97-118.

to analyze their needs, began seeking private consultation to develop proposals through their own committees.[11]

Around the same time, Oscar Newman undertook a research project, supported by the U.S. Department of Justice, at the Columbia University School of Architecture. Newman attempted to correlate design characteristics inherent in the "tower-in-the-park" with increased frequency of crime and vandalism. The study resulted in the publication of *Defensible Space*[12] and had a wide, though controversial, impact.

By the early 1970s, projects realized in New York City through agencies such as HDA and the New York State Urban Development Corporation (UDC) inevitably combined low- or medium-rise housing and high-rise towers on the same site. In 1975, UDC developed an important prototype with the construction of Marcus Garvey Park Village in the Brownsville section of Brooklyn. Designed in collaboration with the Institute for Architecture and Urban Studies, it was a tightly knit, low-rise, medium-density alternative to high-rise housing for lower-income tenants.[13]

For the proposed Taft Houses transformation, the existing site plan is not drastically altered, but the changes are significant. Prior to the construction of Taft Houses, site coverage was approximately 78 percent. Taft Houses, as built, reduced site coverage to 19 percent. The proposal increases the site coverage to 31 percent through the introduction of low-rise linear housing that attempts to redefine the edges of the site along the streets. The new housing forms five straight and L-shaped buildings, physically connected to the towers, combining low-rise and high-rise construction. A number of different spatial configurations result at the site interior but are all at approximately the same scale.

There are some fundamental issues that the studio has not dealt with but that should be mentioned. One is cost. Although a modest design approach

11) For a specific example, see *Form and Public Policy in the United States*, ed. Richard Plunz, New York: Praeger (1980), pp. 209-211.

12) Oscar Newman, *Defensible Space: Crime Prevention through Urban Design*, New York: Macmillan Co. (1972); see also the preliminary report: Oscar Newman and George Rand, "Questionnaire: Design for the Improvement of Security in Urban Residential Areas," Columbia University Project, supported by the National Institute of Law Enforcement and Criminal Justice, U.S. Department of Justice (1970).

13) Museum of Modern Art, "Another Chance for Housing, Low-Rise Alternatives: Brownsville, Brooklyn, Fox Hills, Staten Island," designed by the Institute for Architecture and Urban Studies for the New York State Urban Development Corporation, New York (1973).

was consciously pursued, no actual estimates were made to determine the feasibility of construction. Beyond the initial construction budget, it was assumed that other factors such as long-term maintenance and the operation of social benefits could significantly affect both the long-term cost and the quality of life in the projects. While the proposals attempted to manipulate these factors by utilizing design tactics that would encourage such things as tenant self-maintenance, increased safety, and reduced vandalism, it is extremely difficult to quantify the effectiveness of design remedies in combating maintenance and social problems. Also, significant is the reclamation of the high-rise towers, implicit to all schemes. Ultimately, the existing towers may not be worth a renewed 30-year lifespan, the minimum period required to secure a largescale investment for redevelopment.

A controversial design feature inherent in the infill strategy is the removal of large open space from each project. Even though these areas are often considered the source of critical problems, the simple fact of open space removal, regardless of use in that urban open space, tends to be identified with "public good." Their elimination does affect certain related amenities. It may not be easy to convince the tenants of a high-rise project that there are advantages in reducing the amount of public space within their project site, whether or not an equivalent replacement is guaranteed for the surrounding neighborhood. For example, some inexpensive on grade outdoor parking must be removed to permit the new low-rise construction and can only be replaced by more costly parking structures, although it could be argued that replacement is not necessary, especially if on-street parking in the area is underutilized. In the case of most NYCHA projects, such tenant concerns would be given further credence by the fact that the grounds are extremely well maintained: despite their being fenced off and inaccessible for actual use, the lawns, trees, and planting provide a dramatic relief to the city pavement.

Other difficulties are political in nature. Some residents might fear that their own survival would come into question in projects undergoing major redevelopment. Considering the present state of housing subsidy programs, it would be easy for tenants to visualize a scenario in which redevelopment becomes a means for replacing lower-income families with a higher-income population. This scenario is likely to be particularly threatening if project amenities are upgraded, and the design of new low-rise housing surpasses minimum standards. These kinds of topics were discussed at length in the studio. Several participants felt that project residents should have control over design decisions: in reality, this would undoubtedly be a political necessity.

In the studio work generally, the patterning of the existing sites led to severe physical constraints, especially in the placement of the existing high-rise towers. The integration of new, low-rise linear housing was facilitated in the Taft Houses proposal because the existing site configurations were among the most simple and rectilinear. Other sites were more difficult to organize. Although none were impossible, the use of a different housing form, such as "carpet"-type housing which combines internal courtyards with extended ground coverage and very low building height, might prove more successful for some areas. On the other hand, it is quite possible that many NYCHA sites would present so many physical design problems that they would not be worthwhile to consider for infill redevelopment.

Many of these issues need to be studied more extensively such that the proposals were not intended as an argument for direct implementation. Given the limitations in the scope of the problem and its definition for studio purposes, the work was presented as preliminary design investigations. In fact, throughout the design stages, as many negative as favorable arguments emerged around the question of actual construction. But the proposals do tend to demonstrate that it is physically possible to redevelop at least some high-rise "tower-in-the-park" sites through the introduction of low-rise linear housing within the project boundaries.

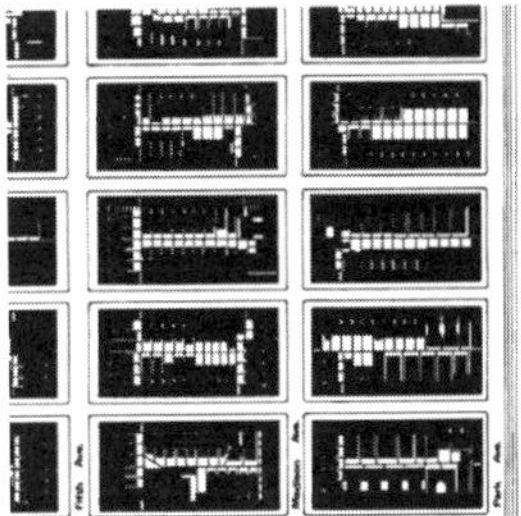

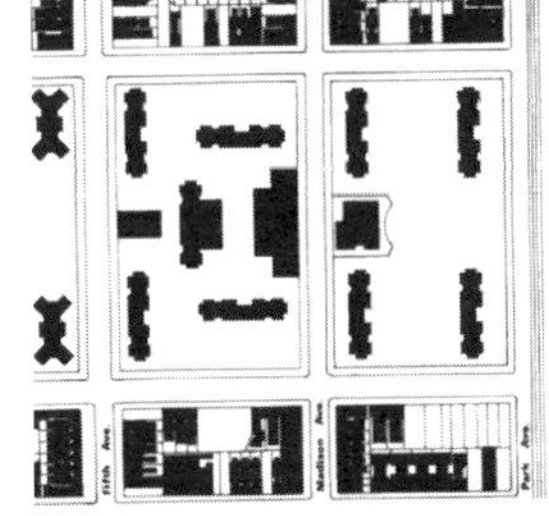

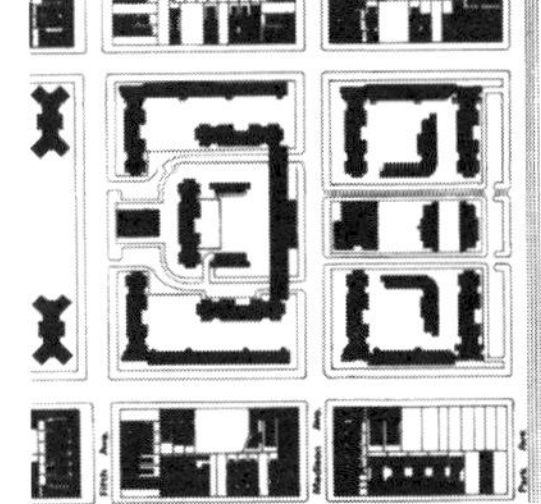

Taft Houses

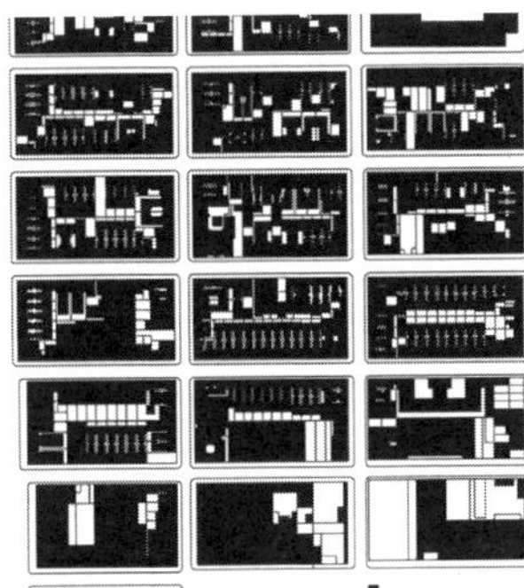

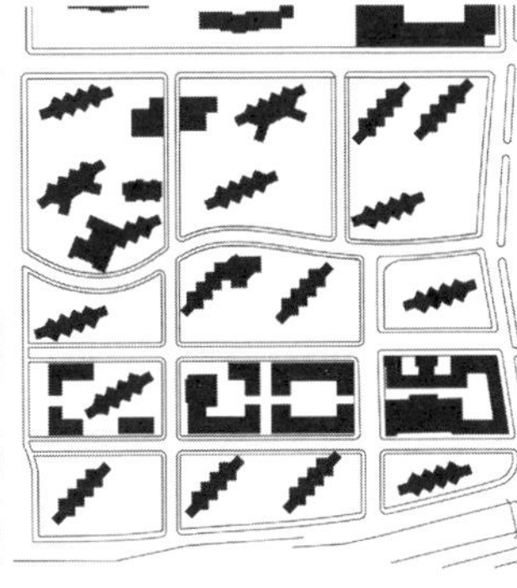

Mitchel Houses

Baruch Houses

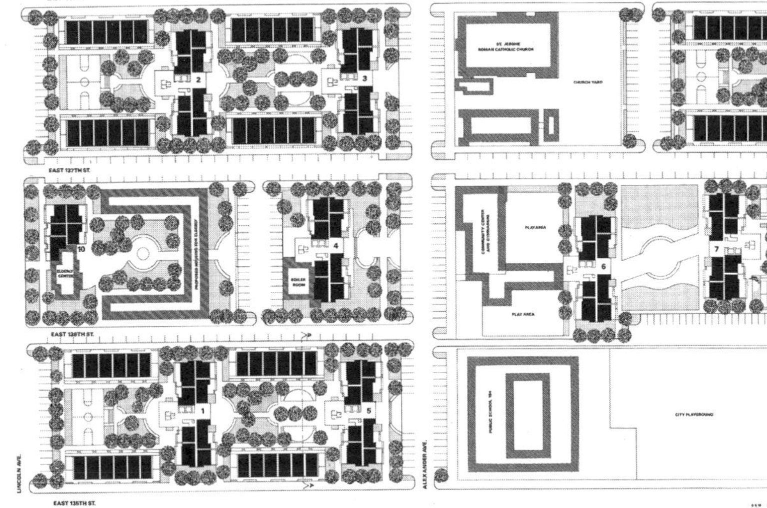

Mitchel Houses Transformation

PLATES C+D

"Tower-In-The-Park Densification" New York, New York

1976. Transformation of NYCA Taft, Mitchel, and Baruch Houses. Columbia GSAPP architecture studio, Spring Semester.

Proposals for redevelopment of New York City Housing Authority (NYCHA) public housing high-rise tower sites built during the 1950s and '60s. Included were Taft and Baruch Houses in Manhattan and Mitchell Houses in the Bronx. For such NYCHA sites, considerations included the mono-functional programming of the sites and the unstructured nature of the open space. The apparent spatial pathologies were partially associated with the severe disjunction from the surrounding built fabric. Corrective restoration of the deteriorating physical structure of the existing towers was addressed concomitantly with remediation of the adjacent sites. Redesign of existing high-rise towers at the lower floors was combined with the design of new, horizontally-organized, low-rise housing and commercial uses that could extend and integrate with the surrounding contexts. A fine-grain neighborhood could be reestablished with an emphasis on maximizing the benefits of a ground-related organization and a hierarchy of spatial scales, and with an emphasis on increasing the viability of the initial NYCHA project investments.

1976. "Tower-In-The-Park Densification," Columbia GSAPP architecture studio, Spring Semester. Faculty: Richard Plunz; Studio Projects as shown: Daniel Ocasio (M.Arch 1976), Albert Smith III (M.Arch 1976), Fredric Bell (M.Arch 1976). Graphic reconfiguration: Patrick O'Malley (M.Arch 1978), Christine Hunter (M.Arch 1978). Isaac Warshauer (M.Arch 2019)

PUBLICATION: Daniel Ocasio and Albert Smith III, "A Prospectus for the Taft and Mitchel Houses, New York City," *Housing Form and Public Policy in the United States*, ed. Richard Plunz, New York: Praeger Publishers (1980), ch. 16; Richard Plunz, "Transformation of the 'Tower-in-the- Park," *Lotus International* 24 (1979), pp. 61-65. Also see Richard Plunz Papers, Department of Drawings & Archives, Avery Architectural and Fine Arts Library.

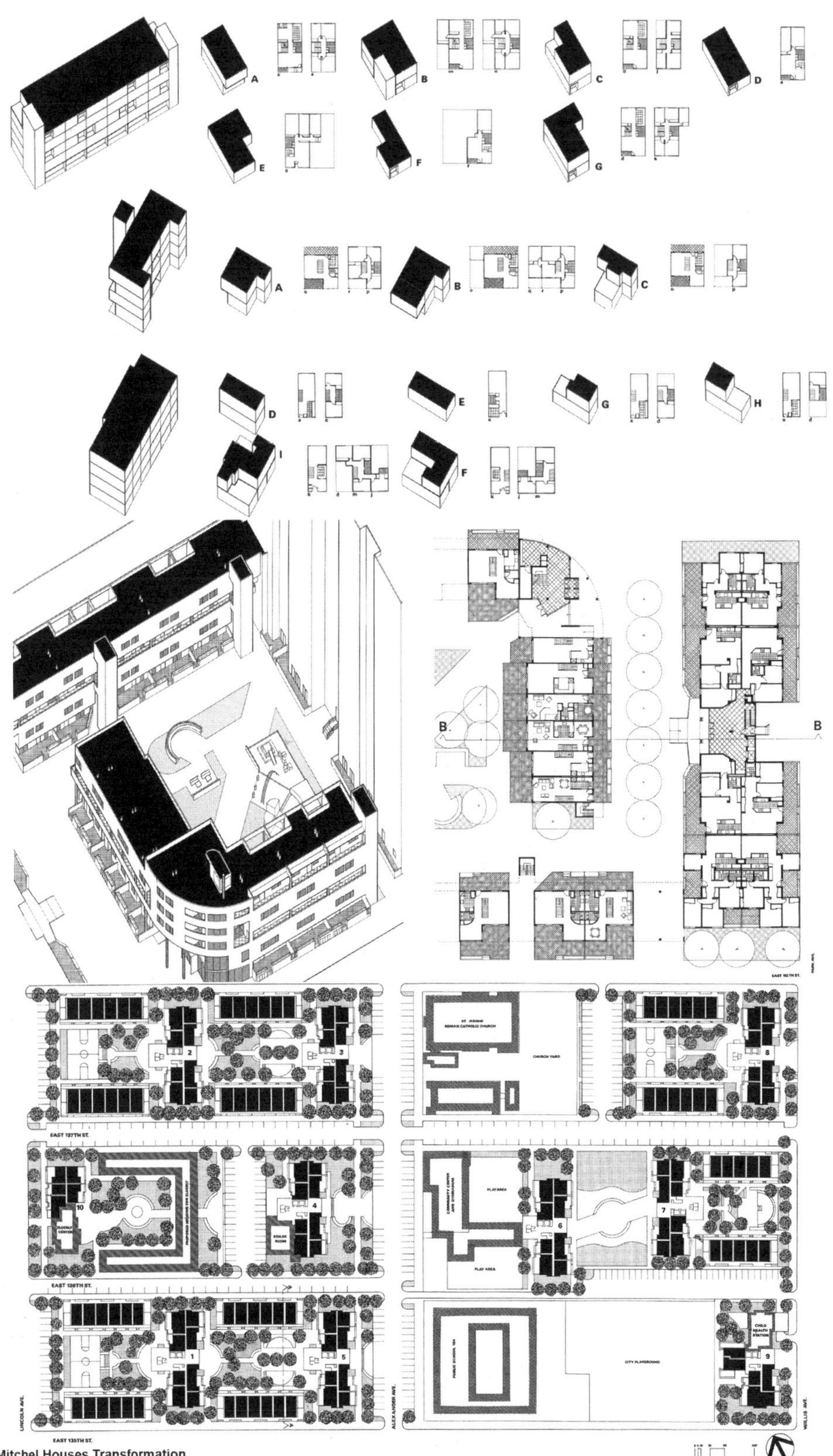

Mitchel Houses Transformation

1983
"NEW YORK RING"

Excerpted from "Il 'Ring' di New York," *Eupalino 1*, with Marta Gutman, Italy (1983), pp. 32-47; also published as: "De New York Ring. Volkshuisvesting binnen het stedelijk grid," *Wonen-TA/BK*, no. 23 (December 1984), pp. 12-26.

The present housing question in New York City involves a broad range of problems and contradictions. The contrast between the housing conditions for the poor and the rich mirrors, if not exceeds, the contrast between the 19th-century slum tenements and the robber baron mansions on Fifth Avenue. There is a shortage of affordable housing not only for the poor but for the middle class as well, which tends to cluster in tight and overcrowded enclaves. At one end of the spectrum, the Upper East Side and Midtown Manhattan areas continue to enjoy a building boom in luxury housing, typified by such projects as the apartment tower being developed over the Museum of Modern Art. These luxury enclaves are expanding through the "gentrification" of additional areas such as Park Slope in Brooklyn or the Upper West Side in Manhattan, where developers have begun to acquire and build on a number of sites once deemed unsuitable for luxury housing. Still, the demand exceeds supply to the extent that the vacancy rate of the upper middle-income areas of Manhattan and Brooklyn has been reduced to less than one percent.[1] This expansion inevitably has displaced the poor to substandard housing in less desirable areas.

At the other end of the spectrum, the destruction of once stable working class and moderate-income neighborhoods during the past two decades has left a "ring" of devastation around central Manhattan.[2] In the remnants of once stable residential areas such as Crotona Park in the South Bronx or Bedford-

1) The press has covered the housing shortage and the problems caused by gentrification from a number of different perspectives. See, for example, Denis Hammill, "Park Slope: The Myth of Neighborhood," *New York* XI (February 13, 1978), pp. 36-40; Dempsey J. Travis, "How Whites Are Taking Over Black Neighborhoods," *Ebony* XXXIII (September 1978), pp. 72-74; J.D. Besser, "Gentrifying the Ghetto," *The Progressive* XLIII (January 1979), pp. 30-32; and Paul Goldberger, "Upper West Side Story: Explosive Growth Near," *The New York Times* (February 4, 1982), p. B1.

2) The identification of the "New York Ring" originates with a design studio investigation at the Graduate School of Architecture and Planning, Columbia University, funded through a grant from the National Endowment for the Humanities. Richard Plunz was Project Director with Marta Gutman as assistant. The authors wish to thank Wiebke Noack for her assistance with the graphic preparation for this article.

THE NEW YORK "RING"
AREA OF POPULATION LOSS
EXCEEDING 40% 1960-1980
0
4000
24000

PLATE E
"Ring Entropy" New York, New York

1981-1983. New York abandonment ring studies. Columbia GSAPP housing research team.

Research into the characteristics of the "Ring" of physical destruction encircling the core of Midtown Manhattan that had evolved by the mid-1960s, encompassing large areas of the South Bronx and Harlem, eastward to Central Brooklyn, and south into the Lower East Side of Manhattan. The most engaging public symbols of this process were the fires that fed the devastation, occurring on a scale previously unknown in New York City. Vast areas of the Ring had experienced a population decline of more than 40 percent, and in some cases more than 80 percent. Causality could be connected to legalized "disinvestment" permitted under the city's "red lining" policy, as well as the effects of community destabilization from the massive public housing interventions of the previous decades. The study envisioned opportunities for rebuilding with innovation in housing typologies similar to precedents in Eastern Europe in the 1920s including the "Red Ring" in Vienna built during that decade.

1981-1983. "New York Ring" Study. GSAPP housing research. Principal Investigator: Richard Plunz; Research Assistant: Marta Gutman (M.Arch 1981). Graphic representation: Wiebke Noack (M.Arch 1984).

PUBLICATION: Richard Plunz and Marta Gutman, "Il 'Ring' di New York," *Eupalino* 1 (1983), pp. 32-47; also published as: "De New York Ring. Volkshuisvesting binnen het stedelijk grid," *Wonen TA/BK*, no. 23 (December 1984), pp. 12-26. Also see Richard Plunz Papers, Department of Drawings & Archives, Avery Architectural and Fine Arts Library.

open land. At the same time, an economic model for housing production which can rebuild such areas simply does not exist. The only current viable housing production is market-value rehabilitation of existing structures or new high-rise apartment buildings within upper-middle-class enclaves.

The existence of the "New York Ring" is the most serious symptom of the city's housing crisis. In total, New York loses from 15,000 to 25,000 units of housing a year,[3] mostly as a result of building abandonment in Harlem, the South Bronx, Central Brooklyn, and the Lower East Side. At one time, diverse terrain and street patterns defined these small moderate-income and working-class neighborhoods. They were knit together by a tight social fabric, mixed-use zoning, and a tradition of privately owned, low-rise, high-density housing. Transportation networks linked the residents to adjacent jobs, cultural activities, and civic institutions in Manhattan. However, between 1960 and 1980, vast areas of the New York Ring have experienced a population decline of more than 40 percent; in some areas, more than 80 percent of the residents have left.[4]

As neighborhood demographic shifts produced conflict, and as government and business policy forced people to seek new homes, housing deteriorated at a tremendous rate. Whatever new housing has been built usually has been government-sponsored public housing for the poor, designed to inferior standards, according to the "tower-in-the-park" ideology. These public housing projects, which are concentrated within the Ring, have made a major contribution to its deterioration because they destroy the continuity of small neighborhoods. They also present a major problem because inferior design and construction have hastened their decline to premature obsolescence.[5] The rows of burned-out tenements, punctuated by empty lots, have deprived the city of needed housing and tax revenue. In the extreme, mounds of brick

3) These figures come from the report, "With Love and Affection: A Study of Building Abandonment," produced by the Women's City Club of New York in 1977.

4) United States, Bureau of the Census, Census of Population 1960, Washington, D.C.: Government Printing Office (1961); 1970 Census of Population, Washington, D.C.: Government Printing Office (1971). 1980 Census of Population, Washington, D.C.: Government Printing Office (1981).

5) For examples of rehabilitation proposals for "tower-in-the-park" housing projects see Daniel Ocasio, Albert Smith, and Richard Plunz, "A Prospectus for the Taft and Mitchell Houses, New York City", *Housing Form and Public Policy in the United States*, ed. Richard Plunz, New York: Praeger Publishers (1980), pp. 201-232; and Richard Plunz, "Transformation of the 'Tower-in-the-Park': Project for the Taft and Mitchell Houses in New York City", *Lotus International* XXIV (1979), pp. 61-75.

are occasionally interrupted by vacant tenements in such areas as the district around Charlotte Street in the South Bronx. Boarded-up windows reveal the flickering lights of squatters who cannot find or afford any other place to live. New York City now owns much of the property in the Ring because property owners have defaulted on tax payments, leaving the city as caretaker for much of the deteriorated building stock.

Devastated as the Ring may be, it will be rebuilt because the existing transportation network makes it accessible to Manhattan such that the existing urban infrastructure makes rebuilding feasible economically, and the city needs to strengthen its tax base. This situation offers an opportunity to propose models for the redevelopment of the Ring that can become the base of the stable working-class and moderate-income communities the city needs so desperately.[6] Before this massive undertaking can happen, a viable economic model will have to rise from the ruins of the existing modes of housing production—both private and public. In addition, this economic model will have to be closely linked to a low-rise, medium-density design model which can respond to the need for some of the amenities of the lower-density suburban house, as well as to the urban context, including Manhattan, which is only a few minutes away via mass transit. Both economics and design will have to complement each other if the impasse is to be removed. In this respect the Ring bears remarkable similarity to earlier European precedents, particularly to the Red Ring in Vienna, especially with the potential for typological innovation; but it also differs.

For the New York Ring, much of the original urban infrastructure still exists and can be reused, despite the intrusions of the "tower-in-the-park" housing projects. Some of the small neighborhoods have resisted disintegration and have remained architecturally and socially intact communities. These provide "islands" around which the new housing can initially develop. Most importantly, the grid of streets and services is still intact. Since little of the service network will have to be built, the production of the new housing will

6) Proposals for rebuilding the New York Ring have ranged in scale from the large planning proposal, "South Bronx Revitalization Program and Development Guide," New York (1980), produced by the South Bronx Development Office, directed by Ed Logue, to the small-scale rehabilitation of tenements and multiple dwellings conducted by the People's Development Corporation. See Roger M. Williams, "New Urban Pioneers: Homesteading in the Slums," *Saturday Review* IV (July 23, 1977), pp. 8-14; R. Schur, "Rebuilding from Within: a prescription for the South Bronx", *The Nation,* CCXXVI (January 21, 1978), pp. 38-42; and Michael Harrington, "The South Bronx Shall Rise Again", *New York* XI (April 3, 1978), pp. 34-38.

be more feasible economically. Also, the grid, which may have appeared to be a neutral fact at the time of its construction, is by now through history and experience charged with memory, meaning, and association. It will root the new housing in the history of neighborhoods once knit by a tight social fabric, mixed-use zoning, and housing with clearly defined public and private realms.

Potentially, a variety of middle-density housing, industry, and commerce can knit the communities of the Ring into the existing grid of streets and services.[7] The innovative new housing will stand in opposition to the anti-urban social and visual monotony of the existing public housing in the Ring because the exploitation of the existing grid will produce formally coherent, functional solutions to the full range of architectural issues associated with housing design. The problem will not have been simplified so as to satisfy only utilitarian necessity as has happened with so many projects of the past few decades. Moreover, the new housing will also have to include some of the amenities of single-family suburban housing, which has been the icon of working-class culture for too long to be ignored. But the model must be essentially new in its outlook, and the government will have to participate in setting the stage, much as it did in the 1930s and '40s for the single-family suburban house. In this respect, the fact that the government owns much of the New York Ring provides a fortunate circumstance.

There are examples of medium-density low-rise housing within New York City, which are useful as historical precedents in looking toward the issue of rebuilding the New York Ring. Perhaps the most instructive precedents were those few neighborhoods within the Ring itself, which experienced their greatest development during the prosperous decade of the 1920s, toward the end of its cycle of development. This prosperity, coupled with the almost explosive infill of higher density within the Ring and beyond, encouraged the development of new types of housing which responded both to new urban ideas and to new technology, such as the private automobile, the modern low-cost kitchen or bath, and the modest self-service elevator. At this time, the prototype for the New York "garden apartment" appeared, usually as a

7) The recent formation of the New York City Housing Partnership, a private, non-profit corporation that promises to build 30,000 units of middle-income housing in the next five years, indicates just how serious the housing problem is. Unfortunately, the partnership, chaired by David Rockefeller, has ignored the problem of housing the working and non-working poor. See Lee A. Daniels, "New City Group to build Middle-Income Housing", *The New York Times* (15 January 1982), p. B1; and, by the same author, "The Rockefeller Proposal for Middle-Class Homes", *The New York Times* (22 January 1982), p. A20.

"perimeter block" structure, with an internal communal green space, not dissimilar in basic type or organization to the superblocks of the Red Ring, although usually smaller.

Those areas of the New York Ring that developed relatively quickly and with some unified overall concepts were successful in addressing certain issues of community design, within the context of the gridiron. Jackson Heights, especially, provides an excellent, if slightly incomplete, model. The soundly-built housing helps give the community an architectural identity while offering a broad range of types and context—from two-family attached houses with discrete garages, to row houses with integral rear or front garages, to a number of perimeter block configurations. A simple functional and spatial hierarchy organized the grid of streets and avenues into a comprehensible whole greater than the sum of its parts. The neighborhood may lack a clear, representational, central space, but architectural and urban coherence gives it a public, symbolic face, which in turn helps shape the neighborhood into a community.

The housing at Jackson Heights remains at the center of the only remaining large intact area of the New York Ring.[8] Similar to the original development of Jackson Heights, the redevelopment proposals for the Ring will continue to rely on the gridiron plan as a basic planning tool, if for no other reason than it remains a viable infrastructure of services and streets which would cost an inordinate sum to replace. Even if it were easy to replace the grid, the more difficult question would be with what; clearly, one model—the disastrous "tower-in-the-park" interventions of the 1950s and '60s—has failed. Thus, the design question is one of how to adjust the grid as a "found device" in order to compensate for some of the shortcomings of the original developments. This "adjustment" focused on spatial and functional hierarchies, characterized by architectural and urban diversity at all scales, which create a broad range of public, semi-public, and private space. By stressing the virtues of urban proximity, these transformations can point toward a series of hybrid housing types that incorporate some of the amenities of the detached single-family house into the context of higher-density urban housing. Also evident is the possibility of rebuilding neighborhoods incrementally to create communities

8) Much of the information on the 1920s circumferential development and the Jackson Heights case study is discussed in greater detail in Richard Plunz, *The Institutionalization of Housing Form in New City: 1850-1950*, to be published as *Habiter New York: La Forme Institutionnalisée de l'Habitation New-Yorkais*, Brussels: Pierre Mardaga Éditeur (1982).

composed of varied streets and public spaces, which accommodate the car while also encouraging the use of public transportation. The variety of house types can also be seen as working toward social mixture, encouraging a population diverse in class, sex, age, and family type, as well as ethnicity and race, and which will be able to find affordable places to live.

Using the Jackson Heights case study as the seminal critique for Ring redevelopment, an ideal model can begin to emerge. It reaffirms that the original urban structure of each of the Ring's new neighborhoods can provide the basis for the new community designs. At their most fundamental level, site proposals for the Ring can be conceived as a set of rules, without determining the exact architectural character, style, or image of the buildings. Instead, within the spirit of the Vienna Red Ring or Jackson Heights, they should govern building height, use, setback, open space, and automobile access, and suggest, in the cases of housing, formal types. This will permit the developer and the individual architect to develop differing approaches for buildings and blocks, and it will encourage incremental rebuilding, rather than massive renewal. Potentially, existing structures worth saving can be incorporated into the new fabric more easily, if the city rebuilds the Ring in increments. That too will encourage varied designs for individual building clusters.

1983 "PROGRESSIVE IDEALS"

Excerpted from talk transcript, "Chermayeff and the Evolution of Progressive Ideals in Urbanism after CIAM," Second Planning History Seminar: "Town Planning, 1930-1960. A personified Debate.," The Center for Urban Historiography, Katholieke Universiteit Leuven, Belgium, April 29, 1983. Richard Plunz Papers, Department of Drawings & Archives, Avery Architectural and Fine Arts Library.

For those who are interested in the criticism of architecture beyond definitions of formal structures to engage the issue of architecture and culture and, more fundamentally, to the relationship between architecture and power, the decade following the Second World War in the United States is a critical one. It was a period of decisive transition in the evolution of theory and practice in relation to architecture and urbanism. The United States had reached its zenith in terms of the expression of its imperial wealth and imperial ambitions. If one believes that architecture is ultimately connected to such power, one cannot be surprised at the force of events within the architectural evolution of this period, when mainstream American culture as we have inherited it today received its greatest impetus. In the period since the 1950s, formal conventions may have changed but fundamental attitudes toward the relationship between architecture and power within mainstream architectural criticism and practice are essentially the prolongation of those that achieved their legitimacy during this period. There can be little doubt that the previous period of transition in architecture—of the 1930s—had germinated an outlook that was quite different from that of the 1950s, and which, had it been allowed to flourish, would possibly have produced a rather different picture for American architecture today. Those earlier ideals were decimated in the 1950s, only to come briefly to the forefront again in the 1960s—and to once again be decimated. The prospects now for a third cycle are not encouraging.

The text by Auke van der Woud, published with the current Congrès International d'Architecture Moderne (CIAM) exhibition at the Rijksmuseum Kröller-Müller in Otterlo, provides a critical evaluation of CIAM Modernism, especially in Europe.[1] But I think that it may also be interesting to shed more

1) Auke Van der Woud, *Het Nieuwe Bouwen – International CIAM*, The Netherlands: Delft University Press (1983).

light on the situation in the United States. The American CIAM provides us with a good example of the kinds of dilemmas and compromises that liberal and progressive architectural lobbies of the period faced. The American CIAM is interesting in that it united both Europeans and Americans, albeit briefly and superficially. This particular hybrid would consequently take its own rather strange direction. Van der Woud mentions some symptoms: for example, the fundamental American complicity in introducing the issue of monumental expression to CIAM—of overshadowing, even, the fundamental CIAM problematic of housing—especially at the critical CIAM 6 meeting of 1947 in Bridgewater.[2] This "American" representation was, of course, the achievement of Sert, Gropius, and Gideon. So obviously, we have by this period, a complex set of affairs, but we must go back to the decade of the 1930s to adequately understand the significance of this transition in the United States.

In the period between the Great Depression and the end of World War II, the outlook and interests of American architects changed considerably.[3] The market crash abruptly extinguished the vast production of building that had resulted from the prosperity of the 1920s. During the next five years, architectural building activity was almost nonexistent. By 1931, the Architects' Emergency Employment Committee, which remained active through this period, was organized in New York City.[4] Similar progressive organizations began in other cities including Philadelphia, Boston, and Cleveland. In the same year, the American Institute of Architects (AIA) convention authorized a lobby for federal employment of architects to which the government responded.[5] Architects, especially the younger generation, had little choice but to join New Deal programs, espouse the New Deal's social rhetoric, and design according to its particular public works type of functionalism. Within the milieu of economic disaster, human suffering, and the uncertainties of European fascism, the profession developed a new social consciousness. As it began to question existing professional institutions, progressive architectural organizations, publications, and schools began to emerge.

2) Ibid., p. 82.

3) Some of this historical material has been previously published in Richard Plunz, *Habiter New York. La Forme Institutionnalisée de l'Habitat New-Yorkais. 1850-1950*, Brussels: Pierre Mardaga Éditeur (1982), ch. 8.

4) "Architects' Emergency Committee," *American Institute of Architects Journal* III (November 1931), p. 14; and "Unemployment Relief in New York," *American Institute of Architects Journal* IV (February 1932), p. 29.

5) Louis LaBeaume, "The Federal Building Program," *American Institute of Architects Journal* III (April 1931), pp. 13-15.

Among the most interesting political developments in the 1930s was the emergence of labor unions for architects and architectural draftsmen employed in private offices or by the government. In relation to progressive organizations, the first and most powerful such union to emerge was the Federation of Architects, Engineers, Chemists, and Technicians (FAECT), founded in 1933.[6] It was considerably more to the left than CIAM, amply reflected in its goals and activities through its affiliation with the Congress of Industrial Organizations (CIO), and with a distinctively socialist bent. It was founded at a mass meeting held in New York in 1933 in response to a "Code of Practice" the American Institute of Architects (AIA) had submitted to the federal government.[7] The code included wage guidelines that were proposed for use under the newly passed National Recovery Act, which scheduled architectural draftsmen with two or more years of experience to receive only 50 cents per hour. Enraged by the meager figure and the apparent lack of concern about the welfare of workers so directly related to the AIA membership, the 1933 mass meeting was organized to fight the code. As the FAECT magazine, *Technical America*, editorialized on the union's fourth anniversary:

> *Almost totally without economic organization, full of illusions as to their role in industry, with strong prejudices against unions or contact with the organized labor movement, architects and engineers suffered the worst kind of degradations and demoralization. Some dared to fight back.*[8]

The FAECT sponsored a number of strikes by architects through the end of the 1930s, against both private and government practice. There were other unions and labor organizations for architects and draftsmen. For example, the prominent Architectural Guild of America (AGA) had an active chapter in New York. In September 1936, through the combined efforts of both the FAECT and the AGA, a major wage increase was secured for 7,000 architects and engineers working for the WPA.[9]

6) The Congress of Industrial Organizations (CIO) led a massive unionization program after 1935, bolstered by the provisions of the Wagner Act, which gave federal protection to organized labor.

7) "Architects' Craft and Code of Practice," *The New York Times* (August 7, 1953), p. 5.

8) "FAECT Four Years Old," *Technical America* IV (September 1939), p. 10.

9) "FAECT and AGA Win Big Increase in New York," *The Architectural Record* LXXX (September 1936), p. 171.

World War II tended, however, to negate the architectural concerns of labor organizations. After the war, these concerns remained sublimated, undoubtedly due to the peculiar political economy of the architectural profession. However, many of the issues raised in the pages of *Technical America* remained with the profession: for example, questions of accessibility of architectural professional services to lower-income groups; increasingly rigid requirements for professional licensing; and changing conditions in academic architectural programs. Conditions in architectural offices were also criticized, particularly the issue of economic exploitation of young architects. The dichotomy between the architect-businessman and the nameless designer draftsmen was a recurring theme. The established architectural journals were perceived with some humor and anger. Many of these same themes were central to the concerns of the Designers of Shelter in America (DSA), founded in 1936 in New York. The DSA professed to concern itself with the welfare of the general population, instead of the elite few. It also stressed that issues of "style", whether Modernist or otherwise, were secondary to issues of purpose and function.[10]

Toward the end of the 1930s, immigrant Europeans escaping fascism began to augment the progressive thinking and activity of U.S. architects. Many of the most prominent newcomers were invited to take academic posts where their influence was enormous. Radical new design programs were implemented by László Moholy-Nagy at the New Bauhaus in Chicago in 1937; Walter Gropius and Marcel Breuer at Harvard University in the same year; Ludwig Mies van der Rohe and Ludwig Hilberseimer at the Armour Institute (Illinois Institute of Technology) in Chicago in 1938; and Serge Chermayeff at Brooklyn College in 1942 and later in 1947 at the New Bauhaus in Chicago.[11] Others, such as Jose Lluís Sert at Yale University, were influential visiting professors. The European influx helped channel American activism into directions that it would not have otherwise taken. Gropius, a figure crucial to the European architectural revolution 30 years earlier, had especially great influence. United States progressives seemingly embraced his ideas. If in retrospect, the results of European dominance are questionable, at the time, the union of the United States and European movements produced limitless optimism about changes that could later occur in architecture in the United States.

10) Simon Breines, "Designers of Shelter in America: A New Society Makes Its Bow," *Bulletin of the Federation of Architects, Engineers, Chemists, and Technicians* III (November 1936), pp. 4-5.

11) A brief description of post-Bauhaus activity in the U.S. may be found in Hans Wingler, *Bauhaus in America*, Berlin: Bauhaus-Archiv (1972).

In the early 1940s, the list of progressive activities and groups continued to grow. Included was the American CIAM, organized with the complicity of Gropius, Sert, Breuer, and others. To some extent, its organization was intended to duplicate its European precedent, with representative sections in New York, Boston, Philadelphia, and Washington. These sections began defining their proposals for American cities, just as their counterparts in Europe were doing.[12] Furthest to the left were probably the Architects' Committee of the National Council of Soviet-American Friendship and the Committee of the Arts, Sciences, and Professions.[13] The latter especially became prominent in the fight against McCarthyism after 1950 but with little involvement from architects.

Perhaps the most prestigious alternative organization was the short-lived American Society of Planners and Architects (ASPA), founded in New York in 1944 with other chapters established in Boston, Philadelphia, and Washington. ASPA's very select membership of architects and theorists included some 70 persons who would shape the direction of United States architecture in the 1950s. During its four years of existence, the executive board included Serge Chermayeff, Walter Gropius, George Howe, Louis Kahn, Carl Koch Jr., Oscar Stonorov, and Hugh Stubbins Jr. Among its other members were Alfred H. Barr Jr., Marcel Breuer, Gordon Bunshaft, Wallace K. Harrison, Henry-Russell Hitchcock, John M. Johansen, Philip Johnson, Edgar Kaufmann Jr., Richard Neutra, I.M. Pei, Jose Lluís Sert, Eero Saarinen, and Konrad Wachsmann. The literature of the ASPA expressed a commitment to urban problems and stressed the necessity for the integration of aesthetics, economics, technology, and sociology within architecture.[14] Immediately after World War II, however, an overwhelming current of conservatism swept the architectural profession, and already by 1948, the ASPA, along with most other liberal and progressive groups and activities, no longer existed.

The obvious question is: How could this happen? How could the transition to conservatism be so smooth, and so complete? What happened to the progressives? At least a part of the answer lies in the nature of the profession

12) Miscellaneous material on the American Chapters of the Congrès Internationaux d'Architecture Moderne (CIAM) may be found with the Chermayeff ASPA papers, Widener Library, Harvard University.

13) Miscellaneous material on the architects' committees of the National Council of Soviet-American Friendship and on the Committee of the Arts, Sciences and Professions may be found in the Chermayeff Papers Archive, Avery Library, Columbia University.

14) Miscellaneous material on the American Society of Planners and Architects may be found with the Chermayeff ASPA papers, Widener Library, Harvard University.

itself. Even as much as the Moderns rationalized away the idea of the "palace architect," that timeless professional persona remained, and they perhaps only slightly changed its hue. The relationship to power, with all of its consequent compromises, in the end, had not changed in spite of the rise of modern political institutions—although the indignities suffered by Tolstoy's architects who were allowed to come to dinner,[15] were considered, one supposes, a thing of the past. This new status, which reached its zenith by mid-20th century, represented the illusion of power for architects, which had limited basis in reality. Architects were not in a position to "help mankind find its identity on earth;"[16] and at least for the American architect-businessman, including most of the recent immigrants from Europe, when the time came to get back to business, everyone stood in line. Some architects had remained in line all along.

During the progressive euphoria of the 1930s, the groundwork was laid consciously and unconsciously for the post-war conservative reaction. Among other things, it was precisely the CIAM Modernism that became one of the key tools in this preparation. It was to be the new "court architecture" —the symbol of the new post-liberal capitalism which was expected to rise out of the economic crisis of the Great Depression. Philip Johnson and Henry Russell-Hitchcock Jr. announced this breakthrough after returning from their "grand tour" of 1930, with the complicity of the forces behind the Museum of Modern Art, newly opened in 1929, and coinciding with the establishment in 1932 of a "Department of Architecture" within the museum, under the directorship of Philip Johnson.[17] To study the "International Style" exhibition catalog is indeed enlightening, with its sinister attempt to cleanse the new European urbanism of its progressive social aspect, while also attempting to discredit the growing radicalization of the profession in America. Most insidious were the distinctions made between "architecture" and "building," and especially between "architecture" and "housing."[18]

The "new monumentality" of Sert, Gropius, Gideon, and others is imperatively credited to these sensibilities as much as to anything else. The "new

15) In *War and Peace*, Tolstoy provides interesting vignettes of the relationship between palace architects and their employers. For example, see part 1, ch.24.

16) Van der Woud, op. cit., p. 148.

17) Henry-Russell Hitchcock and Philip Johnson, *The international Style: Architecture Since 1922,* New York: W.W. Norton and Company, Inc., (1932), p.38; and Museum of Modern Art, *Modern Architecture International Exhibition*, New York: Museum of Modern Art (1932), pp. 198-199.

18) Henry-Russell Hitchcock and Philip Johnson, op. cit., ch. 8.

monumentality" of Modernism became the "International Style" of the new Medicis of the 1950s: the multinationals. Such was the American contribution.[19] As for Johnson, his search for power and legitimacy by the end of the 1930s would lead him to extremes: to the Third Reich in Germany and to Father Coughlin in America.[20] It is hard to imagine a more schizophrenic community than existed among architects: Philip Johnson writing for the reactionary *Social Justice* in 1939, decrying the absence of "real" war;[21] less than five years later, a member of the liberal ASPA; by five years' time after that, the ASPA had disappeared completely.

As the McCarthy era unfolded, the dilemmas that it presented to architects are an important, if neglected, segment of the history of the profession. For liberal architects within a profession that represents a quite fragile public art subservient to the sources of economic and political power, the period forced difficult choices. As Victor Navasky relates in *Naming Names*, his recent book on the Hollywood blacklisting, there was ample evidence "of how deep were the divisions that beset the liberal community in the third great cold war conflict—the war between those who thought of themselves as progressives and those who inhabited what they like to call the vital center."[22] Consistent with tradition, the compromises of the "vital center" were paramount to commercial survival for architects, leaving the progressives adrift. An interesting symptom is the conservative stance taken by the AIA toward public housing after the close of World War II.[23]

The surge of professional conservatism obviously affected architects' stances toward housing design and production. For example, by the end of the war, architects hardly resisted the long campaign by government and industry to legitimize the architectural problem of the modest single-family house.

19) There existed a partially analogous situation between American art and American internationalism. See, for example, Max Kozloff, "American Painting During the Cold War," *Artforum* 11 (May 1973), pp. 43-54.

20) Johnson has renounced his Nazi sympathies of the 1930s. During that period, he also supported the American fascist priest, Father Coughlin, writing for his magazine, *Social Justice*. The journalist, William L. Shirer indicated the extent of Johnson's activity in *Berlin Diary*, New York: Alfred A. Knopf (1941). See also Calvin Tomkins, "Forms Under Light," *The New Yorker* LIII (May 23, 1977), p. 48; Paul Goldberger, "Philip Johnson: A Controversial New Vision for Architecture," *The New York Times Magazine* (May 14, 1978), pp. 26-27.

21) Philip Johnson, "This 'Sitdown' War," *Social Justice* (November 6, 1939), p. 9.

22) Victor S. Navasky, *Naming Names*, New York: Viking Press (1980), p. 47.

23) Richard Plunz, op. cit., pp. 208-209.

Undoubtedly, an invisible carrot over the heads of many architects was the certainty, after years of hardship, of a post-war economic boom. Even more important was the common knowledge that the boom would take place in the trouble-free wilds of suburbia rather than in the increasingly problematic center cities. The public works programs of the New Deal had provided road infrastructure, the essential ingredient for suburbanization, fully formulating the post-war priorities for industrial production. Indeed, long before the American entry in the war, American business was planning for the post-war expansionist period and the priorities for the new American culture were in place.[24] After the war, as far as CIAM ideals were concerned, they could be adjusted quite easily, providing an interesting confluence of motives between architecture and business. The "tower-in-the-park" was ideal for housing the poor; and the "new monumental" Modernist urbanism was the ideal expression for American corporate wealth.

As far as the fortunes of the progressives were concerned (as opposed to the vital center, to use Navasky's distinction), their demise was much more than a casual reflection of the brutality of the stylistic marketplace. There was also the repression of the McCarthy era—a history that is yet to be admitted and clarified in relation to the architecture and planning professions. Architects were not immune, although they were not nearly as affected as Hollywood actors and screenwriters—perhaps a valid measure of the latter's importance in American culture. For the progressives among architects, difficulties did arise. One needs to look no further than the Architect's Committee of the National Council of Soviet-American Friendship, which was active between 1944 and 1946, and found itself listed by the U.S. Attorney General as a subversive organization in 1952. Those on the leadership roster, almost entirely AIA members, were thus prevented from gaining approval for certain government work. Ultimately, some of the membership would renounce their affiliation with the National Council in order to obtain clearance for work.[25]

Of course, from the disintegration of a progressive constituency among architects in the 1950s, a new movement emerged in the 1960s. Its sources were widely varied—so much so that it, as well, would also reach an uncertain impasse, and ultimately a quick and easy disintegration. Among the important foundations for the new movement was the mounting real

24) Ibid, pp. 181-185, 202, 207-208.

25) "National Council of Soviet-American Friendship," Serge Chermayeff Archive, Avery Library, Columbia University.

evidence of the destruction of American urban centers, and the reaction against the widespread ideological basis for this entropy; including political and economic motives and their aesthetic justifications that were so close to CIAM urbanism. For example, the first (and last) anti-nuclear movement among architects came into considerable force in America by the early 1960s.[26] Thereafter, the most important impetus for the reappearance of a progressive constituency among architects became liberal capitalism's social programs of the 1960s, which were born of enormous prosperity, and were revoked rather quickly at the end of the decade.

Now, after the decade of the 1970s just passed, we can look back at the period of the 1940s and '50s and begin to see more clearly how that period functioned in relation to the evolution of American architectural theory and practice. It takes its rightful place within the important cultural criticism of the 1950s—Marshall McLuhan's *The Mechanical Bride*, C. Wright Mills' *White Collar*, John Kenneth Galbraith's *The Affluent Society*, and the like.[27] One hopes that the same slender thread perseveres today, with the same critical dimension and lucidity.

26) Some of the events of the early 1960s are briefly discussed in Marta Gutman and Richard Plunz, "Anatomy of Insurrection," in *The Making of an Architect 1881-1981*, ed. Richard Oliver, New York: Rizzoli (1981), pp. 198-199.

27) Further interpretation at Chermayeff's contribution is found in *Design and the Public Good. Selected Writings, 1930-1980 by Serge Chermayeff*, ed. Richard Plunz, Cambridge: The MIT Press (1982).

1984 "RUMINATIONS ON EDEN"

"Ruminations On Eden," *Adam's House in Paradise*, New York: Storefront for Art and Architecture (1984); also published in *Spazio e Società* 28, Italy (December 1984), pp. 74-76.

The "garden" has been many things in the historical evolution of housing in New York. Most fundamentally, botanical sensibilities have been distinguishably reflective of social class. A classic contrast, much cited in the late 19th century, was between the mansion of multi-millionaire A.T. Stewart and the slum housing at "Five Points." Stewart's marble palace was sited on six city lots at Fifth Avenue and 39th Street, with an appreciable private garden. By contrast, Five Points on the lower East Side was long characterized as the poverty-level housing of the period; it had not a modicum of light and of "nature," in this context consisting of insufficient oxygen and without the hygienic blessing of a sunlight "bath."

For middle to upper incomes, the ideals of the palace, garden, and housing changed over time but never overlapped with the sensibilities of the poor. For example, in the second half of the 19th century, the ideal of a private urban garden diminished for the wealthy as densities rose in Manhattan. For some people, the elaborate apartment building was embraced as an alternative cultural norm, complemented by a country house for summer escape and requisite contact with green nature. Wealthy neighborhoods had their parks and the most luxurious buildings, such as the Apthorp, integrated formal internal garden courtyards, more to be appreciated as urban relief than to be touched.

In the 19th-century world of New York's poor, the issue of the "garden" was perceived literally as one of life and death. In the "pre-penicillin age," nature in housing was the prevailing medical antidote to disease, even if only in terms of obtaining "light and air" in every room, a goal never fully achieved in New York to this day. The progression of different attempts at legislative control of speculative housing for the poor, tenements, between 1867 and 1901 trace the gradual eking out of a minimum exposure to light and air.

For non-speculative philanthropic housing, for which profits were restricted, the incorporation of nature as a real garden appeared from early on, among the most impressive examples being among the earliest Alfred Tredway White projects in Brooklyn, built between 1877 and 1890. In these examples, unlike upper-class projects, the garden is designed to be actively used, with drying racks for laundry and gazebos for play and concerts. Around the same time, the notion of public provision of parks in slum neighborhoods was advanced through reform efforts. An early example was Columbus Park on Mulberry Bend adjacent to Five Points, a slum clearance encouraged by Jacob Riis and completed in 1896. The park replaced one of the most unhygienic blocks in Manhattan.

With the New Deal, philanthropy shifted from private to public. The incorporation of literal nature with housing for the poor was an integral aspect of design ideology, even as the medical imperatives declined. Naturalism in housing moved from the "garden" to "park." The two earliest large-scale public housing projects in New York City bear witness to this progression. The first, Harlem River Houses, was a hard urban project, with its paved courtyards, discrete gardens, and vistas well-defined and integrated with the buildings. The second, Williamsburg Houses, was a series of buildings that tended to float in a sea of green. Ironically, as this aesthetic imperative for nature intensifies, it also became more and more dissociated from buildings. Use by people, especially with the park, has been one of the staple criticisms of that era and ideology in social housing.

Chrystie-Forsyth Streets, once the controversial location of a vast tower project proposal publicized in 1931, is now the site of a controversial tiny garden. Today, constraints on the design of housing are different than those of a few decades ago and, in general, many aspects of the present situation would seem to be synergistic with Adam Purple's "Garden of Eden." Today, massive public housing projects are no longer built, atrophied by both political and economic constraints. The incessant reductions of the last 15 years in direct government subsidy of social housing have been combined with a greater private role in production. From the side of architectural theory, 1960s social criticism of the "tower-in-the-park" has led to other design ideologies. Naturalism in housing has retreated from park to guerrilla patch. In fact, scores of vacant lots throughout New York have been expropriated as neighborhood gardens; sometimes as accommodation from some temporary patron, but more often as ignored enterprise in that the neighborhood situation is officially deemed hopeless anyway. On what basis can such initiatives be opposed? Can anyone afford to be against the improvement of New York in this way?

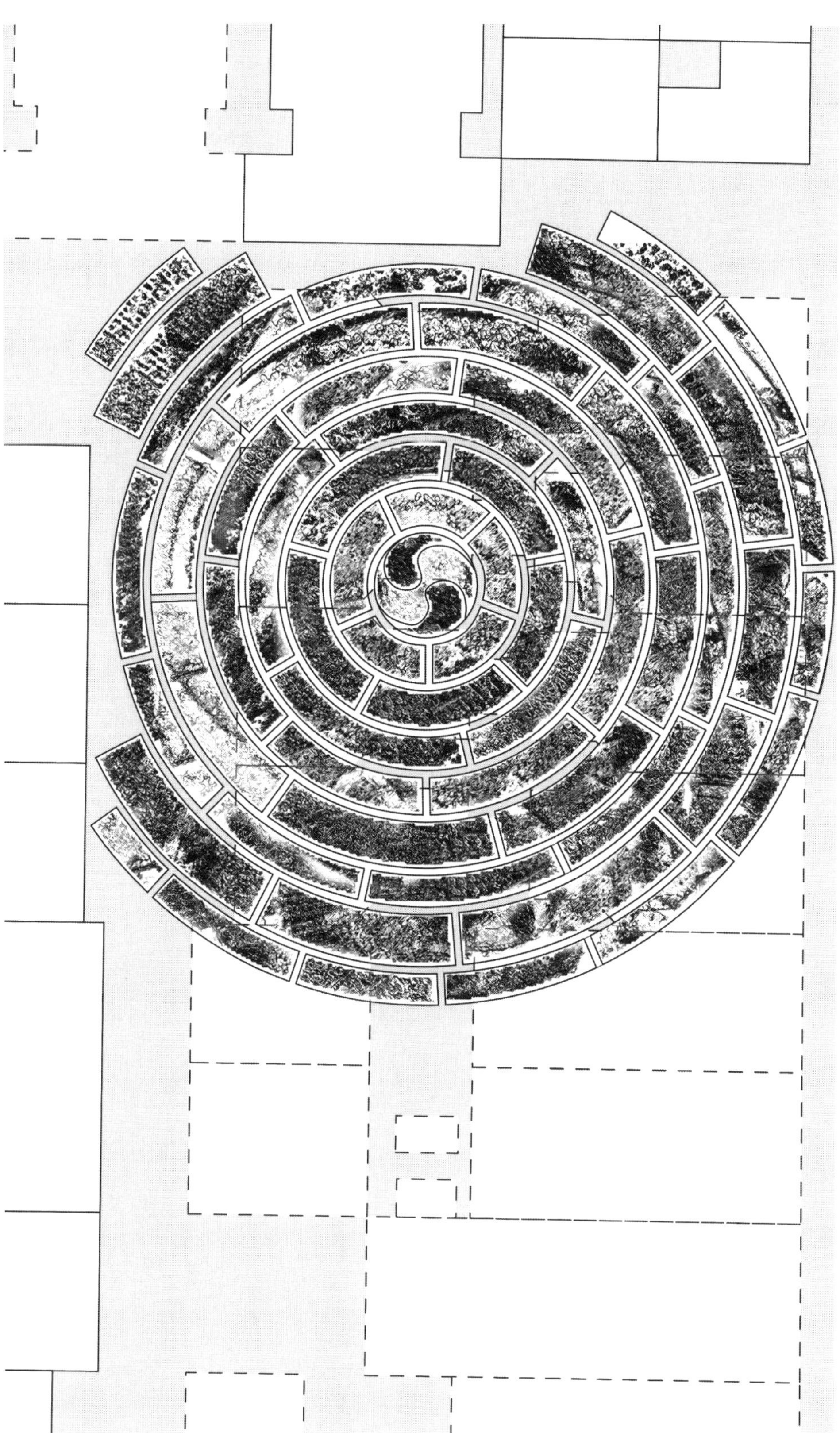

PLATE F
"Garden of Eden" Manhattan, New York

1984. Adam Purple's Garden, Lower East Side Reconstruction. Columbia GSAPP research team, 2017-2020.

Research into the lost potential of Adam Purple's Garden in directing next-generation development on the Lower East Side of Manhattan. For a period of 10 years starting in 1975, Adam Purple, resident of the Lower East Side, constructed his garden on Eldridge Street on the vacant land at the interstices within the rubble of abandoned Old Law Tenements. As buildings crumbled, the rubble became a resource for the construction of concentric rings filled with an extraordinary variety of flora nourished by horse manure transported by bicycle from Central Park South. By 1984, the garden came to represent a heroic symbol of resistance to the destruction as well as of hope for a new urban moment while giving new meaning to urban ecology. The New York City Housing Authority (NYCHA), however, saw an opportunity to build new housing on the site. The Storefront for Art and Architecture initiated a struggle to preserve the garden, with an international invitation for alternative designs that would preserve the space. In a tragic demonstration of bureaucratic intransigence about the fundamental purposes of housing, Adam Purple's Garden was demolished on January 8, 1986.

1984. Project for the Preservation of "Adam Purple's Garden of Eden," Storefront for Art and Architecture. Kyong Park, Glen Weiss, with Richard Plunz and others. Graphic representation: Ashna Raman (M.Arch 2019), Maria Isabel Carrasco (MSAUD 2017), Lucy Navarro (M.Arch 2020).

PUBLICATION: Richard Plunz, "Ruminations on Eden," *Adam's House in Paradise: Lower East Side, New York City*, eds. Kyong Park and Glen Weiss, New York: Storefront Art and Architecture (1984). Also see Richard Plunz Papers, Department of Drawings & Archives, Avery Architectural and Fine Arts Library.

The guerrilla patch is a "Victory Garden" with an edge, and not exactly like the predecessors of the First and Second World Wars: it is "victorious" for the kind of assertion which it represents, and, in this sense, threatening in spite of minuscule scale. Can the Lower East Side afford to discard the power of Adam Purple's assertion? Is the aesthetic initiative alone not worth the cause, as the Lower East Side becomes more and more populated by artists fleeing housing difficulties nearby? No one has argued that the Garden of Eden did not improve its context, that it has no aesthetic value, or that it cannot be integrated within the configuration of the project proposed for the site. In relation to the evolution of housing in New York City, the appearance of the Garden of Eden is of timely circumstance. Its significance is underlined by the history of community design activism in the 1960s by the "green" movements; by the socio-political opposition to over-scaled housing projects; and now, by the issue of gentrification in the East Village and the Lower East Side and by the artist community which has become the inevitable staple in this process in New York City.

It has been observed that in New York art is on the cutting edge of real estate, and it is at this level that the Garden of Eden is an interesting incident. It is here that housing reform and nature meet, beginning with the threat of making a dangerous precedent to the discredited development processes in New York. At the bureaucratic level, the Garden of Eden interjects a level of participation in decision making which was granted and then withdrawn by the very then effective Neighborhood Development Program (NPD) of the Omnibus Housing Act of 1968 and dismantled by the Nixon Administration less than four years later.

The chic of today pervades values that are not fully apparent in the art world. Bohemianism is far from the commercialism of the East Village gallery scene, which is smoothly paving the way for young professionals who need the neighborhood. In Manhattan and elsewhere, this gentrification process is nearly perfect, moving from neighborhood to neighborhood and penetrating the subconscious depths of City bureaucracy. In this frenzy, can the unsolicited and unpaid product of one person's divination survive? Or if it does survive and is protected, can it have any possible meaning beyond cynical usurpation? Mr. Purple's Garden stops us short.

1984 "ACADEMIC RESEARCH"

A version of this paper was originally presented at Recontre, *Récherche et Architecture. Pour un Bilan International*, Ministere de L'Industrie et de la Recherche Paris, June 14, 1984; published as "La Recherche Universitaire en Architecture aux États-Unis," *La Recherche en Architecture: Un Bilan International*, Marseille: Editions Parentheses (1986), pp. 152-158; also published as "Comments on Academic Research in Architecture in the United States," *Journal of Architectural Education* 40:2 (1987), pp. 62-64.

"Research" does not hold an important role in guiding the priorities of the "culture of architecture." Architecture, at least as practiced by the majority of architects in the United States, is of necessity and before all else a commercial enterprise, albeit a less than lucrative one in many cases. Certainly, research is done, but more often than not in response to exigencies of the marketplace, and it ranges from the dictates of energy conservation to the imperatives of style and fashion. Architectural research survives as an *ad hoc* phenomenon which is employed when needed, remaining erratic for most subject areas and, in general, unmonitored and un-institutionalized. The percentage of the yearly total of built environment activity devoted to building research of all kinds is minuscule. However, precise statistics are not available, which is probably symptomatic of the state of research. Recently, the American Institute of Architects (AIA) did attempt to monitor research using computerized data, but that effort was short-lived.[1] There are many research areas that in some way coincide within the realm of building construction and use, but most are simply not of interest to architects, and many others are of interest on a cyclical basis, depending on shifts in the larger economic, political, and cultural climate within which building occurs. In the interest of coherence, and because I am principally involved with the academy, my comments will be directed primarily toward the academic realm of architectural research, to the possible exclusion of other areas which might also be considered.

1) Around 1977, the American Institute of Architects Research Corporation initiated its "Research Information Retrieval System," which was a computerized catalog of architectural research projects in the United States. The system is no longer extant, however. The Research Corporation does still exist, but in a form reduced from its original conception.

The culture of architecture in the United States tends to dissociate "architecture" and "building," and therefore all of the research areas connected with building do not coincide with architecture, and research activity still reflects the old split between "architecture" and "engineering." A large proportion of technical research into building materials and systems is done entirely outside of what might be considered architectural practice. This split has become more pronounced of late. In comparison to 20 years ago, most schools of architecture have considerably deemphasized technical subjects, a condition which is reflected in the nationwide examinations for the licensing of architects. Within professional offices, the consulting engineer is called upon more and more to assume legal responsibility for the technical realm. This is reflected in the typical percentage of the entire building budget devoted to technical systems, which now hovers around 50 percent. In recent years, the split has also heightened between architecture and the "behavioral sciences" after a decade of considerable mutual interest in the 1960s. And the issue of evaluation of building use after construction, which seemed to be an emerging long-term research involvement 15 years ago, has all but disappeared from popular architectural engagement. But as with the engineering split, the behavioral split is consistent with the long-term anathemas of architects. Architects have never been much interested in auto-criticism. This is reflected in the almost total lack of critical architectural press in the United States, and most behavioral evaluations of building are made by non-architects.

The general direction of architectural research has to do with shifts in the culture of architecture, as well as with shifts in the sources and availability of funding for research. The shifts are probably most noticeable within universities as opposed to private or government-motivated research, and where research tends to be somewhat ephemeral anyway - or at least the university does not answer very directly to the pragmatic needs of the marketplace. Very few schools of architecture play even peripheral roles in fulfilling the ongoing need for technical research in building,[2] which is primarily sustained by private or governmental entities. In other words, the university has no concrete research constituency for architecture, and, therefore, what is researched (and valued as a subject of study) tends to shift with the wind even more than elsewhere. In the 1960s, an expanding

2) Schools of architecture such as Berkeley, Michigan, and Rensselaer Polytechnic Institute, which have, at least until recently, enjoyed reputations for high-level and professional building technology research, are quite rare in the history of the profession of architecture in the United States.

academic research domain had to do with the relationship between architecture and urban social problems, and more generally with the relationship between architecture and the behavioral sciences. This reflected the enormous government spending in that period, fueled by the Kennedy-Johnson era social programs. Although schools of architecture were far from the forefront in this development, its influence did filter down to the schools, especially toward the end of the decade, including its influence on academic curricula. Government-sourced impact has shifted, as evidenced by the emergence of areas of more recent importance—historical study, for example.

The government-sourced impacts of a decade or so ago represented a diverse range of concerns, including behavioral research. In 1963, the "Comprehensive Community Mental Health Center Act" was passed by the U.S. Congress, launching a major building program for mental health patients. Due to the specialized behavioral problems involved with the design of such facilities, behavioral scientists and architects were forced into a closer relationship than previously, when the functional relationship between physical environment and behavior by architects was pretty much limited to the level of the "form follows function" dictum. In this new moment, an earlier legacy from the behavioral sciences was tapped, especially from fields such as cybernetics, operations research, and linguistics. Subsequent legislation further encouraged other aspects of behavioral research in architecture, including the Economic Opportunity Act of 1964, followed by the Model Cities legislation of 1966. The relationship between architecture and user began to take on a new dimension. Both of these major legislations mandated the "maximum feasible participation of the poor" in the implementation of programs designed to help them. Both began massive funding toward support of community organization activities and community participation in design of local projects. By 1968, within the context of the general urban disorder of that decade, this tendency had intensified.

With the passage of the Housing and Urban Development Act of 1968 the "Neighborhood Development Program" (NDP) was initiated, which could provide financial assistance directly to community organizations for program development. At this level, NDP was seen as a form of reparation for embittered communities, and it passed a portion of government renewal funds directly to local leadership, sometimes even bypassing municipal authority. From the point-of-view of architectural research, this development meant that communities were given some autonomy in hiring architects and were placed in a position to demand professional work that came much

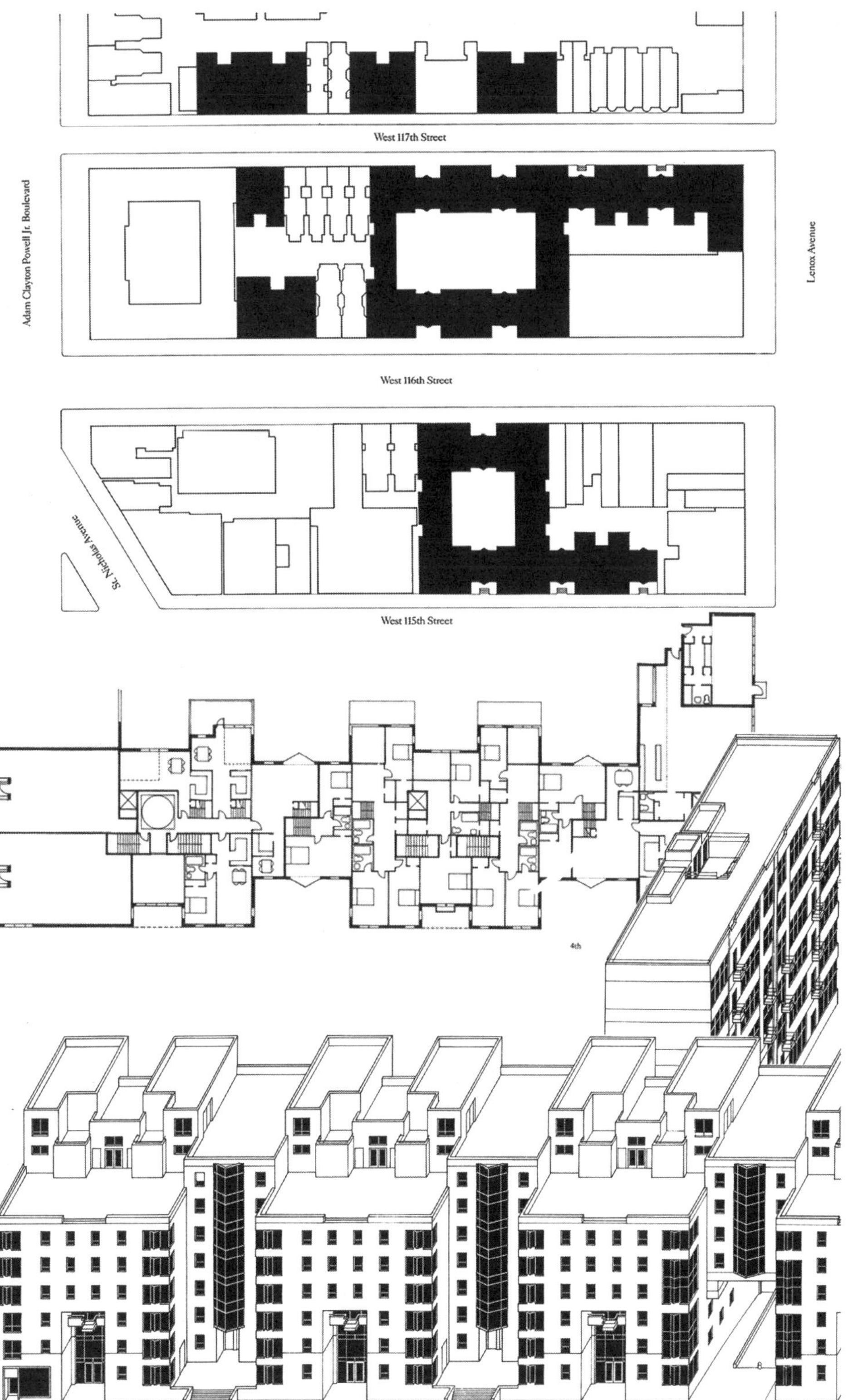
West 117th Street
Adam Clayton Powell Jr. Boulevard
Lenox Avenue
West 116th Street
St. Nicholas Avenue
West 115th Street
4th

PLATE G+H
"Inner City Infill" New York, New York

1985. Entry to "Inner City Infill" competition, New York State Council on the Arts, in collaboration with the Harlem Urban Development Corporation, Manhattan Community Board 15, and the New York Landmarks Conservancy. Columbia GSAPP housing research team.

Proposal for development parcels located in Central Harlem, between West 115th and West 118th Streets, entry to the 1985 "Inner City Infill Housing" competition. The requirements were for 420 units of new and rehab housing, together with 33,000 square feet of commercial space and another 7,000 square feet dedicated to community facilities. Onsite parking was limited to 80 cars. The strategy responded to the scale and continuity of existing brownstone and tenement streets, with adjustments made to the existing block patterns wherever possible to improve light, air, and community spaces. A "kit of parts" could be combined and assembled as a partial or whole system. "Terrace-type" and "infill-type" apartment buildings distinguished between the public space of the street and the private space of the backyards. A third "loft-type" building was introduced on the east-west edges of the interventions to further knit new and old fabrics.

1985. Entry to "Inner City Infill Housing Competition." Project Team: Richard Plunz, Marta Gutman (M.Arch 1981), Ann Kalla (M.Arch 1980), A. Eugene Sparling (M.Arch 1980), with John Ambrose (M.Arch 1986), Blake Auchincloss (M.Arch.1986), Ellen Belknap (M.Arch 1987), Ellen Kuhn (M.Arch 1987), Jylle Menoff (M.Arch. 1986), Maurizio De Vita, Martine Kornier. Graphic representation: Maria Isabel Carrasco (MSAUD 2017), Isaac Warshauer (M.Arch 2019), Lucy Navarro (M.Arch 2020).

PUBLICATION: *Reweaving the Urban Fabric: Approaches to Infill Housing*, ed. Deborah Norden, New York: Princeton Architectural Press (1989). Also see Richard Plunz Papers, Department of Drawings & Archives, Avery Architectural and Fine Arts Library.

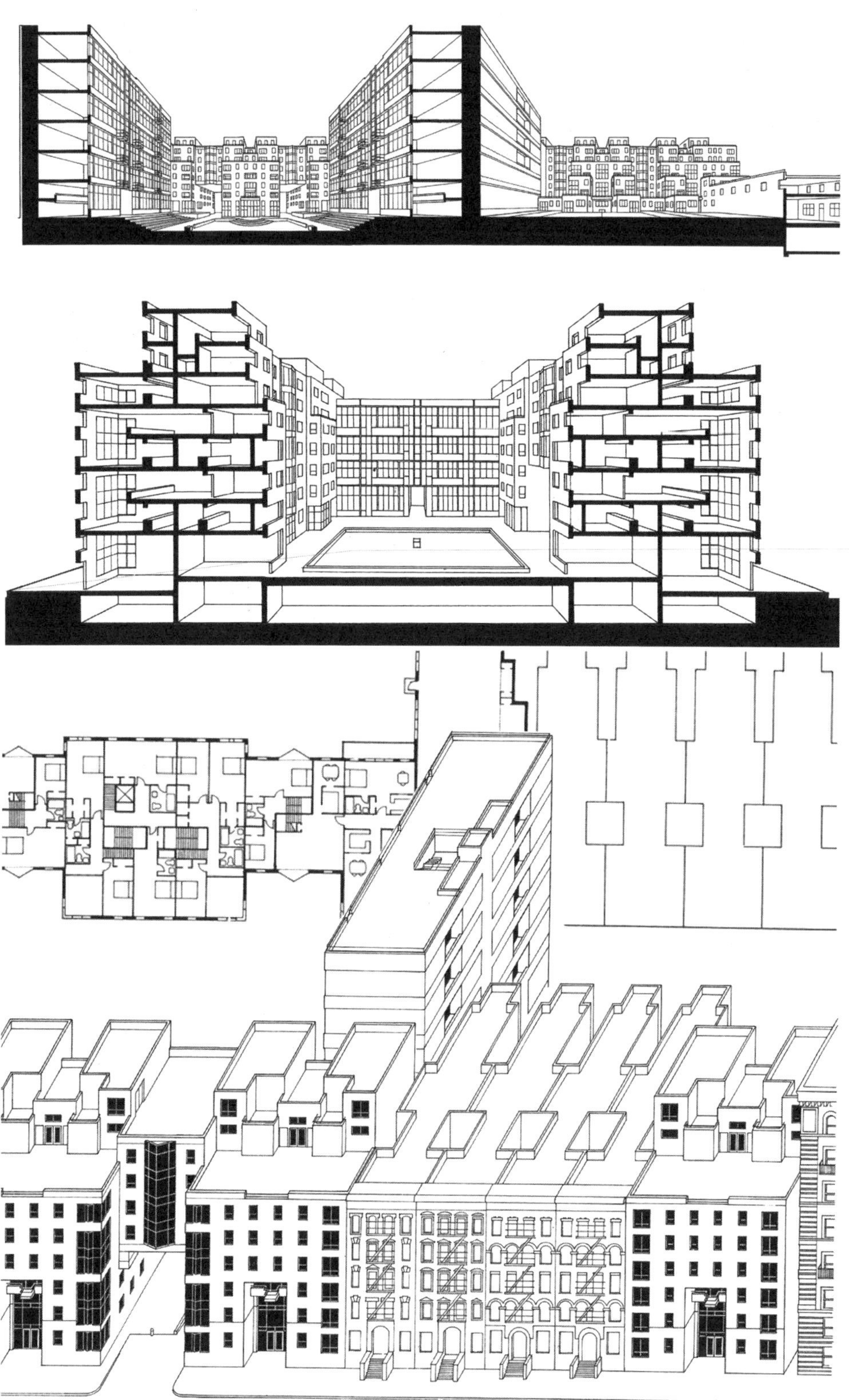

closer to their needs than was traditionally provided by the profession. This approach focused on the development of architectural and urban design interventions that generated a very particular response to the anthropology of urban low-income communities. In effect, architects could function in an "advocacy" role, translating such data articulated by a constituency normally unknown or unrecorded into the professional technical language which was necessary to formulate and implement building projects. This advocacy movement among architects and planners was critical in bringing change in both pedagogy and research to the academy. Advocacy meshed well with the tendency toward behavioral research which was already in development.[3]

This merging of the fields of environment and behavior produced significant new academic research institutions and organizations. One of the earliest and most important was the Joint Center for Urban Studies at Harvard University and the Massachusetts Institute of Technology. Founded in 1959, this institute sponsored a number of now classic studies, especially in the 1960s, and became an important model for the proliferation of academically affiliated research institutes for architectural- and environment- related fields during this period.[4] The expansion of the range of possible architectural activity also led to an expanded range of professional alliances and publications that included involvement of architects. For example, in 1968 with the founding of the Environmental Design Research Association (EDRA), the new generation of architects and designers nurtured on a behavioral sciences perspective could join the ranks of other academics with similar interests.[5]

3) By 1969, more than eight institutions were giving academic credit to architecture students for advocacy related activities, figures cited in "Advocacy Planning. What It Is, How It works," *Progressive Architecture* XIX (September 1968), p.104, out of 92 schools of architecture in the U.S. at that time. By 1971, more than 70 "Community Design Centers" were operating, using financing from private foundations and government monies under the liberalizing influence of programs such as NDP. Figures cited in Walter F. Mondale, "A Congressional View of Community Participation in the Planning Process," *Design Quarterly* 82/83 (1971), p.7.

4) Concrete figures on the scale of such activity are quite impossible to locate, but one source identifies 51 "university-based" architectural research centers by 1972. It also identifies 32 "non-university-based" centers. (Figures extrapolated from William C. Miller, *Architectural Research Centers: An Annotated Directory,* Council of Planning Librarians Exchange Bibliographies, 199 and 333 (July 1971 and October 1972)). These figures are undoubtedly inconclusive. For more general research, another source identifies approximately 240 urban studies research centers by 1970. Figure extrapolated from "Urban Studies Research Centers," *Urban Affairs Quarterly* V (March 1970), pp. 392-560.

5) An EDRA monograph on the field of environmental design research is slated to be published in the near future, by Praeger Publishers, New York.

Previous to the 1960s, no important professional architectural alliance existed except for the AIA, which was heavily oriented toward the concerns of commercial practice.[6] And while EDRA helped fill a critical need, it has remained largely academic, and without appreciable orientation toward formal research in relation to design. The same era also produced important new behavior-oriented journals, from the relatively populist *Design and Environment,* which broadened the concerns of the established architectural press, to the more scholarly *Environment and Behavior.* And in certain noteworthy situations, new university curricula were pioneered that were parallel to traditional architectural programs—for example, the Division of Man-Environment Relations at the Pennsylvania State University. But, again, these tended to minimize the problem of architectural design relative to the perspective of formal research. Within government agencies, conspicuous, if rather momentary, experimental research entities also emerged. For example, the Bureau of Standards within the U.S. Department of Commerce organized an important design research program within the "Institute for Applied Technology," directed by John Eberhard. Within the Health Services Research organization of the United States Public Health Service, important architectural projects were initiated.

Today interest in social-behavioral connections has diminished, partially because government social programs began to be reduced in the early 1970s. For example, in 1974 the Nixon administration abruptly cut all of the NDPs, thereby removing one of the bulwarks of the advocacy movement. Many other bulwarks were also removed in that, for one thing, community politicization had worked too well. Of the more than 70 Community Design Centers in operation in 1971, about 45 still survive,[7] all with considerably reduced programs. That these many organizations still remain, however, is some indication of a continuing commitment in one form or another to the ideals of the previous era. Other remnants survive, including EDRA, and the individuals buried in universities. But the last decade has spawned quite different realms of architectural research activity, most notably related to aesthetic "theory" and to history.

In the United States, historical research in architecture has had a long reign as a mainstay. The earliest publications on architecture, dating from the end of the 18th century, were concerned with history from the rather eager context

6) In the 1930s, a number of professional alliances existed for architects, but they disappeared in the post-war era.

7) This figure has been recently cited by the Director of the "Community Design Center Directors Association," in Salt Lake City, Utah.

of a colonial outpost. Later on, by the latter half of the 19th century, when the profession of architecture became institutionalized, historicism was critical to its legitimization. Technological innovation, which has also been so critical to the development of United States building, was basically left to the engineers. In exchange, architects garnered the right to aesthetic expertise, which led directly to the stylistic marketplace. Probably not much has changed since in relation to the nature of the profession. In periods of change in the stylistic market, historical research has engaged the legitimation of stylistic or ideological tendencies which are "bought and sold;" with the involvement of the academy as an essential component of this equation. The academy produces the "pattern-books" which are needed for such purposes.

Today is a period of intense activity within the stylistic marketplace—so much so that it is reminiscent of that other period in the 1890s, when the United States was reaching toward its first taste of global power, and when the "American Renaissance" chose Academic Classicism to symbolize that power. It is curious that now, in a period of relative decline for the United States, Academic Classicism again surfaces, although in a far more marginal way. But the complicity of the academy with the marketplace is critical now, as it was then. And in both periods, the market reflects all manner of related social phenomena, such as the relationship between political left and right. Behind the current revival of classicism lurks fundamentally conservative political ideology.

In the 1890s, the relationship between academic historical research and the architectural profession differed from today in that historical material was supplied to architects by the then-emerging disciplines of archaeology and art history—by researchers who were professional academics, and presumably interested in knowledge more for its own sake than for the promotion of a particular stylistic credo. In the past decade or so, the field of historical research in architecture has been embraced by architects alone—that is by those trained as architects rather than as historians, and in some cases, by architects who continue to practice architecture while practicing history on the side. There are now two kinds of historical research—one academic and the other for the marketplace. Already 40 years ago, in a talk on "Architectural Research in America," Talbot Hamlin, the prominent historian and critic who taught for decades at Columbia University, identified these two polarities as "antiquarianism" and the "search for new style inspiration."[8] As Hamlin notes, this polarity is probably very American. It is considerably stronger today than in 1944.

8) Talbot Hamlin, "Architectural Research in America," *Art in America* XXXIII (October 1945), p. 185.

As with behavioral science research in the 1960s, the government has played an important role in nurturing the recent prominence of historical research. Government support for cultural pursuits increased as support for behavioral research decreased. In relation to architecture, perhaps the most visible such support has come from the National Endowment for the Arts (NEA), which was established by Congress in 1965, along with the National Endowment for the Humanities (NEH). By the mid-1970s, NEA support for architectural projects and research totaled more than $1 million dollars a year and has since risen sixfold. In comparison to the lack of other major funding sources, this budget has made NEA a very substantial patron, especially for research which otherwise would lack funding. Together with NEH and with a multitude of smaller agencies at the state level (such as the New York State Council for the Arts), a positive climate was created for certain research areas, including history. These agencies tended to consider academic research pursuits to be legitimate concerns for professional architects, and because they were relatively accessible and egalitarian, opened up the study of history and theory on a scale not previously known in the United States.

This period has seen access to funding both at an individual level as well as on an institutional scale. In New York, it is likely that without these generous government subsidies the Institute for Architecture and Urban Studies could not have thrived as a kind of "alternative academy." And the Institute, with its extensive lectures, classes, and publications has had a great deal to do with the changes in architectural culture in the last decade. Its journal, *Oppositions,* provided an important public forum for architectural theorists. At this point, academic journals seem to abound, with scores of schools of architecture publishing their own magazines, each filled with "history" and "theory."[9]
In 1954, there was only one, which was *Perspecta,* published at Yale. Perhaps no better indication of recent new activity exists than in publishing statistics. There are approximately three times as many books in print on architecture in the United States today than in 1958, and it is fair to speculate that most of this difference has been supplied by history books. This development would have pleased Hamlin, who in 1944 complained that "commercial publishers, almost without exception, were prejudiced against architectural works—especially historical works. Whatever the improvements have been, even university presses look askance at such books, unless they are backed by whacking subsidies, but with limited resources for such."[10] And United States'

9) This increase is estimated through examination of the numbers of entries under "Architecture" in *Books in Print* between the years 1958 and 1983-84.

10) Talbot Hamlin, op. cit., p. 192.

book publications for architecture are still paltry in comparison, for example, to Italy, where such activity is remarkable for its scale and diversity. Hamlin's characterization of United States architectural periodicals, as having "almost eliminated solid critical or historical writing in favor of style propaganda or the mere presentation of buildings" remains largely true for mainstream publishing today.[11]

The lack of substantial critical research into building practice is perhaps even more notable today than in the post-war decades, when the academy was less involved with the historical "search for new style inspiration," not that historicist buildings had entirely disappeared. The decade of the 1950s was biased more toward the pragmatics of building, and research by architects tended to focus on issues related to technology and construction. As well, architectural curricula, in the transition away from Beaux-Arts pedagogy, reconsidered the purposes of historical study and, in that period, de-emphasized historicism while still leaving the teaching of history to historians.

Unfortunately, the value of much of today's historicist activity rests only with fashion, in the same way that much of the social activism of the 1960s in architecture had to do with radical chic. In relation to academic research in architecture, this observation points toward certain structural problems within the discipline as a whole; and, most importantly, toward the ambiguities within schools of architecture in relation to their purpose and autonomy. The evolution of the academy toward a contribution that goes beyond a service capacity for the perpetuation of private practice has never really occurred, although there have been spasmodic lurches in that direction during the 1930s and '60s. This service role is again being reinforced. The promise that the university held 15 years ago to serve as a base for professional involvement with architecture between private practice and teaching has diminished. The domain of the academy has retreated again toward its traditional role of the technical institute for staffing private offices, after an interesting period of less parochial involvements.

In the United States, one finds as strong as ever the cultural prejudice that the only legitimate activity for the architect is private practice rather than, say, academic research, for which there are few resources anyway. This condition is reinforced by the laws that license architects to practice, which require a three-year period of "apprenticeship" after completion of academic

11) Ibid., p. 190.

curricula before one can complete the examinations and legally be called an architect. This stands in contrast to much of Europe, where academic training is considered worthy enough for bestowal of the title of architect. In the United States, apprenticeship guarantees a rather modestly paid labor force for private firms, which is a desirable form of self-benevolence. But as for the academy, this practice devalues the importance of academic activity, or of any architectural pursuits which lie outside of the narrow confines of professionalism and the Ayn Randian myth of its mystique. Within the culture of architecture, an unlicensed architect is considered an aberration.[12] The academy remains disjointed, unable to legitimize fully its own evolution outside of the commercial marketplace.

Finally, for architectural design, perhaps the least recognized but most pervasive academic research in architecture occurs within design studio curricula. In the United States, conventional architectural pedagogy centers around studio teaching in groups of 12 to 20 students, involving a kind of Socratic dialogue for a particular problem of building type or context. A kind of formal research in architecture is engaged, which, even if unscientific, is none-the-less rational and productive. In fact, it must be admitted that some of the most interesting research in design emerges from the academic studio setting—from 14 good minds exploring alternatives. Unfortunately, this energy is rarely directed outside of the studio itself toward any larger coordinated body of knowledge. But in relation to my own research, this resource has been invaluable, especially with the paucity of other recourse.

12) Recent studies have shown that approximately one-half of architecture graduates never complete licensing examination, choosing instead careers outside of conventional private practice. They remain "hidden" from the mainstream culture of architecture. See Robert Gutman and Barbara Westergaard, "What Architecture Schools Know About Their Graduates," *Journal of Architectural Education* 31, no. 2 (1978), pp. 2-11.

1985 "LET THERE BE BLIGHT?"

Excerpted from "New York: La modifica delle tipologie residentiali nell'ultimo decennio," *Urbanistica 79*, Italy (May 1985), pp. 102-111; also published as: "Modelli e tipologie residenziali a New York," *Roma, Parigi, New York. Quale urbanistica per le metropoli?*, ed. D. Cecchini, G. Hermanin, and M. Talia, Rome: Gangemi Editore (1986), pp. 225-235.

The fundamental changes of the last decades in housing production within New York City can be summarized briefly in a few statistics. First, the population of the municipal area has decreased, from a high of slightly more than 8.1 million at the end of the 1960s to 6.95 million today.[1] Housing production has suffered a decline of far greater proportions, from a high of 51,399 units added in 1963, to less than 5,000-unit totals in the past several years.[2] This decline is reflected in both private market housing and publicly subsidized housing. There has also been a large dynamic between modes of production. For example, in recent years rehabilitation numbers have become far more significant than new housing. Until the late 1960s, reuse played a minor role in social housing programs, involving less than 2,000 units per year. By the mid-1970s, rehabilitation climbed to almost 100,000 units and has since dropped off to a few thousand.[3] The long-established public housing program for new production of social housing was effectively terminated in 1974.[4]

The value of the above statistics is limited, in that they must be carefully correlated with geography. The distribution within the various physical precincts of New York City is very uneven. In the past decade or so, outlying areas such as the South Bronx or Brownsville-East New York in Brooklyn have seen enormous reduction in both population and housing stock in relation

1) Michael A. Stegman, *Housing in New York: Study of a City, 1984*, New York: New York City Department of Housing Preservation and Development (February 1985), p.29.

2) *New Housing in New York City 1981-1982,* New York: New York City Department of City Planning (December 1983), pp. 6, 26.

3) A figure based on all programs used to stimulate rehabilitation, including direct intervention and tax abatement. See *Housing Database. Public and Publicly Aided Housing*, New York: New York City Department of City Planning (August 1983), vol. 1, Tables A-2, A-5.

4) For a general summary of social housing programs in New York City between 1928-1982, see Ibid., Table A-1.

to elsewhere.[5] At the other end of the spectrum, certain areas of Manhattan, for example the Upper West Side, and more recently the East Village, have experienced enormous renewal and displacement involving an influx of affluent new population. Substantial government subsidies have at least indirectly contributed to this phenomenon, at the expense of the production of social housing. Midtown Manhattan has experienced large commercial building activity in the past decade that, among other things, reflects the changing industrial base of the city. The importance of the new professional "worker" is reflected in the changing housing stock of Manhattan and select other areas, especially in Brooklyn. Amid this evidence of new affluence exists an unprecedented display of poverty. For example, combined public and private institutions are now housing 20,000 "victims" each night in the winter cold. These are figures that match or exceed the conditions of the Great Depression in the 1930s.[6]

There are also recent shifts in prevalent housing typologies that must be placed within the larger context of the last 25 years.[7] In a sense, the present situation represents a certain conclusion to this period of housing production. For example, the design of social housing in the early 1960s witnessed a turning-away from the orthodox post-war urbanism of the "tower-in-the-park." With the effective fall from power of Robert Moses in 1960, design sensibilities shifted, reinforced by the years of municipal administration under Mayor John Lindsay when housing design experimentation occurred that attempted to see high-rise housing within an urbanistically integrated view. This 1960s generation of design was of generally unprecedented quality for social housing, possible partially because social housing programs began to move into the middle-income category, with increased subsidies

5) According to the U.S. Census figures, the population total for the South Bronx (below the Cross Bronx Expressway) has dropped from 499,346 in 1970 to 266,089 in 1980, or almost one-half reduction. Some census tracts within the same area were reduced by up to 90 percent. Within the same approximate area, 67.6 percent of the remaining occupied buildings are adjacent to abandoned buildings, and 41.2 percent have maintenance deficiencies, which is the highest rate in New York City. In the same area, 54.7 percent of the population is below the official poverty level, which is also the highest rate in the city. See the U.S. Census and Stegman, op. cit., Tables 7-2 and 7-5.

6) The total number of homeless is estimated at more than 34,000 persons. See the following: Deirdre Carmody, "Clerics Find City Lags on Plans for Homeless," *The New York Times* (November 21, 1984), p. B1; William R. Greer, "Record Number Seek Shelter on Frigid Night," *The New York Times* (January 11, 1985), p. A1.

7) For a general history of housing design in New York City, see Richard Plunz, *Habiter New York. La Forme Institutionnalisée de l'Habitat New-Yorkais. 1850-1950*, Brussels: Pierre Mardaga Éditeur (1982).

over the earlier programs. Precedents were set, engaging drastic change in the conventions of social housing design, with the reintroduction of low-rise housing as a legitimate form for social housing, in spite of its historical "tenement" associations. The fight for West Village Houses, which lasted for approximately 15 years between 1960 and 1975, was the milestone in this development. This project was advocated by Greenwich Village residents to replace a tower-in-the-park project proposed for the same site and was reinforced by new ideological directions advocated by figures such as Jane Jacobs, with the argument that the new towers would be the "blight," rather than the older low-rise fabric.[8] The old so-called blight became the new order.

All of this aside, in the present period one must point to what appears to be the most intense activity of the municipality; this, directly and indirectly, having to do with maintenance of present social housing stock at current levels (as opposed to expansion) and with facilitation of renewal in Manhattan and select other areas for middle- to upper-income residency. This shift is partially pragmatic, in that, after 1974, national government subsidy for public housing became limited, and other subsidy was shifted towards the mechanisms of the private marketplace, making large-scale initiatives more difficult than before. Within these constraints, the New York City municipality is now the largest single landlord in New York, with much of this prominence having to do with programs designed to rescue buildings that are in the process of abandonment by private owners (through tax arrears and lack of maintenance). In Brooklyn alone, the municipality maintains 2,000 such buildings.[9] The New York City Housing Authority, which owns the public housing projects, has almost 600,000 tenants, which is a number about equal to the population of San Francisco. As for New York's middle- and upper-income constituency, the process of so-called "gentrification" is being facilitated in its spread from the Upper East and West Sides for example, into the East Village and the Lower East Side through public municipal intervention, including unspoken incentives to private investment.[10] A good case in point is the Clinton or the Lower East

8) The West Village struggle is well described in Stephen Zoll, "The West Village: Let there be Blight," *Dissent* III (Summer 1961), pp. 289-293. The other essays in this volume offer a vibrant commentary on the culture planning in New York at the apex of the "Urban Renewal" era.

9) Figure cited in Matthew L. Wald, "Saving Aging Housing: A Costly City Takeover," *The New York Times* (November 27, 1983), p. A1.

10) The incentives are actually not so unspoken. For example, see Anthony DePalma, "Can City's Plan Rebuild the Lower East Side?," *The New York Times* (October 14, 1984), Sec. 4, p. 6.

Side redevelopments proposed by the municipality, which will reinforce the already heated real estate market there.[11]

After the Lower East Side, Harlem is the last remaining enclave for a low-income black and Hispanic populations in Manhattan. Already, there are signs from both the municipality and private developers of increasing interest in Harlem.[12] Mayor Edward Koch has on occasion publicly stated that those who cannot afford to live in Manhattan should expect to have to move.[13] It can be assumed that his point can apply to Harlem as well as to elsewhere unless there is massive political resistance. The latter looms as a possibility, as the community leadership begins to sense the inevitability of their housing situation if the present cycle is allowed to play itself out without interference from the community. Threatening prospects are raised in that, if completed, the upper-middle class would be back in Manhattan, and the poor in the suburbs, isolated in pockets of discarded and substandard single-family houses of the post-war era. The earlier geographical distribution would become reversed with the poor no longer concentrated toward the urban center, and the middle class no longer at the periphery. Apart from the obvious issue of housing quality, this transformation could have a devastating effect on the political power base of the minority population.

As for developing areas like the Upper West Side, the evidence of large-scale change is everywhere. For example, the massive Lincoln Towers project, built in the early 1960s with public subsidy as lower middle-income housing, is soon to be sold by the present owners and is also certain to be reorganized as a cooperative, which in New York terms means enormous profit for the new owner, and is synonymous with a change to a new upper-middle income tenantry.[14] This completes an evolution in that area that began almost three decades ago with the planning for Lincoln Center, which was seen as a

11) Buckhurst, Fish, Hutton, Katz, Planning and Development Advisors, *The Special Clinton District Planning and Zoning Study*, New York: New York State Urban Development Corporation and New York City Community Board #4 (June 1, 1985).

12) Popular interest in Harlem real estate has been stimulated by recent articles such as Craig Unger, "Can Harlem be Born Again?," *New York Magazine* (November 19, 1984), pp. 28-36.

13) One of the more notorious quotes attributed to Mayor Ed Koch was: "We're not catering to the poor anymore ... there are four other boroughs they can live in. They don't have to live in Manhattan." See Arthur Brown, Dan Collins, and Michael Goodwin, *I, Koch*, New York: Dodd, Mead, and Company (1985), p. 290.

14) Michael deCourcy Hinds, "Lincoln Towers Up for Sale, Called Likely Conversion," *The New York Times* (December 2, 1984), sec. 8, p. 7.

necessary bulwark for the redevelopment of the Upper West Side. Elsewhere in Manhattan, for example in Soho and Tribeca, such redevelopment is also passing its most intense phase.

In Soho, the 19th century industrial buildings are converted to upper-income residency, after having passed through a period of occupation by artists. Through this formula, the New York art "scene" established a chic public presence, which then paved the way for permanent occupation by young professionals. The municipality gave its support through an initial lack of enforcement of building codes and other legalities of residential occupation.[15] Now, in the final stage, these constraints are being reintroduced. Elsewhere the municipality perfected the reoccupation process, most notably in Tribeca, the East Village, and now in Brooklyn. But areas outside of Manhattan remain problematic and spotty. For example, the municipality recognizes the danger of letting the loft conversion phenomenon heat up in Brooklyn or Queens to the extent that it did in Soho or Tribeca, in that the lofts still play a critical role in the industrial economy outside of Manhattan.[16]

Mayor Koch's advice that those who cannot afford Manhattan should expect to leave has come to apply to the middle class as well as to the poor; in the other boroughs; Brooklyn especially is experiencing an influx of a young, relatively affluent population fleeing the high rents of Manhattan. Areas of impressive 19th century rowhouses such as Park Slope or Brooklyn Heights have long been redeveloped. Adjacent areas are quickly following. This points to the shortage of middle-income housing in New York City, which ironically, co-exists with the phenomenon of abandonment and destruction, exacerbated by social problems and racial prejudice that makes much of the outer Boroughs inaccessible to the white middle class which is leaving Manhattan. And in the past decade, little housing in this category has been built in the boroughs. The last large, private multifamily building built in Brooklyn was completed 15 years ago.[17] The Department of City Planning is now studying ways to stimulate private housing production in the boroughs,

15) For a documentation of this process in the East Village, see Rosalyn Deutsche and Cara Gendel Ryan, "The Fine Art of Gentrification," *October* 31 (Winter 1984), pp. 91-111.

16) Kirk Johnson, "City Scrutinizing Lofts in Brooklyn," *The New York Times*, (November 18, 1984), sec. 8, p. 6.

17) According to David Van Dor of the Zoning Study Group within the New York City Planning Commission, the last multi-family apartment building in Brooklyn was built 15 years ago at Ocean Avenue and Avenue S, interview with Richard Plunz and David Smiley (November 27, 1984).

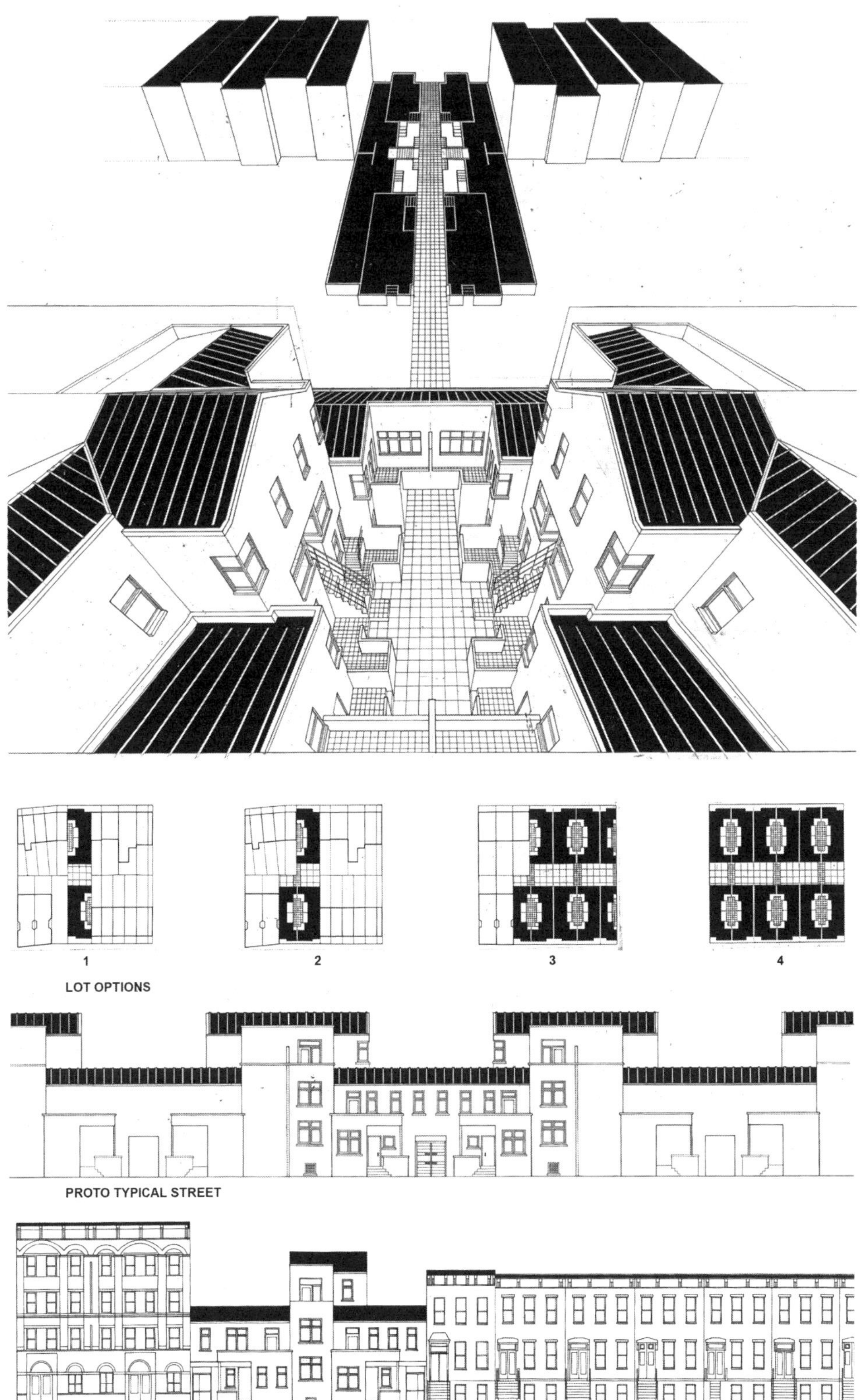
1
2
3
4
LOT OPTIONS
PROTO TYPICAL STREET
EAST 144TH STREET

PLATE I
"Ring Prototypes" New York, New York

1987. Court-type infill design prototypes, South Bronx, for "Vacant Lots" initiative, Architectural League of New York, in collaboration with the New York City Department of Housing Preservation and Development. Columbia GSAPP housing research team.

Proposal for housing infill prototypes on vacant lots in New York City as response to the devastation within New York "Ring." Hybrid housing types challenge the constraints of the traditional New York row house block, reknitting the fabric where partial buildings still remain. A courtyard strategy is applied to six typical site configurations in the Mott Haven neighborhood in the Bronx. Applications can include single- or multiple-lot sites at varying dimensions. Two plan types accommodate lot widths ranging from 25 to 33 feet. Building heights are limited to two or three stories, providing the possibility of less expensive construction than for greater heights. Several of the configurations permit individual ownership of the houses, with flexibility for the provision of attached rental apartments. Another more complex arrangement provides for a communal dwelling or "Great House" for non-nuclear families. In effect, the prototypes were meant to offer a critical alternative to the proliferation of small house typologies encouraged by Section 235 of the National Housing Act and local government.

1987. "Ring Prototypes. Court-type Infill," GSAPP housing research. Richard Plunz, Principal Investigator; Project Team: Stephen Day (M.Arch 1988), John Flynn (M.Arch 1987), Suenn Ho (M.Arch 1988), Nancy Josephson (M.Arch 1988), Mark Rosenbaum (M.Arch 1988), Marcia Smith (M.Arch 1988), Darius Sollohub (M.Arch 1988).

PUBLICATION: Richard Plunz, "'Ring' Prototypes: Courtyard-type Infill," *Vacant Lots*, eds. Carol Willis and Rosalie Genevro, New York: Princeton Architectural Press (1989), pp. 30-31; *Progressive Architecture* 69 (January 1988), p. 37. Also see Richard Plunz Papers, Department of Drawings & Archives, Avery Architectural and Fine Arts Library.

most notably through incentives built into a new zoning law. This law would encourage low- to medium-rise housing of the type which is no longer economically feasible for middle incomes in Manhattan.[18]

As for the specifics of housing typologies in the last decade, it is useful to review the upper- as well as the lower-income opinions, in that these illustrate the spectrum of current practice. By far, the most significant new housing production is for the luxury market, reflecting the drastic reduction in government support for new social housing, which since 1977 has lagged behind private production. Most of the new luxury housing is confined to the mid-section of Manhattan, and involves cooperative ownership, whereby the tenants buy shares in the building corporation from its developer, based on the size and location of the apartment. In addition, they pay a monthly maintenance cost for their apartment. At this point in the economics of luxury housing production in New York, this form of ownership is very lucrative for entrepreneurs, both for new construction and for redevelopment of existing buildings. For the tenants, it provides the possibility of building up equity at such times as now when the market is expanding. The prices of cooperative apartments are still increasing, fueled by a shortage of supply.[19]

The actual apartment design standards of the luxury-level housing are far lower than one might suspect in relation to the cost of the investment. What the tenant buys is the security and prestige of the location and the quality of services within the building—of course, all of this contributes to security of the investment, which in itself is worth the high price. Only 10 years ago, the New York cooperative market was in a severe recession—cooperatives were considered, at best, a risky investment.[20] That situation has changed in the extreme, abetted by the fact that New York real estate has moved definitively into the international arena, making the risk of another period of decline less appreciable.

A Trump Tower penthouse recently sold for $15 million. Business has been so brisk for Donald Trump that he has raised the prices several times in

18) Sandy Hornick, Arne Kotlin, Tony Levy, and David Van Dor, "Quality Housing and Related Zoning Text Amendments," New York City Planning Commission memorandum (April 17, 1985); Alan S. Oser, "Restructuring Zoning to Spur Apartment Construction," *The New York Times* (June 2, 1985), Sec. 8, p. 7.

19) Kirk Johnson, "Pace of Co-Op Conversions Slackening," *The New York Times* (December 2, 1984), Sec. 8, p. 1.

20) The extreme escalation in apartment sales prices in Manhattan co-ops are an indication of this revival. Between 1974 and 1984, the average price per room has increased by more than six times. See Ibid.

the past year or so. The $15 million penthouse was only $10 million a year ago.[21] At the same time, Trump with his lawyer, Roy Cohn, persisted in a legal suit against the municipality, insisting that loopholes in the laws on tax abatements permitted him a $20 million cut in his taxes on the building. The municipality counterclaimed that the abatements were intended to stimulate lower-income housing, rather than luxury housing. In court Trump and Cohn triumphed over the city, to receive the subsidy. Cohn proclaimed that he had provided a "shot in the arm" for the real estate industry.[22] Trump's victory reinforced public perception that the laws really help upper-middle-income housing, in the face of so blatant a violation as the subsidy for Trump's Tower, not to mention indirect subsidy for his purchase of another large parcel under consideration for development of the abandoned railroad yard in the Upper West Side known as the "Lincoln West." The site was recently purchased by Donald Trump for a development intended to rival Battery Park City in scale. He bought it for $95 million, or the cost of a few penthouse apartments in his Trump Tower.[23] Indeed, the question of "blight" remains manifest in many forms, and not just limited to the South Bronx or Central Brooklyn. It is alive and well on Fifth Avenue in Midtown.

21) Tony Schwartz, "The Show Must Go Up," *New York Magazine* (December 24-31, 1984), pp. 48-49.

22) Ultimately the municipality lost its case in court. See Ronald Smothers, "Tax Relief Is Said to Benefit Luxury Housing," *The New York Times* (December 1, 1980), Sec. 2, p. 1; Clyde Haberman, "Ruling Supports Tax Abatement Asked by Trump," *The New York Times* (May 21,1982), p. B3; E. R. Shipp, "City's Denial of a Tax Break to Trump Is Ruled Improper," *The New York Times* (December 15, 1982), p. B3; Sydney H. Schanberg, "Strictly Beau Monde," *The New York Times* (December 18, 1982), p. 27. N.B. Recently it has been revealed that in 1980 a settlement was reached for $1.375 million in class action involving Trump over conditions involving illegal workers in demolition of the Bonwit Teller building, the site of the Trump Tower in Manhattan. See Charles V. Bagli, "Trump Paid $1 Million in a Labor Settlement Over Signature Tower," *The New York Times* (November 28, 2017), p. A17.

23) Martin Gottlieb, "Trump Set to Buy Site of Lincoln West Project," *The New York Times* (December 1, 1984), p. 1. Donald Trump has been pleased with his Lincoln West negotiation, pointing out the low cost of the 150 acres, in comparison to the selling price of a single penthouse apartment in his Trump Tower. See Tony Schwartz, "The Show Must Go Up," *New York Magazine* (December 24-31, 1984), pp. 48-49. "World Class Guy" for example, was a term used by Donald Trump to describe the ideal architect for his Lincoln West project. That architect turned out to be Helmut Jahn of Murphy/Jahn. See Martin Gottlieb, "Trump Set to Buy Lincoln West Site," *The New York Times* (December 1, 1984), p. 1; and "An Architect Is Named for Trump City," *The New York Times* (January 23, 1985), p. B3.

1989 "DIAGONAL'S SEGMENTS"

Excerpted from "La Diagonal, Segmenti. Diagonal's Segments," *Lotus International* 64 (1989), pp. 98-107.

An invited entry to the competition "Housing and the City" sponsored by the Collegi d'Arquitectes de Catalunya and the Quaderns d'Arquitectura i Urbanisme provided a unique opportunity for research by a team from Columbia University. The competition brief required completion of the Avinguda Diagonal, which was an integral part of Ildefons Cerdà's original Ensanche plan of 1859, but was never implemented in the Poblenou quarter. This section of the Diagonal links the Placa de les Glòries to the west with the seaside at the east. At the center is the village of Poblenou, a 19th century industrial settlement since absorbed into the fabric of the city. Most of the original industrial activity is now marginal, and with the exception of only a few buildings, the path of the Diagonal has been cleared. The intimate village character of Poblenou remains, however, in spite of recent transformations, and its industrial tradition continues in the form of many small-scale artisan and retail activities. The competition brief proposed further consolidation of the Poblenou quarter with the city through development of new housing, using the completion of the Diagonal as a catalyst for implementation. More generally, the competition also sought to explore the issue of housing as an element that goes toward forming the urban landscape... in the face of dynamics that seem to restrict the city to the role of accumulating services.

The most significant way that our proposal has engaged this question is at the conceptual level, involving the qualitative aspects of infrastructure. It raises the question of exactly how a "plan" is to be generated beyond normative models of movement and context. At this level, we have proposed that the character of the infrastructure cannot be generated simply through historical memory; or through rationalized movement systems and typing of buildings; or even through the sensitive placing of monuments. We have argued that the actual fabric of the housing is at least as important in terms of determining the real quality of the city. We sought a certain ambiguity between the new housing and the existing Poblenou quarter such that each could define the other, rather than superimposing a simplistic elaboration of *a priori* models.

The quality of cities is always greatly indebted to the character of their housing fabric, and this is especially true in the case of Barcelona. The extraordinarily powerful poetry of the Ensanche is derived from the Cerdà plan conception. However, it is also a consequence of the fit between the plan and the nature of housing within, at once constrained and liberated by the conventions of market mechanisms, with this infinite variation tamed by the forces of building economics and a particularly strong cultural conception of what Louis Wirth called "urbanism as a way of life." In our cities something of this spirit has been lost in the massive projects of recent decades. In general, the new urban fabric is becoming universalized in an uninteresting way, and more importantly, in a way that can be very destructive to cultural sensibilities that should be preserved. Barcelona has much to lose in this tendency.

At the Poblenou, in particular, we felt that the fabric of the housing was a critical issue, within the overall complexion of the city. The Poblenou is unique within the Ensanche, and we felt that it should remain unique, and as a predominantly residential quarter of the city. In spite of the existence of the Diagonal, there seems to be no gathering of extraordinary forces which would demand creation of a monumental scale and fabric. Perhaps this scale should be encouraged elsewhere in Barcelona, but the real strength of the Poblenou is that it is quiet. We did not want to disrupt the normative qualities of a place where daily life goes on, and, in this respect, the Poblenou has an important history. We sought to enrich the possibilities of its daily life through the configuration of the housing, including the reintegration of workplace such as the community once maintained. The character of the entire Diagonal, then, moves from the open vertical city of the Zona Universitària on the west; to the dense traditional perimeter blocks of the typical Cerdà gridiron; to the new horizontal city of Poblenou; and eastward to the Mediterranean.

The proposal is obviously not complete in any sense, but we sought to present a concrete image of the possibilities of our thinking. The method which we pursued is consciously developed. The site was divided into six relatively arbitrary segments, partly derived from the geography of the area, and partly from the composition of the study team. In this, we were fortunate that the team was well-matched to the site. When we say that the segments were "arbitrary," we mean in the positive sense that we did not want to prematurely bias our starting point with some quickly conceived notions of infrastructure and parceling. We wanted to find as "neutral" a beginning as possible. We assumed that the boundaries we chose could be adjusted,

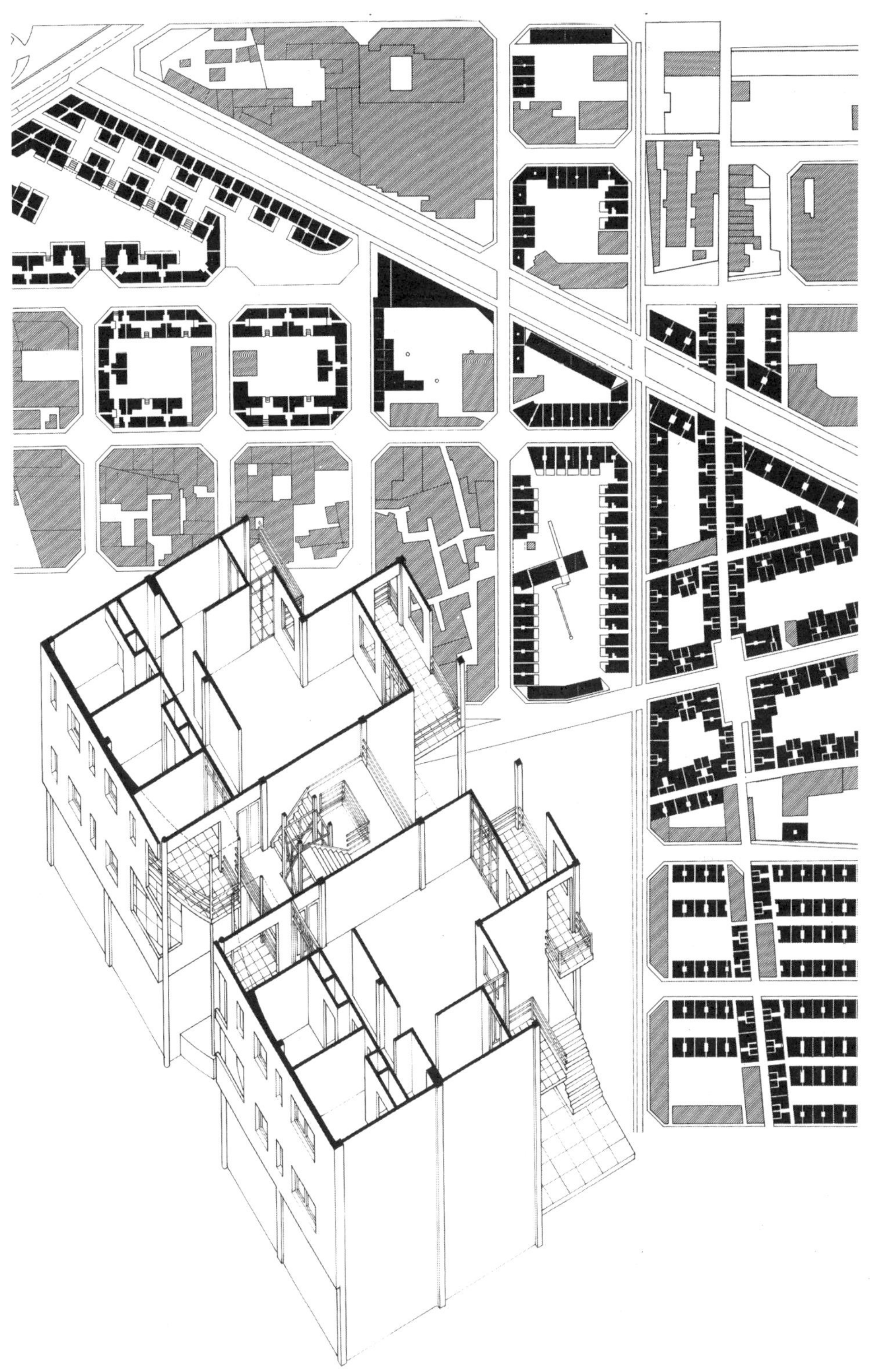

PLATE J+K
"Segmentary Urbanism" Barcelona, Spain

1988. Invited entry to "Housing and the City" initiative, Collegi d'Arquitectes de Catalunya and the Quaderns d'Arquitectura i Urbanisme. Columbia GSAPP architecture studio, Fall Semester.

Proposal for the completion of the Avinguda Diagonal, an integral part of the original Ensanche plan of Ildefons Cerdà (1859) but never implemented in the Poblenou quarter. The site strategy transcends simple rationalization of movement systems and monumental markers to include the actual fabrics of the housing as infrastructure. The intimate village character of Poblenou is reinforced, with housing as an element that goes toward forming the urban landscape in the face of dynamics that seem to restrict the city to the role of accumulating services. A certain ambiguity is sought between the new housing and the existing Poblenou quarter such that each could redefine the other, rather than a superimposition of *a priori* models. The site is divided into six parcels, partly derived from the geography of the area and "arbitrary" in the positive sense of finding as "neutral" a beginning as possible. In a second iteration, the initial proposal parcels could be adjusted or even radically changed after a systematic evaluation process, as an alternative to a top-down master plan.

1988. "Barcelona Poble Nou Segments," Columbia GSAPP architecture studio, Fall Semester. Faculty: Richard Plunz; Projects shown: Holly Hollmeyer (M.Arch 1990), Jun Sung Kim (M.Arch 1990), Luis Estrada (M.Arch 1992), Marisa Oliver (M.Arch 1990); Other project team: Leslie McBride (M.Arch 1990), Stella Zavrou (M.Arch 1990), Joel Towers (M.Arch 1990), Henry Urbach (M.Arch 1990), Meta Brunzema (M.Arch 1990), Suzanne Niego (M.Arch 1990), Ethan Nelson (M.Arch 1990), Emily Roth (M.Arch 1990), Jun Sung Kim (M.Arch 1990). Graphic reconfiguration: Isaac Warshauer (M.Arch 2019), Lucy Navarro (M.Arch 2020).

PUBLICATION: "La Diagonal, Segmenti. Diagonal's Segments," *Lotus International* 64 (1989), pp. 98-107. Also see Richard Plunz Papers, Department of Drawings & Archives, Avery Architectural and Fine Arts Library.

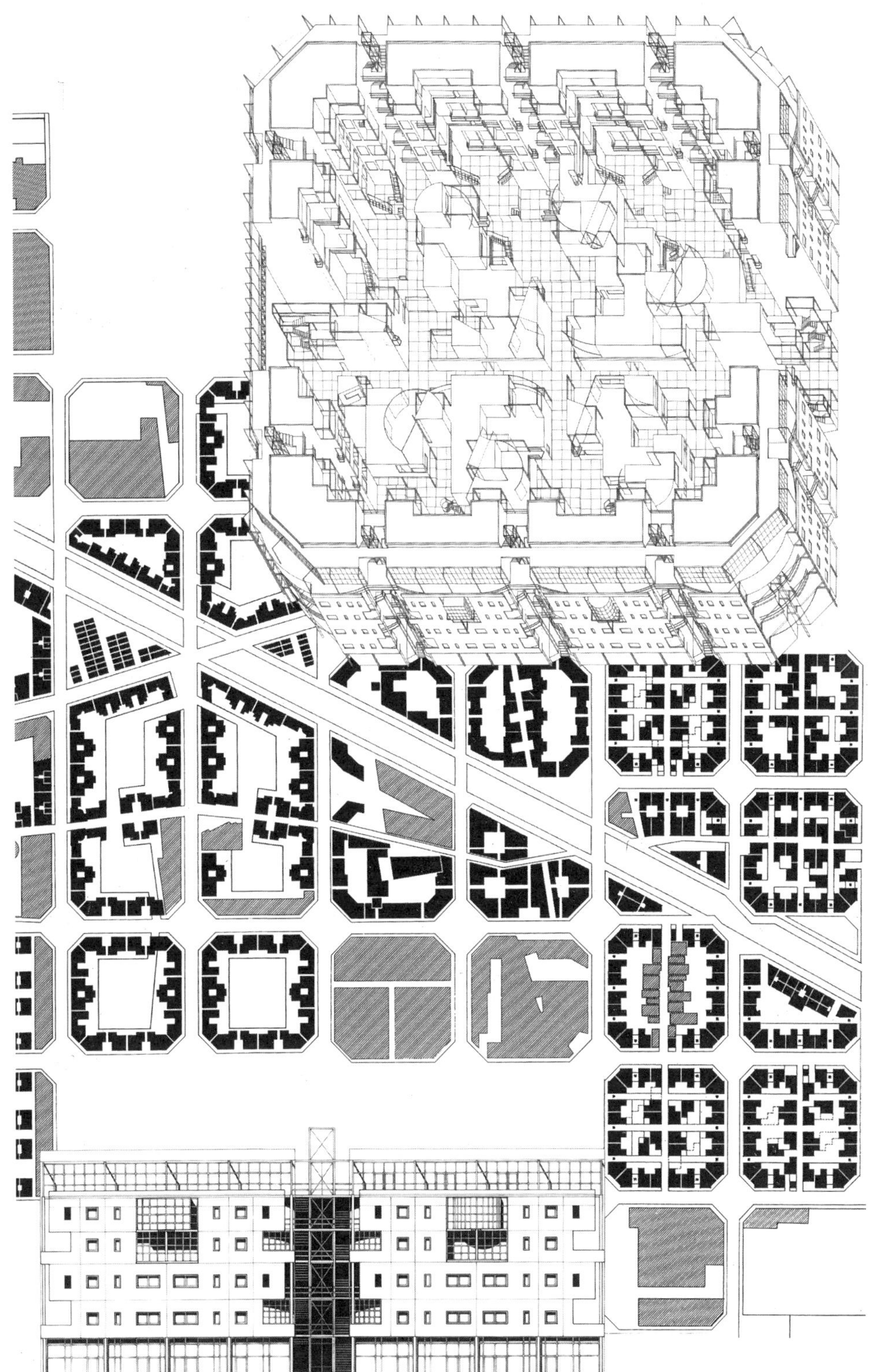

perhaps even changed radically in a second design phase after a systematic evaluation of what we have already completed.

The segments were purposely made to embrace the Diagonal, rather than following its tendency to cut the fabric. It was seen as an urban "room," with multiple readings and functions. It is a linear park and a variant on the *Rambla*, with its character changing emphasis as it moves through each "segment," the variation defined by changes in the housing types as well as the functions along the way. While our proposal includes the possibility of elaborate public and semi-public parks and gardens, the large park of the original Ensanche plan was eliminated. This is not to say that large parks are not needed elsewhere in the city, but at Poblenou we felt that sufficient such space was already planned along the seashore within walking distance of the entire site. Apart from this obvious consideration, we also resisted the temptation to over-scale public open space for another reason: we felt it to be important to integrate open space more intimately with the housing fabric, such that the possibilities for innovation in the form of the housing itself could be enhanced. Most apartments have a private outdoor space and access to a shared semi-private space within several minutes' walk. Our exploration, therefore, was an attempt to find alternatives to what we saw as problematic conditions within much recent housing found in the city. One is the overbuilding within the existing Ensanche blocks, using tall buildings in situations which can only function well for the conventions of lower fabric. In this case, however, at least the street remains intact. Another more pervasive situation involves the isolated high housing block set in minimal open space such that no obvious benefit is obtained, while the traditional fabric of the city is eroded.

As a team, when we visited the site, we were quite taken by the intelligence of the critique of the new housing which was given by some of the residents of Poblenou. There was nothing scientific about this investigation, but we tended to meet people who lived in the older housing, which is more conducive to contact with the street. Some of that housing was still extremely good, and they knew it. They recognized the need for housing in Barcelona, but a large part of their opposition to the Diagonal project was focused on a fear of what the new housing would be; that is over-scaled blocks with no contact with the ground, etc. These considerations are hard to refute, and, as architects, we have an obligation to explore alternatives.

Our investigation, then, focused on housing types that could address some of these concerns. No building proposed is more than eight stories;

most are five or six and some only three. We followed the density norms which have been proposed for the site (these figures include streets and other public space): 90 dwellings/hectare; 1.2 floor area ratio; and 6,000 dwellings. In fact, these constraints were quite low, and our proposal increased the scale to 8,150 dwellings. It could easily be denser still, and a second development phase would surely reflect this possibility. But the larger point is that the standards already proposed by the City of Barcelona for the Diagonal development are so advantageous—so conducive to design innovation—that it would be tragic for this opportunity to be lost to the inertia of convenient conventions, which have no real meaning for the specifics of this particular context.

Our architectural resolution avoided the trap of linear thinking - that is, that one must begin with abstract rules and end up with detailed buildings, from the general to the particular. The opposite way is equally valid—one can begin with the particular and end with the general. Our overall "plan" at the end of this process is a three-dimensional framework of parceling, building bulk, configurations of movement and use, and the like. This framework evolved out of the smallest detail as well as the largest detail.

As the spirit of this investigation began to clarify itself, along with its implications for a new kind of urbanism of accumulation rather than reduction, the importance of the consideration of historical memory took shape. The rich texture of our proposal could be invented only through a kind of anthropological understanding of the historical development of Poblenou, which places this new intervention as one more step in a long evolution. The richness of possibilities inherent to the original village structure; to the Ensanche gridiron; and finally to the Diagonal itself, were represented without the recognition of memory. Frequently, new interventions lack this level of invention, and today it seems especially true that the spatial significance of the original Ensanche has sometimes been rendered meaningless through improper weakening of the gridiron. At times, the Ensanche loses its identity altogether. The "pre-grid," "grid," and "diagonal" were important geometries to overlay and understand; but for our investigation the most crucial question was the compositional means—that is, how to make the housing work rationally in relation to these geometric forces. This consideration engages the question of "housing types." Our choices have been influenced by historical memory in the sense that they attempt to respect a certain "culture of housing" in Barcelona. Diversity is reinforced through the incorporation of a number of serviceable existing structures, whose configuration may be a starting point for new formal delineation. The housing types are influenced by adjacencies such as existing streets and buildings. At the scale of the individual apartment, the same variety is foreseen, both in size and amenity. And this variation is also produced in part in response to the conditions of the site itself.

Our most strongly felt goal was to provide a holistic vision of a rather specific nature at Poblenou while offering a clear alternative to the standard residential development practice that already exists in the city. We presented not only a design process but a development process. Too frequently these two realms are isolated from each other: a "plan" is made and then "implementation" is begun, which becomes at odds with the plan. One can foresee a much more integrated process in which many architects rather than one are merging into a plan and several developers are merging into implementation—an organic process that can be no less than the way cities have always been built, that is, incrementally. It has been in the modern period, with the increasingly unified capitalization of projects, that the unitary scale of urbanists' thinking has become not just ineffectual but dangerous in its side effects. In this consideration, we attempted to point toward an alternative, or at the very least, to put forward a provocation for a better understanding of this Diagonal initiative.

1990 "CRANE URBANISM"

From the report "Proposal for Redevelopment of the Cité du 5 Juillet, Bab Ezzouar, Algiers," with Tahari Mohamed Lamine, Rafiq A. Malik, Paul Vermeulen. International Workshop "Housing Strategies and Urban Coherence," United Nations Center for Human Settlements and Katholieke Universiteit Leuven Post Graduate Center Human Settlements, Algiers, December 1-12, 1990.

The eastward displacement of the city of Algiers, along the bay, started as early as before independence in 1962 with the building of collective housing on some colonial agricultural estates, following the Constantine Plan. The flat land facilitated the deployment of heavy prefabricated building systems, at the time in an experimental phase of development and symbolic of progressive ideals in housing production. Eastward development remained a basic principle of the post-independence city plan by Oscar Niemeyer, and of the consecutive official plans in the 1960s and '70s. The remaining fertile farmland is still a valuable resource today, interspersed with large housing estates. A pattern exists of isolated pieces: collective housing estates and clusters of private allotments, including industrial and educational facilities together with the former colonial settlements.

A result of Niemeyer's involvement in Algiers was the construction of the University of Science and Technology—Houari Boumediene (USTHB), designed by the architect himself. Later, the municipality of Bab Ezzouar was planned as an "urban support" for the university. Another proposal resulting in an eastward displacement for Algiers was the relocation of the main railway station from the historical center to Bab Ezzouar, near the Constantine railway junction. In Niemeyer's plan, this position, approximately in the middle of the bay, was to be at the new center of the capital. Today, the eastward development is being challenged by alternative planning proposals and sensitivities, allowing for the preservation of the old city center's importance. The project for relocation of the railway station still persists, however, as a remnant of previous planning ideals.

The municipality of Bab Ezzouar is characterized by a network of traffic arteries, which separate and isolate large housing estates as "islands" of habitation within a "sea" of traffic, agricultural, and residual space.

Currently, there are approximately 5,000 dwellings. Any further development should address the question of connecting these islands, considering which of the divides bridge "archipelagos" and which are irreversible. For example, the Autoroute de l'Est, with its green corridor, is a major east-west divide that does not allow any urban continuity. It cuts Bab Ezzouar into two discontinuous sectors: an irreversible condition, which must be accepted in any redevelopment scheme. This reality dictates the logic of defining the northern half of Bab Ezzouar in relation to the sea resort of Bordj El Kiffan. The southern half, which includes the university, can be considered another entity. Our proposal concentrates on the southern sector and assumes that the green corridor separating it from the Autoroute de l'Est is to be maintained as a boundary. The north-south corridor of the major airport Autoroute is also an obvious divide. In contrast, several other north-south roadways are seen as connective arteries. The road along the east side of the university campus has the potential to become an urban boulevard, and the road separating the Cité du 5 Juillet and the Cité des 2025 Logements could logically become a street.

The southern sector of Bab Ezzouar comprises eight or more built-up islands within the sea of roads and residual space. These include the university, the original Cité estates, and several more recent operations, which attempt to use the private marketplace to improve on the earlier projects. While these recent projects have increased the quality of the individual dwellings, the old mistakes remain in relation to site planning, and new islands bear no attempt to bridge to the older islands. A new language of infill building is needed that can address the question of the identity and continuity of the overall sector. Perhaps the one exception could be the university, which due to the extremely low proportion of building in combination with the rather rigid nature of its physical plan, may be best left untouched as a "Central Park," surrounded by dense walls of buildings along its motorway edges. This pattern is prefigured by the boulevard along the northern edge of the campus, already densely built, thus making a fairly high frontage overlooking the vast, impressive emptiness of the campus. Whatever other architectural value one may attribute to Niemeyer's campus plan, the stretched, horizontal buildings set against a dramatic mountainous background do offer a striking image. It may be the only spot in the area where some relationship between buildings and landscape is felt. When contrasted with a dense fabric, this scenery may gain urban significance.

Of the several Cité estates within the southern sector of Bab Ezzouar, the Cité du 5 Juillet is one of the most problematic from a design point of view.

The housing is uniform, constructed with a Soviet prefabrication system.[1] The site composition is an obvious example of "design by crane," which is to say that the public space is generated by the radius of the construction cranes, which were used to assemble the prefabricated buildings. The entire composition is surrounded by a belt of fallow land. Wind and dust blow through the spaces with scant protection gained from the loose configuration of buildings. Through the center of the site, a curvilinear road spanning east to west has gradually developed into a central spine with some shops and other community uses. Recently, a public bath and a mosque have been added along the road, toward the center. Local circulation throughout the project is generally confused and disorienting, with little possibility to move efficiently from one area to another caused by the difficulty in differentiating between the various spaces.

The prefabricated housing consists of approximately 175 slab segments comprising almost entirely five-story walk-ups, with the exception of a few three-story sections. The segments are joined linearly in vaguely spatial gestures, but the position of the buildings is largely indifferent to the road system and, more generally, to the open spaces. Points of spatial interest do arise at the narrow pedestrian corridors in between perpendicular buildings. A few large, privately-owned extended-family houses with workshops underneath are under construction behind the apartment slabs near the central spine. This new type of building responds to totally different space standards and even, arguably, to a different society. It is introduced without any planning concerns and hardly brings any differentiation within the coarse image of the estate. Both types of housing coexist but exhibit no physical relationship. Due to the indifference of buildings to roads, privacy problems occur at the ground-floor apartments. Sometimes these have been protected against visual intrusion with a "wall" of vegetation, but these private "gardens" are inaccessible from the interiors of the apartments, making them rather disjointed in their use. All buildings have cellars, most of which are filled with foul water springing up from the swampy soil. Residents complain of the smell and health hazards from the mosquito infestation, not to mention the general nuisance and danger, especially to children.

1) N.B., references to the details of the system have kindly been shared by Olga Aleksakova of Buromoscow, and Adjunct Assistant Professor at Columbia GSAPP. Details of the panel assembly are found in, <http://pstu.ru/files/file/adm/fakultety/kaloshina_proektirovanie_ustanovki_montazhnyh_kranov.pdf>.
The crane itself was СБК-1 with different modifications, a copy of a German WOLFF. See <http://www.techstory.ru/krans/bash/sbk1.htm>.

The proposal for redevelopment of the Cité du 5 Juillet concentrates on four critical concerns: 1) valuable but derelict land at the circumference of the Cité adjoining the boundary roads; 2) ill-defined public spaces; 3) incoherent ground-level pedestrian and vehicular circulation; and 4) substandard hygienic and privacy conditions of the ground floor dwellings. The proposal envisions that the sea of empty land between the boundary roads and the Cité will be infilled with a dense fabric of low-rise houses penetrated by entry "gateways" to the interior. This new fabric allows considerable variation within its loose gridiron organization. At the outer edges, i.e., on the major roads, houses may have shops or workshops. Towards the interior, single-story and two-story houses are intermingled. The houses have inner private courtyards, and their entrances are organized around small public squares. Other typological and architectural features such as extensive balconies, canopies, and roof terraces are drawn from the contemporary vernacular. At the interior, additional apartment slabs complete the existing Cité. They clarify the articulation of the open spaces and place new long continuous building as a backdrop to the ragged rhythm of the existing slabs. The scale of the large public spaces in between the slabs is principally maintained. Contrasted to the network of small squares in the surrounding low-rise fabric, they acquire new significance.

The existing configuration of circulation within the Cité is reorganized. A new gridiron of pedestrian and vehicular streets is cut through the slabs by removing some ground level apartments. In this way, the discontinuous and haphazard existing circulation is opened up in order to give more overall spatial and social identity to the place. In functional terms, movement is facilitated rather than impeded. This new internal circulation is linked to entry gateways of the new low-rise perimeter. There is, in this strategy, a systematic collision and intermingling of both systems: of the existing slab grid with the new low-rise grid. This confrontation becomes the catalyst for rebuilding. At the scale of the dwelling, all ground-floor apartments are redesigned to properly link with adjacent outdoor space. This reconstruction is to be coordinated with rectifying the cellar-flooding problem. In some cases, the ground-floor dwellings are extended into the low-rise grid and are transformed into courtyard houses woven within the slab. At the other side of the slabs, i.e., into the large public spaces inside the Cité, ground floors are occasionally extended to accommodate social facilities of a domestic character: nursery, launderette, party room, etc. Furthermore, the roofs of the slabs are appropriated as additional private outdoor spaces. The pathways of the low-rise grid connect with the narrow corridors in between the slabs or, alternately, new gateways piercing the slabs are provided when rebuilding the ground floors.

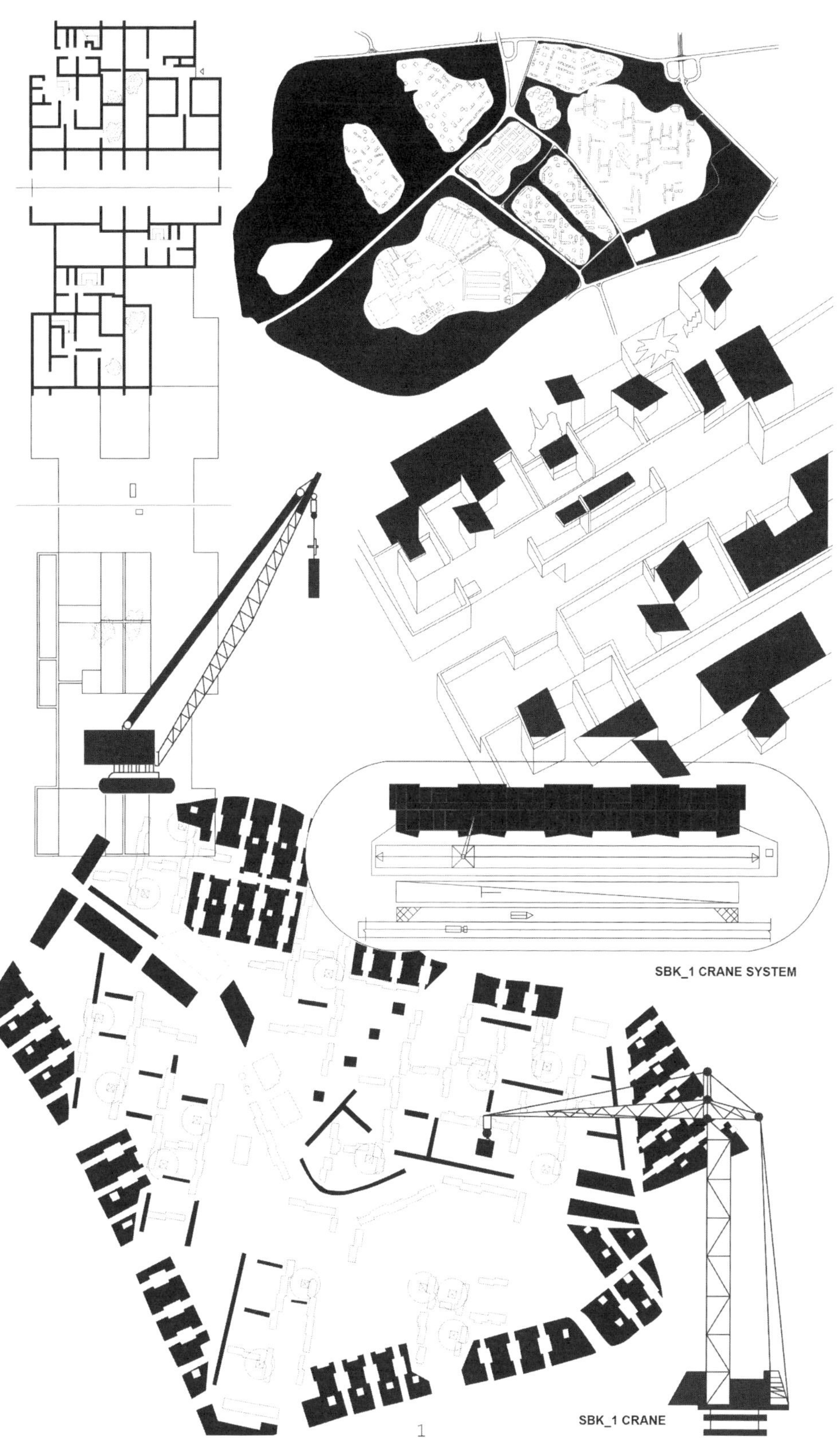
SBK_1 CRANE SYSTEM
SBK_1 CRANE
1

PLATE L

“Crane Urbanism” Bab Ezzouar, Algiers

1990. Proposal for densification of El Bab Ezzouar, Algiers. International Workshop on Housing Strategies and Urban Coherence Algiers, organized by the Post Graduate Center for Human Settlements at the Katholieke Universiteit Leuven with the United Nations Center for Human Settlements..

Proposal for site densification of the Cité du 5 Juillet housing in the Algiers satellite town of Bab Ezzouar to reconfigure a linear prefabricated panel system developed in the Soviet Union and built in the 1970s. The existing public space was organized around the placement of СБК-1 cranes or equivalent in order to produce the most efficient assembly operations. In consideration of the unease provoked by the harsh logic of the site plan, the proposal argues that remediation requires a radical redesign centered on four considerations: 1) valuable but derelict land at the circumference of the estate adjoining the boundary roads; 2) ill-defined public spaces, 3) incoherence of the ground-level pedestrian and vehicular circulation; and 4) substandard hygienic and privacy conditions of the ground floor dwellings. The linear configuration of the housing slabs is countered with new courtyard housing that defines the precincts while better responding to the climate and local building traditions. This new “infill” language addresses the question of the identity and continuity of the overall sector. The collision of the existing slab grid and the new low-rise grid emerges as the most interesting of spaces.

1990. “Algiers Bab Ezzouar Proposal,” United Nations Centre for Human Settlements, Katholieke Universiteit Leuven Post Graduate Centre Human Settlements. Project Team: Richard Plunz, with Mohamed Lamine Tahari, Rafiq A. Malik, Paul Vermeulen. Graphic reconfiguration: Maria Isabel Carrasco (MSAUD 2018), Lucy Navarro (M.Arch 2020).

PUBLICATION: “Atelier Bab Ezzouar / Workshop,” *Alger 1990. International Workshop on Housing Strategies and Urban Coherence*, eds. Han Verschure and André Loeckx, Leuven: Post Graduate Centre Human Settlements, Katholieke University Leuven (July 1991), pp. 46-47. Also see Richard Plunz Papers, Department of Drawings & Archives, Avery Architectural and Fine Arts Library.

The edges of the Cité are given absolute definition with the wall of lowrise houses. The wall is double-sided: from the outside, it gives the boundary roads a coherent street front; from the inside, the encircling of the Cité enhances its integrity as a single place. The resulting configuration does not correspond with conventional images of urbanity. The uncompromising fabric provided by crane design is transformed into a new urbanism, through aggressive development of the leftover spaces that the crane could not reach. Whether this approach could be applied to other inhabited islands nearby is, to a large extent, still an open question. But in any event, the clearly articulated edges of the new Cité du 5 Juillet can be a stimulus and an obvious invitation to the vacant spaces on the other side of the roads.

During seminar discussions, this proposal was met with two criticisms of an ideological nature: 1) it failed to address technical matters such as condition of the infrastructure and financing of the operation, which should be settled before moving to the level of architectural ideas; and 2) the architectural proposition should be the direct outcome of a social survey of the present inhabitants. This design team, to the contrary, felt that this criticism, while claiming to be "realistic," tends to defend the status quo, which, as far as Bab Ezzouar is concerned, is without vindication. An approach is needed that is aggressively resistant to the status quo. Any proposal for this context cannot be the mere sum of technical, economic, political, or social data. In this case, an aggressive architecture must control the technical means. Can "realism" exclude the imagination? Should architects not defend themselves in assessing the quality of space as economists can defend numbers? If it is clear that environments like the one under study have come about without any concern for spatial quality, should architects today abdicate once more? A consensus emerged that the unease provoked by the harsh logic of such environments cannot be met with architectural timidity.

1991 "BETWEEN EDGE AND FABRIC"

"Battery Park City. Between Edge and Fabric," in *Between Edge and Fabric: Battery Park City*, ed. Roy Strickland, New York: Columbia University Graduate School of Architecture, Planning and Preservation (1991), pp. 2-7.

Since 1962, five proposals have been advanced for the Battery Park City landfill. At first glance, the wide divergence in these schemes appears to be a simple reflection of the considerable volatility in architectural design ideals, in so far as urbanism is concerned during the last three decades. But, under the surface, they are also an interesting commentary on the lack of a clear conceptual ideal about how the edge of Manhattan might be configured in the approaching era of reformulation. What makes the issue so interesting is that it is a structural one, at the heart of the identity of the city and its culture. Involved is how New Yorkers express themselves through the physical artifact, which is the centerpiece of their environment. This self-image appears to be in transformation, and the redevelopment of the city's water edges is an important symptom of the change.

Only once before in the city's history did an equivalent transformation occur. An indication of this earlier transition can be found in the iconographic views that New Yorkers have used to represent their environment, contrasted in the first and second half of the 19th century. In the period before mid-19th century, a favorite published image was the view from the water, with a foreground of ships and masts dwarfing an inconsequential built fabric behind. This formula changes in the following decades, with representation shifting from inside out, with buildings and fabric dominating the edge in spite of the economic importance of the port. The views from the tall building, imagined or real, across a vast hive of humanity, became the favored icon. This new generation of self-image said much about how New Yorkers interpreted their environment; and became the ideal to which the privileged culture of the city aspired. The upper-middle class embraced the high building as a dense living environment like no other urban culture, and they still do.

It is often remarked by inhabitants and visitors alike that New York does not seem to be a city on water. From the point-of-view of its residential fabric, it is not. There was never the equivalent of the great houses of the Bosporus in Istanbul, or of the Canal Grande in Venice, or the Groenerei in Brugges. The difference is that New York's metropolitan formation (from 1850 onward) was as a modern port with modern industry, which completely usurped use of the waterfront. In the whole scheme of things, all other development was secondary. And so, it came to be, for example, that Manhattan was ringed by piers, industrial building, and rail connections, with the residential development toward the center.

Early on, the planning of Central Park reflected this condition. It was set aside after 1850, just as industrialization was coming into full force. The coincidence is significant. Central Park could only be implemented on such a grand scale because the land was basically worthless, in comparison to the valuable waterfront. Of course, the initiative of Central Park was also related to the urban parks movement and to the question of the general malaise that surrounded urban industrialization within United States culture. But Central Park was also a real estate operation, which sought to give value to "worthless" land through creating a unique public amenity that could attract luxury private development. Beginning in 1857, Central Park was transformed overnight by Olmsted from squatter settlements to a residential showplace with a thinly disguised objective of making Fifth Avenue into the most elite address in Manhattan, and by consequence in the nation. The strategy worked. It has been repeated elsewhere, and it is still with us, now at the water's edge. But Central Park was more powerful than anything that followed.

With the implantation of Central Park, the morphology of modern Manhattan was firmly established: that of a luxurious center and of a marginal periphery in terms of residential real estate, and the opposite in terms of commercial and industrial property. In the Manhattan psyche, Central Park became "waterfront," a kind of "green" sea. Bourgeois aspirations placed Manhattan on a park, rather than in the sea. Water was its lifeblood, but not its soul. This centrical organization is proving very difficult to transform. Even as recently as the Moses era, the same pattern held, in spite of waterfront development. The edge of Manhattan came to be dominated by highways instead of piers, and marginalization remained. By and large, this pattern has remained, with few exceptions. It has only been in recent decades, in the transition to a post-industrial economy, that this pattern has begun to shift. But the new displacement is not without its perplexities in so far as the character of the new residential fabric is concerned, and there is no culture of living on water to turn to. In many ways, a large part of the identity of any city lies within its residential fabric, rather than its monuments. When the basic premises of its fabric shift, uncertainties ensue. The Battery Park City experiment is interesting for its confrontation with this dilemma.

To be sure, by now there have been a number of waterfront precedents for residential development. Among the earliest was the Riverside Park development in the 1890s, which fueled the growth of the Upper West Side. It was not a redevelopment project in the sense that the site supported only marginal uses prior. It needed the rationale of water, although the park was cut off from actual contact by the West Side rail line. It was a precursor to recent thinking on waterfront development in the sense that it was used to establish luxury residential fabric, following the logic of marketplace and geography. But the fabric was a wall of housing against the park rather than a more integral combination of housing, park, and water. It functioned on the Central Park model, yet it could not supplant Central Park. It gives evidence that there cannot be an equivalence between the center and the periphery. Today, the strategy persists to make the water edge the soul of the island (or at least to develop it to upscale middle-income pretentions), but the question is the nature of a hierarchy, rather than an equivalence with the center.

The evolution of a residential ideal at the water's edge continued between the 1930s and the 1960s, when Manhattan's water edges were the depository of social housing: this was, of course, during the de-urbanization period when New York as a residential environment was generally devalued by the culture at large, and low incomes and water could mix. No one else claimed the waterfront. Beginning with the Harlem River Houses, completed in 1937, there was an interesting succession of waterfront projects subsidized as social housing. All exhibit in their own ways the problems of integration of housing and water edge. Harlem River Houses, for example, had a riverfront playground, at least until Robert Moses' completion of the East River Drive in 1940, which cut the project off from the water edge. Unfortunately, this was a generic problem created by Moses' new roads, which cut the island off from its water edge. On the Lower East Side, a number of social housing projects were completed along the East River by the 1960s, adjoining Moses' East River Park, all encountering the same problem of the roadway.

By the 1970s, milestone projects such as Riverbend and 1199 Plaza in East Harlem along the Harlem River were completed, ranking among the best subsidized housing to be built in New York City. But these, of course, had to accommodate the East River Drive, which cut them off from direct river access. With the completion of Waterside further south, however, an attempt was made to engage the roadway, while building on pylons over the water. The pedestrian bridges of Battery Park City did not manage to further resolve the problem of the roadway—in this case, the West Side Highway cuts it off from the rest of Lower Manhattan. Only in the area of the Upper East Side from Carl Schurz Park southward, an enclave of some of the most expensive housing in the city, did Moses make a substantial effort to integrate the housing, road, and water edge through a series of cantilevers covering the roadway.

The evolution of proposals for Battery Park City reveals an ambiguity of conviction. The earliest plan of 1962 placed freestanding towers on a platform-like configuration of open space, which still attempted to maintain some commercial maritime uses. The model was the *Ville Radieuse*, which continued in the next proposal of 1966. A 1969 scheme moderated the severity of the first two with a more variegated and continuous massing: a "village" with a touch of New Brutalism. In 1975, the next approach retreated slightly, combining the sensibilities from all of the previous schemes. All of these proposals were estranged in both physical and cultural terms from dominant upper-middle-income housing ideals of Manhattanites. Their image spoke of "social housing" rather than social aspiration, and one can well imagine the confusion that they all presented, at least in terms of marketing.

The premise of the Battery Park City plan as implemented is obvious: it is an extension of the gridded Manhattan fabric; no more and no less, with an elaborate public edge at the water. It is intended to combine the best of the two worlds: the traditional New York apartment house of the city's most affluent period with the amenity of the water, always present but heretofore not integrated. This approach seemed to represent a secure solution after several decades of more radical readings of the problem: the gridiron as a primary instrument of continuity, infilled with a simulacrum of the time-proven fabric of Manhattan's best residential areas.

It is an approach that has proven to be prudent and efficacious: a tasteful reproduction of fabric that occurred elsewhere on the island in a different time and through different means. But reproduction is not a simple matter. The *ad hoc* spontaneity of the great building booms along Park Avenue, Central Park West, or West End Avenue had to be capsulated into the constraints of the late-20th century economy, albeit with subsidies.

It was done with a certain aplomb, but fraught with angst, official and unofficial, as the northern phase of building nears. The "triumph of urban design," as the public space has been called, has not produced an equivalent triumph of fabric, in so far as the housing is concerned. The apartments are far smaller than what exists all over the Upper West Side. The problem can be dismissed as economic, but in this context, with the subsidies which were present, it is a substantial question. Perhaps there was too much subsidy in the realm of public space and too little in the realm of the residential space. The subsidy question is crucial in relation to the fabric. The space dilemma can be seen as a predictable consequence of the attempt to reproduce a "marketplace" fabric in an era when the marketplace cannot produce large apartments.

But the question does not end here. Even had larger apartments been realized, the insistence on a 19th-century sensibility could only lead to certain 19th-century problems in terms of density and coverage. Ironically, the characteristic landlocked Manhattan fabric is placed on a spectacular water edge, to which it has difficulty responding. There is little integration. Simultaneously, the public, commercial, and civic amenities, which come so easily with the density of the center, cannot be easily reproduced, if at all, at the edge. It is a centrical fabric placed on the edge, without an edge, and without the amenity of the center. Some of the culprits in this puzzle are easy to know. The die was cast long ago: isolation by virtue of the edge location, enforced by the road. Chances are that these problems will not be substantially overcome. But once fully understood, a better conceptual framework for an edge may be forthcoming. Saturating the edge with public uses was properly resisted. The edge cannot compete with the center. There have been many proposals: in 1975, a convention center; in 1978, a heliport; in 1981, an amphitheater for performing arts; in 1987, a visitor center, a ferry terminal, and a large office tower; in 1988, an arts center.

The World Financial Center was the one that stuck, probably appropriately. Manhattan's edges are its "suburbs." Battery Park City seems destined to follow this mode: a "suburban" edge for Manhattan, and a target for suburbanites from further out, who want a reduced version of what the interior of Manhattan is, and the pleasures of a two-minute walk to water. The isolation may be the most desired attribute. The price may be a sacrifice in living space: the subsidized apartment of an upper-middle-class family in Battery Park City may have to be smaller than the subsidized house of a lower-middle-class family in the South Bronx or Central Brooklyn.

But this also may be too easy. Can the city afford the segregation? The real question is that of the prototype. What will happen with the next big pieces of edge: for example, the 16th Street yards on the West Side; or all of the old Westway edge; or even Hunters Point in Queens, which seems to be proceeding along the Battery Park City model? There will be a lapse before these projects are completed, and one hopes with uncertainty about what form they will take. The next phase of Battery Park City can be a crucial proving ground. The problem should be studied and restudied, again and again, by many people, as research in which design invention can be a catalyst for positive development.

1993 "ARCHITECTURE AND COMMONPLACE"

Excerpted from talk transcript, "Architecture, Culture, Commonplace, Criticism, Counterculture," colloquium on Architectural Historiography and Critique in honor of Geert Bekaert, Katholieke Universiteit Leuven, December 3, 1993. Richard Plunz Papers, Department of Drawings & Archives, Avery Architectural and Fine Arts Library.

We may well be entering into a period of widespread disillusionment within the field of architecture, at least from the perspective of the so-called developed world, evidenced by the high-style precincts of Western Europe and North American, which have been so visible during the past decade or so. Certainly, the unemployment statistics for architects in cities like New York, London, and Milan are rivaled only by the crisis of the Great Depression, now six decades past. This condition is now spreading, sufficiently for a malaise, which by no means ends with the economy. Somehow the evolution of architectural theory is also proving to be less than fulfilling, especially given the hope born in the 1960s that a body of critical theory could reenergize the culture of architecture in the wake of the reductivist wasteland of the commercial Modern Movement as it had evolved after World War II. It is less than reassuring that, in spite of the fact that we have more writing on architecture and a larger media apparatus than ever before, this activity simultaneously becomes more and more removed from the central activity of architects. It becomes more and more removed from the primary enterprise of building, which is to provide shelter.

Perhaps we are taken aback when Geert Bekaert speaks of discovering the "poetry of the commonplace," in that so much of the intellectual activity of the past decade or so has been involved with exactly the opposite. Bekaert has described this activity as "the practice of theory formation." He writes that much of it "questions nothing, amounts to nothing, is deadly dull." He adds the consolation that it would not be so bad as "a form of entertainment, if architecture had not been the first victim…"[1] What he signals will undoubtedly be a period of reaction to much of the recent activity of the so-called "thinking

1) N.B., Geert Bekaert, the prominent Flemish architectural critic, who was for many years editor of architecture series for *Mardaga*, and of *Archis*, retired from professorship at Katholieke Universiteit Leuven in 1993. This and other passages from Bekaert are from notes taken of a talk by Bekaert, "Commonplace and Poetry," given at the Graduate School of Architecture, Planning and Preservation, Columbia University (October 6, 1993).

architects" or theorists. I believe that this reaction, rather than being destructive, will be essential to the further evolution of theory. I am therefore concerned about what form this reaction takes. I am fascinated by the situation of architectural theory during this prolonged crisis of global restructuring within which we now find ourselves. The crisis will continue for some time, and it will continue to affect architecture as it has come to be practiced in Western culture. I am deeply interested in architecture, and not so interested in iterating a litany of accusations and disgruntlements. As I see it, there are too many other things to do. Many things may change in Western culture for the better.

Perhaps much of what we see in the world of architecture is no more absurd than what we find in the rest of the world. Some absurdities will change of their own accord. I am not so sure that, for example, those who have created the cottage industry of contorting, distorting, ripping, twisting, and snarling developments in contemporary philosophy will not themselves end up in the same dustbin as the previous generation (by less than a decade), which performed a similar operation on the Beaux Arts in the name of Postmodernism. I can only hope that, to paraphrase the famous line of Eric Gill, architecture will be quite capable of "looking after herself," when the time comes.[2] We can imagine, for example, that buildings now, as always, will continue to be judged on their spatial qualities. What does concern me is that probably there can be no such thing as a virtual or "theoretical" building; that so-called theory is beginning to labor at cross-purposes with building; that we grow more concerned with developing a "culture" for architecture at the expense of architecture itself; that this culture is a subterfuge of the media which can never go deep enough into the issues which it poses. In this, I find contemporary relevance in Herbert Read's admonition in 1945 concerning the Nazis, "that the more conscious they became of culture the less capable they were of producing it."[3]

I would like to focus on the possible nature of the reaction which Bekaert's critique portends, and to begin it may be interesting to linger slightly longer over Herbert Read's admonition from that now distant period at the height of the last global restructuring: during the Great Depression and the Second World War. Politics were on critics' minds then, and I think we can find some useful correlations with the period in which we will find ourselves. I have always been interested in the crisis of that time, especially in the questions of

2) Eric Gill, *Beauty Looks After Herself*, New York: Sheed & Ward (1933).

3) Herbert Read, *The Politics of the Unpolitical*, London: Routledge (1945), p.58.

cultural identity which were related to the monumental crisis of the war itself. Read's angst about the misuse of "culture," as expressed in his interesting little tract, *The Politics of the Unpolitical*, always seemed to me to be quite to the point. Certainly, today we find the same subjugation of culture.

Now the world is different, but the impulse is similar. In 1945, Read's reaction represented a continuity of Anglo-Saxon socialist thought from Morris on. In Read's view, "culture" was seen as a naturalistic outcome of a society's evolution, most fundamentally of the "commonplace." This term is not his: he called it "pots and pans," and he argued that the "best civilizations of the past may be judged by their pots and pans."[4] The nemesis of Read's ideal could be found in Nazi Germany with its vast *Reichskulturkammer*, "charged with the specific task of supervising cultural activities of every kind."[5] It sought to fabricate a culture toward larger political goals. For sure, 1945 was a distant time compared with the world today, but one has to wonder if there are not certain similarities with our own culture "industry" on both sides of the Atlantic. Has the *Reichskulturkammer* simply been replaced by a more insidious form of control, through multinational money with its own requisite cultural tyranny? Or consider, for example, the nationalism implied in the recent appearance in many countries of the "Culture Czar," as an extension of cultural identity. Toward what end is this necessary? Why has even so academic and obscure an entity as "critical theory" been so glamourized and commercialized? In such enterprise architects have been in the vanguard. So, we cannot entirely exclude the impetus for "theory formation" in architecture in recent years from these questions. Does it represent a straightforward commercialization, or is there a deeper significance? Or does this activity develop simply because architects have little else to do? I do not know, but I doubt the latter. The fundamental role of architecture in our society is changing. And there are some obvious problems. Why, for example, is there so little real criticism amid this explosion of theory? And, for example, why does the post-occupancy evaluation of built work remain so unimportant? We all know that once the "shots" are taken, and the building is enshrined in publication, no one cares what happens to it. At this level, we do indeed have the virtual building which takes on a life of its own. The question is how to combine this growing world of the "virtual" with the shrinking world of the "real."

4) Ibid., p.67.

5) Ibid., p.60.

Having posed this question, I will digress for a moment to the 1960s, a period relatively close at hand, when, unlike today, we were starved for "theory formation." For that matter, theory, as it relates to architecture, was considered something new. There were only a few standard texts around, which had been created by the ideology of the Modern Movement; or in one or two cases, some had withstood the purges of the Modern Movement. Everything was dominated by the orgy of the marketplace, with architects participating in the feeding frenzy at the trough of an uncritical commercial practice.[6] This dereliction created a severe counteraction, and new ideals and work began to appear. As students, how excited we were when the new critical writing by architects first burst forth; when we discovered the writings of Team Ten in Europe, for example, or the Metabolists in Japan. These were architects who actually assumed some moral responsibility for their work and who were capable of generalizing about it to form a coherent critical body of theory. How important was the *Team Ten Primer* or the little Metabolist book on *Investigations into Group Form*? We were fascinated by the vital discussions recorded by Oscar Newman in his documentation called *CIAM '59 in Otterlo*. How amazing was the book, *Community and Privacy* by Chermayeff and Alexander, in which architects finally took on the issue of the ruthless de-urbanization carried out in the United States on an unprecedented scale in the previous decade; not only that, but *Community and Privacy* began to explore the power of cybernetics as a design tool when the computer age was still prenatal. I could mention several others: for example, Jane Jacobs' study, *The Death and Life of Great American Cities*, which was another crucial precedent for cultural criticism related to questions central to architecture.

Of course, what I am describing amounts to a rather meagre quantitative output in comparison to the remarkable quantity of writing about architecture which is produced today. And I think that in many ways this exponential increase is good. I do not wish to demean this development in any way. It is the building side of our production that concerns me. It seems that writing about architecture has moved more and more to usurp the building of buildings as a principal architectural activity, at least among the so-called "thinking architects." Some architects have even made careers by "refusing to participate," as they say. We have even arrived at a moment when some

6) There was an important undercurrent of critical writing during this period, but its presence was far from prominent compared to today. Most of it came from Europe rather than North America. For a recent anthology of this period see, Joan Ockman with Edward Eigen, *Architecture Culture 1943-1968. A Documentary Anthology*, New York: Columbia University Graduate School of Architecture, Planning and Preservation: Rizzoli (1993).

Columbia faculty, for example, are motivated to argue that architecture as "text" is more important than architecture as "building." For that matter, they are also capable of stating that the academic environment of the school is more "real" than the environment of the so-called real world (presumably the streets of New York). And so forth.

An obvious question is, how did we get to this state of affairs so quickly? I can offer one observation. My generation had the unique opportunity to criticize the practice of building from a privileged position as architects who were trained to build before all else. Speaking for myself, I was in the last class of architects, I believe nationwide, to graduate with a degree that could also qualify for the appellation of "professional engineer." It was with this kind of background that we participated in the process of unraveling pedagogy. We did so with the luxury of having already obtained that which Bekaert calls that "Old Science" of architecture.

How we questioned could afford to be distant. In my case, my master's thesis was only related vaguely to building, attempting instead to delve into the first generation of cybernetic theory which had just begun to emerge. Like so much of what I see today, it was probably nonsense, and totally indulgent of what Bekaert also calls architects' almost pathological "temptation to 'borrow' and follow the dictates of other, younger sciences." We lacked sufficient critical perspective on this activity. We did not anticipate that we were not going to be the final generation of "old science architects," and that we were creating a questionable legacy which would have an unfortunate life of its own, with its own consequences. Now we find ourselves losing the old science and spawning a young science, which has insufficient context. Tragically, we now find the brightest persons within a generation who, never trained to build, must deny the importance of this activity to architecture. They fill our schools as faculty. In a real sense we have created this specter which now haunts us. Perhaps even because of our culpability, we are unable or unwilling to see the situation for what it is. We rationalize things: that to learn of building is better left up to the marketplace, anyway, in that the commercial offices are better equipped to train; that the academy should concentrate on building the capacity for a critical view. This kind of rationalization does not work so easily. Rather than providing a critical view of the marketplace, we are left even more victimized by it.

There are other ways that the situation of the 1960s was different. Certainly, in 1968 my idea of what sources the new theoretical inroads would invoke was very different from what has followed. We had great faith in the ability of the social sciences to help establish a basis for a better understanding of the old dilemma of how to correlate form with meaning, either in the functionalist or in the metaphysical sense. In part this interest owed a great debt to emerging post-structuralist thinking at that time, which was brought to bear on our concern with re-examining the dialectic of "form and function" following the new work in linguistics. There was also the impulse to turn to the "primitive" or "archaic" as less self-conscious models which could somehow help illuminate each attempt to further rationalize the act of design. In this respect, Aldo van Eyck's discourse on the Dogon and Pueblo was an instructive precedent for our study. We wanted to do the same, but with invention of a theoretical base from which to proceed.

In particular, I turned to certain developments in anthropology and to the idea that building is as important a part of material culture as pots and pans. I began to immerse myself in long-term studies of a variety of existing environments: East Coast ghettos; a Turkish village; a town near Naples; and, more recently, an Adirondack Mountain hamlet. Some of these became lifelong projects. I did not want simply to borrow and artfully collage the work of famous people. I wanted and still want to go back to origins, to the commonplace, and to try to build a new dimension in terms of understanding the functionalist impasse. I felt that this would be a necessary step if we are to move beyond simply trying to make buildings do what they do. I sought new ways of finding underlying patterns of social activity which could become catalysts for formal intervention. I know this sounds naive, but at least it did provide contact with society. It could be comforting.

What I envisaged for architecture was essentially engagement with a social contract; with a political process by which architects, in return for their special status within society, would return a certain immediate social good, as well as a certain reflection of that society, for whatever it could be worth. This is not at all the same as reproducing the values of a social elite. I felt that as architects, we have lost track of our obligations to society, couching our flagrant self-interests only vaguely behind the facade of culture and art; that is high culture and high art. In this sense I understood completely Eric Gill's other famous phrase, "To Hell with Culture..."[7] During the 1980s, I think that the self-interest among architects has been idealized and justified to a degree unprecedented since the beginnings of the Modern Movement. But now the sands are shifting again, or more accurately, the marketplace has collapsed.

7) Eric Gill, op. cit., p.47.

Talk begins again of subjects that have been taboo since the 1960s, and even the pillars of high-style talk of shifting to something else. Just how this shift occurs should be important to reflect upon. As Bekaert has asked, "What do we know of those fantastic 1960s?"

I said earlier that I would not digress into disgruntlements, but the shift back to a more or less activist arena does bring with it some questions. The first has to do with whether or not the academic underpinnings of architecture can actually make the shift from a "virtual" to an engaged reality. If we look at the situation of New York, for example, we see a city with growing disproportion between rich and poor. We see an academic and critical establishment that has increasingly aligned its interests with the former, and has even found talk of an activist response to the reality of the city's problems to be an antagonism. Put succinctly, the new academicism in architecture follows an agenda that is very far from the everyday life of the city: or from the commonplace. This sensibility pervades the whole of the glamorization of theory, which has evolved in the last decade. Glamour, theory, and ghettos do not mix well. On this point, I am reminded of a curious exchange that I had last spring at the ECO-TEC conference held at the Dia Art Foundation in New York, which has plenty of money and a fancy building in Manhattan.[8] The crowd was trendy, pretty much white people, architects dressed in black, that kind of thing. I talked about New York and the problems of "de-densification," one of the issues which I have come to focus on during the past decade; about that growing belt around Manhattan which houses the growing poor population of the city, and about the degradation of both that environment and people's lives who have to inhabit it: what Camilo Vergara has called the "New American Ghetto." My slides were not so pleasant. They showed the uncomfortable side of the city: the South Bronx, Harlem, and Central Brooklyn, where practically a majority of New Yorker's live, the commonplace, as it were. There was some umbrage at my remarks. My reply summarized my concerns about this mentality.[9]

The alienation and mediocrity of the design of social housing is precisely an inevitable consequence of the kind of intellectualization that has plagued architecture for some time now: what Bekaert has described as the use of "architecture or the architectonic means ... applied in order to make a statement, to argue something that is alien to architecture, about which it has

8) "ECO-TEC New York International Forum: The Ecology of the Artificial," Dia Center for the Arts and Storefront for Art and Architecture (April 24-25, 1993).

9) For a complete transcript of this exchange see "The Social Ecology of De-Densification," Richard Plunz Papers, Department of Drawings & Archives, Avery Architectural and Fine Arts Library.

nothing to say, that is outside its scope. Architecture ... reduced to a theory which can never be anything but rather vulgar and simplistic." Housing fell from favor precisely because it could not be reduced to a theory. It is time to move beyond this attitude, and especially beyond the media, which has more culpability than anything else in producing our current situation.

What of the critical establishment is far from critical? We know, for example, that its present disposition will by and large be far from tolerant of the kinds of engaged involvement that housing requires of architects. This question brings to mind a recent controversy at Columbia when a student was denied the possibility to do a master's thesis on housing for elderly gay and lesbian residents, based on the argument that there were limits on the power of architecture to solve social "problems." I do not understand exactly why we can tolerate this kind of outlook, except that we are prisoners of our own values and of our own worlds. It is safe to assume that not one of the Columbia design faculty has been to Pitkin Avenue in Central Brooklyn, or to East 138th Street in the South Bronx. Of course, this is not entirely their fault. They are busy. If they go there, they can be killed. The world of the poor is growing, and it is more isolated. So, I do not blame them entirely.

What I do find extremely annoying, however, is representation of the situation as anything other than it really is. In this respect it is especially annoying to find architects of my own generation suddenly polishing up their political credentials from the 1960s, as if that could alleviate those years of neoliberal dereliction in the 1980s. The 1960s revival is well underway in architecture as well as in the garment industry (even bell bottoms are back). This revival has been given official credence in the *New York Times* last February when its architecture critic presented the Rem Koolhaas project for the library of the Sorbonne in Paris as "reaching back to explore the social mythology of the 1960s at the place where it all began."[10] A local Koolhaas competitor quickly moved to claim the same territory, reaffirming his own experience with the "events of May." And in a lecture, Koolhaas faults architects of his generation for being disengaged from urban issues; for maintaining a stance that is marginalized; for not being able to break from the mold of the "counterculture," which was central to their origins. But I would argue that it is even worse to "marginalize" the 1960s through its co-option by fashion. If that is to be the end result of our next great period of "social engagement," then better to let the 1960s sleep until the right time comes along.

10) Herbert Muschamp, "Some Unfinished Business on St.-Germain," *The New York Times* (February 14, 1993).

1993 "BEYOND DYSTOPIA"

Excerpted from talk and discussion, "The Social Ecology of De-Densification," ECO-TEC International Forum 2: "The Ecology of the Artificial," sponsored by Storefront for Art and Architecture and the Dia Center for the Arts, New York City, April 24, 1993; partially published in "Beyond Dystopia. Beyond Theory Formation," in *Mortal City*, ed. Peter Lang, New York: Princeton Architectural Press (1995), pp. 28-35. For a complete transcript, see Richard Plunz Papers, Department of Drawings & Archives, Avery Architectural and Fine Arts Library.

My images include studies of Mott Haven in the Bronx made between September and November 1991.[1] It is the poorest Community Planning District in New York City. It is a place that tends to defy even the notion of dystopia. It indicates that ghettos and the so-called "theory formation" of recent traction in architecture and cultural studies in general do not necessarily mix. This became apparent during a subsequent exchange with other participants, which was instructive by way of contextualizing the images.[2]

My interest is in the social ecology of built form and certain processes within this realm. I won't talk about Manhattan. We will look at the rest of the city—that is, what surrounds this island. It is the real city, in a way, the places where we don't tend to go, and this part of the city has been undergoing a process that entails de-densification. The process, or rather the mechanism, was developed beginning as far back as the thirties but implemented by the fifties with the transformation of our cities and culture, basically as a whole, into suburban urbanism, if you will. The old urbanism of the city, and especially the "hidden" city of the boroughs, changed drastically, and we'll look at some of the consequences.

You can consider this to be a kind of series of notations in slide form. Included is the ring of destruction around Manhattan, marked by the notorious arson

1) This analytic work was done by Columbia architecture students with Richard Plunz as critic, and with the collaboration of Eden Muir of the architecture computer laboratory; Camilo José Vergara, photographer; and Leonard Hicks, UNIDOS Community Organization, Mott Haven. It was shown with the "New American Ghetto" exhibition at the Storefront for Art and Architecture, also designed by the students (November-January 1991).

2) From discussion at the Second International ECO-TEC Forum sponsored by the Storefront for Art and Architecture and the DIA Center for the Arts (April 24-25, 1993).

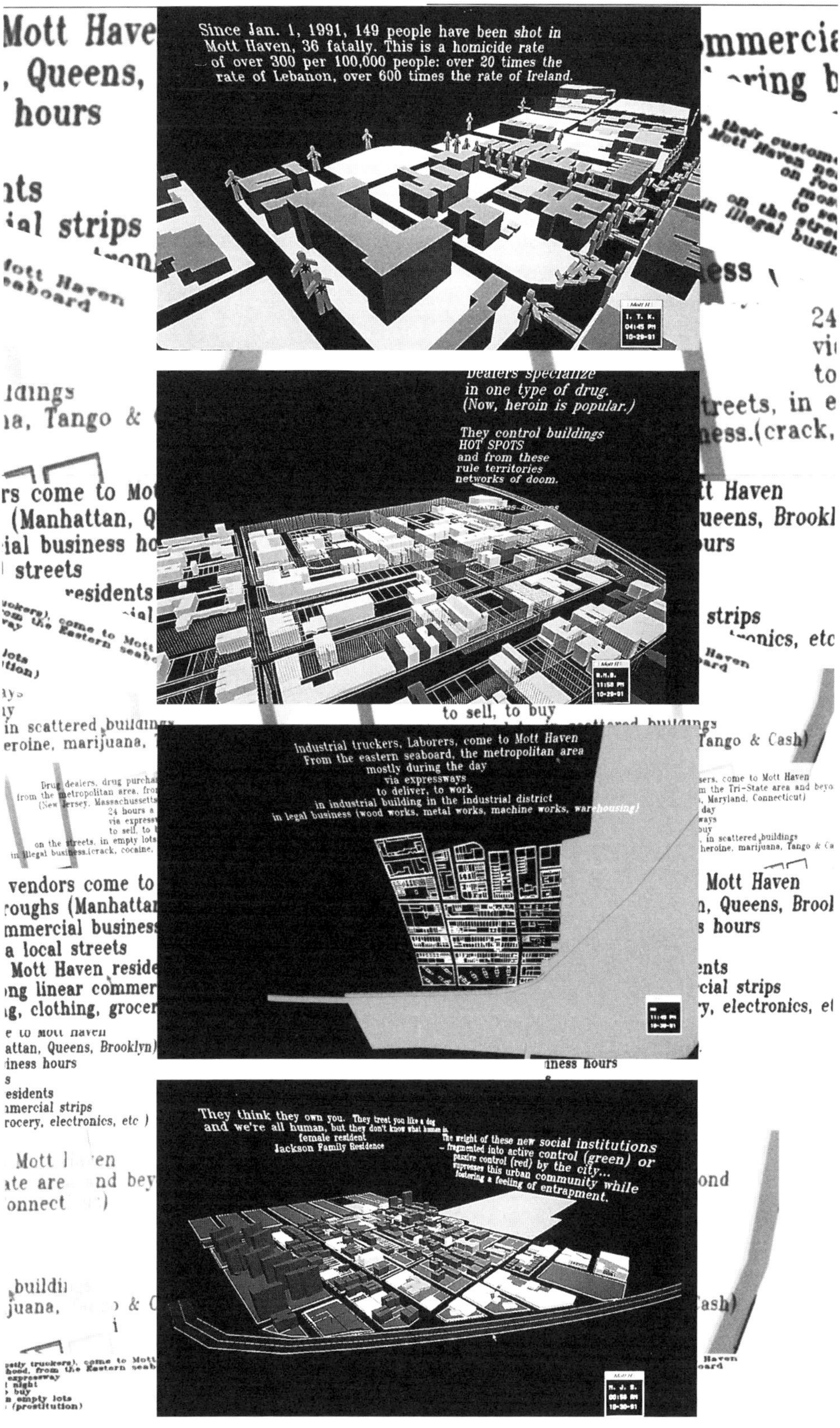

Since Jan. 1, 1991, 149 people have been *shot in* Mott Haven, 36 fatally. This is a homicide rate of over 300 per 100,000 people: over 20 times *the* rate of Lebanon, over 600 times the rate of Ireland.

Dealers specialize in one type of drug. (Now, heroin is popular.)

They control buildings HOT SPOTS and from these rule territories networks of doom.

Industrial truckers, Laborers, come to Mott Haven From the eastern seaboard, the metropolitan area mostly during the day via expressways to deliver, to work in industrial building in the industrial district in legal business (wood works, metal works, machine works, warehousing)

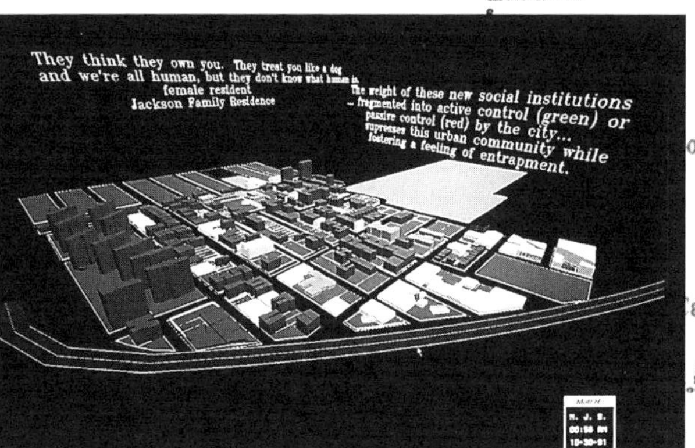

PLATE M
"Beyond Dystopia" Bronx, New York

1991. Mott Haven, Bronx mapping studies. In collaboration with the UNIDOS community organization and GIST, Inc. Columbia GSAPP architecture studio, Fall Semester.

Research into the social dysfunction of the Mott Haven neighborhood in the South Bronx during a period of violence when residents suffered the effects of extreme poverty, exacerbated by the crack cocaine epidemic. Among the poorest census tracts in the nation, daily life in this neighborhood was documented in detail. Phase two developed in-depth consideration of remedial architectural design interventions. This first digital architecture studio at Columbia University incorporated spatial modeling made with GSDL 30 software generated on Silicon Graphics IRIS workstations. Projects were exhibited with the New American Ghetto exhibition, also designed and installed by the Columbia University student team at the Storefront for Art and Architecture (November-January 1991).

1991. "Mott Haven Study," Columbia GSAPP architecture studio, Fall Semester, first GSAPP Digital Studio. Faculty: Richard Plunz, in collaboration with Camilo Jose Vergara, photographer, Leonard Hicks, UNIDOS Community Organization, Mott Haven, and the Columbia University GSAPP computer lab under the direction of Christos Tountas with Eden Muir. Digital representations shown: Ian Kinman (M.Arch 1993), Rachel Blakeman (M.Arch 1992), Mary Jane Skinner (M.Arch 1992), Minsuk Cho (M.Arch 1993). Other project team: Gonzalo Benavides (MSAAD 1992), Karla Maria Rothstein (M.Arch 1992), Toru Tsukida (MSAAD 1992), Stephanie Shapiro (M.Arch 1992), Hyeon Seo (MSAAD 1992), Yosef Habib (M.Arch 1992), Chris Kilbridge (M.Arch 1992), Shelly Brock (M.Arch 1992), Vera Bernardi (MSAAD 1992). Graphic representation: Maria Isabel Carrasco (MSAUD 2017), Lucy Navarro (M.Arch 2020).

PUBLICATION: Richard Plunz, "Beyond Dystopia. Beyond Theory Formation," *Mortal City*, ed. Peter Lang, New York: Princeton Architectural Press (1995), pp. 28-35. Also see Richard Plunz Papers, Department of Drawings & Archives, Avery Architectural and Fine Arts Library.

and other devastation of the late sixties and seventies; it is the area in which the social ecology has changed drastically and is being re-built in drastic new form—what Camillo Vergara calls the "New American Ghetto." You can see by the early seventies the amount of destruction in the South Bronx below the Cross-Bronx Expressway and the re-introduction of open space through the erasure of buildings, including in Mott Haven and Crotona Park. And, from a study last year, you can see an indication of the changing social ecology of these areas. For example, you see the fires in Mott Haven, where there are buildings with five or six fires per year. Then you see, for example, the homicides mapped in that same area, with thirty-six deaths within nine months. Here is a map from the study that we did in the early eighties, documenting the degree of devastation within the entire "ring." The areas in black lost, I believe, more than 50 percent of their population since the late sixties. There has been more loss since then. At that time, I was quite excited about the prospects of rebuilding, which could be done along enlightened and rational lines; a prospect is now pretty much out of the question.

What got destroyed was, by and large, good buildings. A typical example is the building in the Grand Concourse designed by Andrew Thomas in the twenties; it was good enough to be published in *Architectural Record* at the time, and certainly very decent middle-income housing. I just happened by one day, to catch it being demolished through the typical process of arson and insurance arrangements. I'm told that perhaps I'm too conspiratorial, but it is true that the banking interests, at the highest levels, redlined these areas and investment was withdrawn, which led through the cycle. It's a complex process, but between 1970 and 1980 the city lost one million in population, which devastated large areas. This is coupled with problems of racism, with economic issues in terms of basic changes in the economic well-being of the city, such that we see here, now, literally the return to farmland by the early eighties.

As to the question of balancing this dystopian view with a more positive outlook, I do not feel this need. The challenge is not to create an illusion of balance when that balance is so out of kilter with reality that, to me, the responsible thing to do, at best as an individual, is point to reality. I don't know how many in this room have been to Pitkin Avenue recently, or within the last twenty years, or to East 138th Street. That's the problem. So I could show other kinds of things but I thought it would be interesting to put up some slides of the city. I don't know what the percentage is now but, the last I saw, the official percentage of people in poverty in New York was 40 percent—that's official. We're in a very small part of Manhattan, so we shouldn't fool ourselves as to what we are and where we are; we can always gild everything over with evidence of good deeds but it seems to me that the handwriting is on the wall as to what this city is, to what many American cities are, and we can either deal with that or not. I try to stay active, in my own way, but the architecture profession certainly hasn't had much to do with this question for quite a while.

It is an interesting juxtaposition for a lot of reasons. The Bronx, to me, is a fascinating place; you stand back and look at this thing—of course, I have the luxury of being able to be fascinated and not having to live in total fear of my life or under completely atrocious conditions of one sort or another—and you see an area that went from farmland to literally back to farmland, in some large areas, in 60 years. Tell me one other city in the history of the world where you have this kind of stuff.

1994 "NEW DEAL DE-URBANIZATION"

Excerpted from "Architects and the Corporate Agenda for De-Urbanization," paper, Society of Architectural Historians Annual Meeting, Philadelphia, April 28, 1994. Richard Plunz Papers, Department of Drawings & Archives, Avery Architectural and Fine Arts Library.

Common knowledge would have it that the massive de-urbanization which occurred in the United States after World War II just "happened" in the sense that a post-war economy configured by American cultural values emerged indigenously in 1950, in turn producing the phenomenon of the mass suburb and its requisite consumer culture. In reality, this explanation is grossly insufficient. Indeed, the post-war economy was "designed" together with a reconfiguration of American cultural values focused on the potentials of new consumer markets.[1] This change entailed a long and intensive campaign by an amalgam of government and big business. Initiated as early as the 1920s, the draconian economic crisis of the Great Depression intensified the campaign, which called for radical moves to correct the wayward course of capitalism. Central to this correction was the question of urbanism. The decentralization of the 19th-century industrial city became the chief tool in the new economic planning. Beginning with the New Deal, the programs and infrastructure became the basis of the post-war dislocation from city to suburb.

The relationship of architects to the de-urbanist agenda is of particular interest. By the 1920s, the profession had evolved to an important role as purveyors of urban material culture, with the de-urbanist agenda requiring redirection of the culture of architecture. Because the General Electric Company was one of the key corporate players in this transformation of the United States political economy, it provides an interesting beginning point for interrogation of this process. In the 1920s General Electric had already worked long and hard to enter the new domestic market. In 1930, the company had inaugurated a new leadership dominated by President Gerard Swope and Vice President Charles

The author is indebted to Michelle Kriebel (M.Arch 1995) for her generous research assistance for this study.

1) *The American Consumer Market: A Study by the Business Week,* New York: McGraw-Hill Publishing Company (1932), section 1.

Edward Wilson.[2] The latter was specifically in charge of further developing company consumer products. By 1932, G.E. was already the single largest producer of consumer electrical goods, with an ever-increasing proportion of its research and development resources devoted to that arena.

The principal question for the 1930s was how to create more and more demand for consumer products, not only to rescue private business but also to sustain the huge public investment in national electrification infrastructure. General Electric understood that it could create a closed circle whereby increased supply of appliances could force utilities to further increase electrical production because of increasing public demand. This in turn would increase the need for the heavy-generating equipment such as turbines and generators, which the company produced. Each new threshold in electricity generation would in turn force utilities to promote the use of electricity in order to consume the new output. De-urbanism became a catalyst in this equation in that shifting large-scale domestic consumption from city to suburb would cultivate a heightened consumerist lifestyle. In the 1930s, the collaboration of government and big business gave concrete form to this strategy.

By 1935, it was clear to G.E. that only through its sales of consumer products would the company continue to survive the Depression. As Business Week put it, "New and newer devices kept G.E. in the black."[3] Staple products were also Depression-proof. For example, the sales of light bulbs, manufactured by General Electric, doubled nationwide between 1922 and 1934.[4] Between 1929 and 1934, in spite of the depth of the Depression, the domestic consumption of electricity increased by 30 percent nationwide, even though there was only a 3.5 percent increase in the number of domestic consumers.[5] This expansion had everything to do with the growing market for consumer appliances.

Housing typology was a crucial consideration. In 1935, the government encouraged aggressive business inroads into housing production. The economy still seemed despondent, even as the new consumer products kept proliferating. The New Deal had been effective in setting up a government apparatus with which General Electric and other big business could

2) "G.E.'s Third Generation: Wilson and Reed," *Fortune* (January 1940), 21:102.

3) "Appliances: New and Newer Devices Kept G-E in the Black," *Business Week* (October 19, 1935), pp. 28, 30.

4) Ibid. p. 38.

5) Howard Florance, "'G.E.' or Westinghouse?" *Review of Reviews* (September 1935), 78:38.

"cooperate" in order to achieve an economic breakthrough. Central to that apparatus was the Federal Housing Authority (FHA), created by the National Housing Act of 1934.[6] It was created more than anything else as a vehicle to stimulate the economy through creation of jobs in the building industry, which was seen as a key economic sector to this strategy. General Electric's strategies merged very well with those of government agencies. In effect, General Electric and the FHA formed a partnership in terms of promoting a single-family house market.

For government and business alike, there was an enormous logic to the vision of a major cultural shift involving post-industrial production tied to the rebuilding of cities along de-urbanist lines: stimulating short-term employment as well as long-term demand for consumer goods. These initiatives required a market for consumption and profitability. The purpose of the FHA was to administer the financial infrastructure, which could salvage the hemorrhaging banking industry by encouraging the use of credit for building. Housing was the target because it was the only clearly identifiable need that could be established within the building industry. Moreover, housing production was directly related to mass employment, including the consumer products industry.

In 1935, about 52 percent of the U.S. population were renters.[7] Convincing the majority population to either buy a home or improve or replace their homes came through reassurance that this could be affordable rather than foolhardy, given the state of the economy. On August 9, 1934, the FHA created its "Better Housing" program, which became the primary vehicle for transforming public opinion.[8] This was a national mobilization which entailed an initial emphasis on "home improvement," but quickly shifted to convincing the renting majority to buy new homes. The FHA housing ideal was exclusively limited to single-family houses, confirming this most invasive bias of all. A 1935 FHA publication entitled "How to Have the Home You Want" was typical, showing only images of single-family cottages, as if ownership even of a townhouse was out of the question.[9] Perhaps more important than the marketing of a

6) Federal Housing Administration, *The FHA Story in Summary, 1934-1959*, Washington, D.C. (1959), pp. 8-9, 12.

7) Federal Housing Administration, *United States Housing Market. Housing Statistics and Market Quotas*, Washington, D.C. (May 1935), Table III.

8) The FHA provides descriptions of the beginnings of its "Better Housing" program in U.S. Federal Housing Administration, *First Annual Report*, Washington, D.C. (1934), pp. 10-11.

9) Federal Housing Administration, *How to Have the Home You Want*, Washington, D.C. (November 1935).

house type was the more hidden dimension of encouraging home-focused consumerism in general. No company was more aggressive than General Electric, which by then was already the largest single producer of household appliances.[10] In 1935, it engaged the "Better Housing" campaign immediately and pervasively, seemingly in perfect sync with that of the FHA.

General Electric entered the housing field with a major media event: an architectural competition sponsored with *Architectural Forum* in 1935. It was for a small suburban cottage, which could meet FHA standards in order to secure the requisite FHA mortgage guarantees. In its promotion of the competition, General Electric frequently cited its relationship to the Federal Housing Administration. Also mentioned was the Bureau of Home Economics of the U.S. Department of Agriculture, giving further evidence of the extraordinary government complicity. In one sense, General Electric was acting no differently than the thousands of other large and small businesses nationwide, which also responded to the challenge of the FHA. However, the competition stands out as unique as it was a carefully orchestrated effort to identify G.E. consumer goods with the ideal of the single-family house, blessed as a social good by the government itself. It was also the first aggressive attempt to involve the mainstream architectural profession in this agenda. In April 1935, *Architectural Forum* devoted an entire issue to the competition results under the rubric of "House for Modern Living."[11]

The extraordinary amount of prize money was witness enough to the importance that General Electric and the FHA attached to gaining the cache of involvement of the architectural profession in a building type, which up to that time was largely considered the sole province of builders. The prize money totaled a staggering $21,000 (almost $431,000 in 2022 currency) at the height of the Depression, for design of a small cottage.[12] An individual

10) According to *Moody's Investment Survey* (October 19, 1933), General Electric ranked "as the largest producer of electric household equipment in the United States," p. 426.

11) "A House for Modern Living," G.E. Competition Issue, *Architectural Forum* 62 (April 1935). Entries were also published in *The House for Modern Living. 107 Small House Designs New York*, Harcourt, Brace and Company (1935). A copy of the exhibition panels exists in the Drawings Collection, Avery Architectural and Fine Arts Library, Columbia University.

12) The competition, including the prize money, was announced simultaneously in several professional journals and elsewhere. "54 Prizes – $21,000," *Architectural Forum* 62 (January 1935), pp. 8, 11-18; "G.E. Competition," *Architectural Forum* 62 (February 1935), pp. 19-20; "The House for Modern Living," *Architectural Forum* 62 (April 1935), pp. 275. Also see: *Architectural Record* 77 (January 1935), p.18; *Pencil Points* 16 (January 1935), pp. 4, 5, 9; *Architecture* 71 (January 1935), pp. 5-6.

architect could win up to $5,000 of this amount (more than $102,000 in 2022 currency); what better way to interest the architects than to organize a competition at the height of the Great Depression when many were literally selling apples on street corners?

General Electric's choice of *Architectural Forum* as a collaborator in the competition was a strategic one. Of the available architectural press, *Architectural Forum* was by far the most connected to big business and was read by an audience far wider than architects alone. In 1932, *Architectural Forum* had been acquired by Henry R. Luce, Board Chairman of Time Inc., who described his agenda for a post-industrial economy in terms similar to the discourse that pervaded government and big business: "... I have been increasingly conscious of for some time—that the next great industrial effort which this country shall witness will be in building and all affiliated trades."[13] Officially, General Electric was the "sponsor" of the competition, and *Architectural Forum* was responsible for conducting it.

The competition program was an accurate reflection of emerging bourgeois values in the United States as the corporate world perceived them and appeared to depart from the rather populist aura of the early FHA promotions. A certain Bliss Family needed a house for each of two stages in its development: as a young couple with one son; and later on, as a more affluent couple that has also gained a daughter. Mr. Bliss is described as "a young and energetic engineer of thirty-two [who] enjoys tennis and golf, and occasionally takes a week hunting or fishing. Evenings are spent enjoying a book; or a quiet game of bridge with his neighbors." This client is special: Mr. Bliss belongs to an elite postindustrial cadre of the General Electric workforce, far removed from the mass of employees on the factory floor. The stereotyping of Mrs. Bliss reinforces this ideal. While she is said to be "educated at the same university as her husband, [and] has specialized training in home economics and child training," she remains in the home. She does her own housework for two good reasons: "first, financial circumstances preclude an all-time maid; second, she actually enjoys the work."[14] The upward economic and social mobility of the Bliss family is an accurate reflection of the "American Dream." By the time of the arrival of the daughter, the son was 14 years old. More space was needed, including quarters for a live-in maid, which they now could afford. They now

13) Robert T. Elson, *Time Inc: The Intimate History of a Publishing Enterprise, 1923-1941*, New York: Atheneum (1968), p. 187.

14) Program excerpts were published in "The House for Modern Living," *Architectural Forum* 62 (April 1935), pp. 275-276.

required a two-car garage, "as Mr. Bliss uses his car to drive to the office and back, and the other car is necessary because the school and shopping center are some distance from the house." The FHA was said to approve their loan for a new house, thus prefiguring a scenario that plays itself out millions of times in the United States in the post-Depression decades.

There were almost 10,000 registrations for the competition. Of these, 2,040 projects were submitted.[15] This was billed as a record for any architectural competition ever. The 10,000 registrations contrasted with the 2,971 AIA members in 1934, an indication not only of the extraordinary interest in the competition, but also the degree of interest from architects estranged from the mainstream.[16] Each of those 10,000 received the General Electric "product file box [of] reference data [on] all G.E. products used in home construction," which presumably they studied even if they did not end up submitting a competition entry. The file box was quite elaborate and featured prominently in all of the competition advertisements. This meant that some 10,000 registrants and their associates had the opportunity to contemplate the merits of a new society, which would require suburban cottages, two cars, and daily commutes to and from work and shopping centers. They would contemplate the consumer goods that would accompany this new lifestyle. *Business Week* described the General Electric pitch toward architects as a breakthrough in the small house campaign:

> *The idea of G.E. in encouraging electrically equipped buildings is obvious. But there are helpful ramifications that do not appear on the surface. Each architect competing is sent a reference file. In it are booklets (many prepared for the event) which give full particulars for measurement and installation of household electric items which G.E. manufactures. This file will remain in the offices as a valuable aid in future home designs.*[17]

Each architect was required to attach a list of the appliances used, keyed to the plans. The Grand Prize in the small-house category, won by Hays and Simpson, listed 32 appliances. Their list gives a good idea of the extensive consumer products production already in place at General Electric, presumably taken from the free file box. These products were scrupulously

15) "The House for Modern Living," *Architectural Forum* op. cit.; and "New American homes," *General Electric Review* 38 (July 1935), p. 347.

16) Figures were given in *American Institute of Architects Annuary* (1934-1935).

17) "GE's Electric Home," *Business Week* (February 2, 1935), p. 30.

located in plan and enumerated as follows: clock, cleaner, sun lamp, radio, fan, waffle iron, toaster, percolator, chafing dish, coffee maker, mixer, hot plate, iron, ventilating fan, heater, infrared lamp, razor blade sharpener, curling iron, disc stove, heat pad, washer, flat plate, solder iron, water heater, gas boiler, air conditioner, condenser, workshop, stove, dishwasher, refrigerator, lamps and radio tubes. Actually, this list was relatively modest. Another entry that received a Mention in the large-house category enumerated some 79 appliances; another employed 76; another 55; another 50; another 47; and so forth. Richard Neutra, who took a Second Prize, limited himself to 21 appliances, which was fairly typical.[18]

For General Electric, the competition was only one small incident within its strategy for transforming United States housing. Although the company seemed to have considered the idea, it resisted the temptation to enter directly into housing production. Instead, most of what it had done was related to "public relations" promoting consumer culture, a field that General Electric had pioneered since 1923.[19] Rather than actually constructing housing, the company was brokering exposure for its products. Local builders were offered incentives for using G.E. products in their houses that were built using the FHA as an economic catalyst. G.E. furnished local builders with a choice of plans from 18 of the winning schemes produced by the competition, which had presumably become company property. It furnished credit to its local electrical dealers for sales of G.E. appliances to the builders. It also provided help for the builders in selling the houses through company advertising. The FHA did the rest.

By 1941, the company remained the largest producer of household appliances, with sales reaching $100 million. From its corporate offices in Schenectady, Vice President David Prince organized the scheme to transform its production to conform with the exigencies of the new post-war consumer society based on the experience of the 1930s. His "Committee on Planning" was already planning for the new post-war economy in a big way even before the war was declared and surely anticipating the positive effect of the upcoming war itself on its economic well-being. The war would definitively move General Electric beyond the economic malaise of the 1930s, and it would be followed by a "Cold War" of even more economic consequence. The Committee on Planning was flush with

18) Plans are found in "House for Modern Living," *Architectural Forum* op. cit., p. 284, 346, 393, 349, 357-358, 303.

19) For a brief history of General Electric's development of public relations techniques see: "The Public Is Not Damned," *Fortune* 19 (March 1939), pp. 83-88, 109-110.

optimism about the future. The consumer society and national security were a potent combination. The Committee on Planning defined their new opportunity in precise terms: the 1940 national production of $8.3 billion in consumer durable goods would increase to $13 billion at the close of the war and expand enormously from there.[20]

A kind of affirmation of the success of General Electric's 1930s adventure came in 1949 when G.E. became one of the principal targets in the anti-trust investigation of the House Committee on the Judiciary. The House Committee had discovered some of the symptoms of the massive shift that the United States economy had undergone in G.E.'s business practice during this previous era of consolidation. There was nervousness about the destiny of the nation. The electrical and automotive industries represented this shift, which came to symbolize the recovery. The complicity of General Electric in the creation of a new economy was seemingly without bounds. There was fear that the company had become too aggressive. Its monopoly extended from the production of incandescent light bulbs, for example, to large-scale consumer product distribution. The Committee cited that between 1925 and 1941, for example, General Electric had acquired "at least 56 wholesale distributors of electrical appliances and suppliers" in its attempt to fully control the market that its products were creating.[21] What the congressmen neglected to discuss was the enormity of the cultural transformation that represented a far greater transgression of monopoly power than the shrewd merchandising techniques. G.E.'s monopoly involved an unprecedented collaboration between big business and government, which was the real cartel.

Early on there were concerns about the dangers of de-urbanization. In 1937, the National Resources Committee of the Department of the Interior published "Our Cities," a report made to President Roosevelt. The report presented a convincing picture at that time of the continuing importance of the city in the economy and culture of the nation. Prominent was the effect of the electrical and automobile age.[22] The report stated that America was still a nation of 45 percent urban-

20) A detailed description of the activities of the Committee on Planning was published in "G.E. Does It," *Fortune* (March 1942), p. 28.

21) "Study of Monopoly Power." *Proceedings of the Subcommittee on Study of Monopoly Power of the Committee on the Judiciary: House of Representatives, Eighty-First Congress, First Session,* no. 14, part 2-B, Washington, D.C.: U.S. Government Printing Office (1950), p. 1204. See also, the General Electric response: Charles E. Wilson, *Big Progress and Big Business Go Together*, Schenectady: General Electric Company (January 1950).

dwellers, with only 14 percent categorized as "suburban."[23] In its recommendations, the committee argued against "wholesale decentralization," in that it would be too costly in economic terms. It argued for "judicious reshaping ... by systematic development and redevelopment."[24] Clearly, however, decentralization did come to dominate post-war urbanism. Indeed, by the mid-1930s there was enormous naivete afoot—or worse, cynicism. The naive position was that if the economy recovered, whatever else transpired could be absorbed in the end. The cynical position was to take the money and run. Even as the anti-trust hearings were being held on General Electric, General Motors and Standard Oil were busily buying and destroying the tram systems in more than 50 North American cities in order to sell their buses and petroleum products. This process was occurring within the congressional districts of each of the Committee Members themselves.[25] In fact, when they traveled to their home districts, they could hardly avoid the evidence. But there was the temptation to look the other way. Only in 1974, during the interlude of the "oil crisis" did Congress finally send a reprimand, well after the damage.[26]

Today the question of the future of United States "urbanity" remains, but it is clear that it is already from a far different perspective than in 1930. Eighty percent of the built environment was made after World War II,[27] and by 1992, more than half of the nation's population was suburban.[28] This would seem to indicate that a historical understanding of how our urbanity became so radically transformed should be more than an academic exercise, especially now, as we enter our second post-industrial phase.

22) U.S. Department of the Interior, National Resources Committee, Research Committee on Urbanism, *Our Cities: Their Role in The National Economy*, Washington, D.C.: U.S. Government Printing Office (June 1937), p. 30.

23) Ibid., p. VII.

24) Ibid., p. 84.

25) "A Study of the Antitrust Laws," *Hearing Before the Subcommittee on Antitrust and Monopoly of the Committee on the Judiciary: United States Senate, Eighty-Fourth Congress, First Session*, S. 61, part 8 (December 9, 1955).

26) "The Industrial Reorganization Act," *Hearings Before the Subcommittee on Antitrust and Monopoly of the Committee on the Judiciary: United States Senate, Ninety-Third Congress, Second Session*, S.1167, "Part 4: Ground Transportation Industries," p. 2414. For the complete record see Ibid., including "Part 3: Ground Transportation Industries" and "Part 4A: Appendix to Part 4."

27) James Howard Kunstler, *The Geography of Nowhere*, New York: Simon and Schuster (1994), p. 260. Kunstler also makes the observation that, given the force of suburban displacement from U.S. cities, from the closer "vantage point of 1950, the destruction has been incredible—as though World War II had been fought in Schenectady, New York, rather than Bastogne," p. 255.

28) Roberto Suro, "Where Have All the Jobs Gone? Follow the Crab Grass," *New York Times* (March 3, 1991), Sec. 4, p. 5.

1998 "REASSESSING '68"

Excerpted from talk transcript, "One City One View. Reflections on a Few Appropriate Texts and Images," in conference on "Reassessing '68 in New York and Paris: Activism, Architecture and the Academy," Buell Center for the Study of American Architecture, Columbia University, May 2, 1998. Richard Plunz Papers, Department of Drawings & Archives, Avery Architectural and Fine Arts Library.

My take has to do with New York City and presumably American urbanism in general, coincident with the events of 1968. It is impossible, however, to discuss the situation of New York in the 1960s without reference to the 1930s, which were the watershed for the rest of this century as far as the American city is concerned. It was the 1930s that saw the enabling of the American post-industrial de-urbanist program, projected by the crisis strategizing of the New Deal. In the ensuing decades, it would transform American urbanism to a degree that makes any definition of "city" today far different than the urban agglomerations of the 1920s. The dispersal of the American city through sub-urbanization, and its counterpart, the de-urbanization of the old urban centers through urban "renewal," ranks as our most expansive social experiment of the 20th century. The consequences of these policies were no different for New York than for other American cities, although relative to the 1920s, a certain critical mass does survive here compared with other places: by comparison, the erasures in Detroit come immediately to mind. Relative to '68, direct reference must be made to the spatial-cultural adjustments, which occurred as fallout to this century's great de-urbanist experiment which indeed was principally realized by the end of the 1960s. The events of '68 represent the most cataclysmic of the cyclic "adjustments" to the de-urbanist imperative.

The urban changes were monumental. The 1960 census, for example, revealed that in the 10 years since 1950, more than two-thirds of the 15 million inhabitants of the immediate New York City region had changed homes: 10 million of 15 million persons. This extraordinary displacement had everything to do with the out-migration to the suburbs and with this came the trauma of those left behind, the poor urban majority who were extraneous to the economic strategizing. With the middle class removed, cities became a class battleground, arguably more than ever before, and perversely reinforced by government policy as never before. The poorest of the poor who were left behind were relocated into the products of the euphemism of urban renewal, which were the deurbanized new neighborhoods of public housing with their towers-in-the-park: naturalistic mirages which sought to erase from view both the city and its social flotsam and jetsam. The projects were the final evolution of the so-called high-Modernist dream; now brought into economic subservience. In this sense, they represent the end of a cycle. The flotsam and jetsam were also the ones who soldiered the Vietnam adventure. We should not lose track of the one foundational fact: that we were a predominantly urban population that was transformed into a fundamentally suburban population. By the 1960s, the culture of New York City and by extension, Columbia University, was caught in the middle of this transformation: an economic one before all else, in which the transformation of the old industrial city became a crucial component. A radicalized culture of consumption could not evolve from urban densities and propinquities. Such was the logic that it was a short step from the "tower-in-the-park" to a gym in the park.

At Columbia, faculty and students alike could not avoid seeing the urban adjustments around them. They were the refugees from suburban culture, and they were the refugees from the crumbling neighborhoods of internal devastation. It would have been convenient for both sides to be in denial as to what they found. Their dream of refuge could not easily be shattered, but it surely was by 1968 as the litany of devastation unfolded. Perhaps some came from the families of East Tremont in the Bronx, already obliterated in 1955 by Moses and his Cross Bronx Expressway. Perhaps some came from the Grand Concourse, which witnessed a panic exodus in 1967, with many of those who could not make it to Long Island or Florida ending up in Co-Op City, recently completed. Perhaps they came, even, from the Upper West Side, whose fabric was ripped apart by de-urbanist schemes of all kinds, dominated by Robert Moses' spine of urban renewal stretching from San Juan Hill on the south up to 125th Street and beyond. Positioned within this context, Columbia had become an "acropolis" in the most severe sense: a "citadel" amid its changing social landscape and a cultural *non sequitur* as far as the city's renewal was concerned. There is a fine line between citadel and fortress, and that line was definitely crossed in the architectural elaboration of the McKim plan by '68.

To the south was unfolding the new cultural world represented by Lincoln Center, a new kind of acropolis designed to vicariously service the needs of the suburbanized middle class: easy-in and easy-out by automobile without even touching the city. This latter condition connects to the issue of the new urban economy, so astutely understood by Guy DeBord in his 1967 text, *The Society of the Spectacle*, in which the city of consumption ultimately must consume itself. "Culture" and "consumption" become intertwined in ways which led not to growth, but to entropy. And the British economist, Ezra Mishan would elaborate in his classic 1967 work, *The Costs of Economic Growth*, that this process had no self-regulation. The causation between the automobile and urban entropy could not be broken. Nonetheless, the automobile was fundamental to short-term economic growth. For Debord, the same held for the causation between the "spectacle" and urban entropy. The destruction of San Juan Hill for Lincoln Center provides a window on Debord's perception, and in particular, the circumstances of the filming of West Side Story in 1959. The film was shot on the future location of Lincoln Center: at San Juan Hill, before its imminent erasure. Boarded-up buildings provided the setting within which Stephen Sondheim could situate his script, a story based on the real neighborhood of years past. This was an early precedent for the new urbanism of the virtual. It also pointed to a fundamental omission in architectural pedagogy from the 1950s onward: that architecture was as much about "unbuilding" as about building.

Urban battlegrounds emerged in unprecedented numbers in the 1960s. By then, urban inhabitants had gained long experience in resistance to the de-urbanization—experience which only reached the academy by 1968. In New York, the resistance had been intense for three decades. Included were the major battles like Stuyvesant Town in the 1940s; the Cross-Bronx in the 1950s; or the West Village in the 1960s. There were literally scores of others sandwiched between: the clearance of San Juan Hill, for example, or the clearance for Governor Alfred E. Smith Houses on the Lower East Side. Closer to Columbia, on the Upper West side, was the infamous clearance for Manhattantown, which became embroiled in the definitive scandal which unseated Robert Moses from leadership of the all-powerful Mayor's Committee on Slum Clearance, beginning his demise.

It was not until 1968 that resistance turned to violence. Columbia became a catalyst. The rest of the city was rather late in the game. Perhaps the balance of power was simply too overwhelming. Even James Baldwin's powerful 1960 essay, "Fifth Avenue Uptown," would be published in *Esquire*, an empowerment of tragic irrelevance. Perhaps New York was quiet because the civic tradition of organized resistance was long established; or perhaps it was because of the urban form of the city itself and its density and propinquity. It was not New York, but rather the diametric urbanism of Los Angeles, that first spawned the violent phase of resistance: the Watts riots of 1965 were quickly mirrored in more than 30 cities by the time of Detroit in 1967. By '68, the discontent had definitively spread to the nexus of power, put in evidence by the skirmishes at Chicago. The urban insurrections were all about the structural social inequities which had been built into de-urbanization. For the poor, the enormous general prosperity of the 1950s and '60s only served to underline this condition. And the Kennedy- and Johnson-era localized economic initiatives like the Neighborhood Development Program (NDP) demonstrated the disparities: one of the reasons why they were so abruptly terminated during Nixon's first years. In this sense, 1968 represented the end of a cycle.

During the 1960s, the academic literature of resistance gradually expanded to architecture. Of particular interest was the work which reached out to innovation in other disciplines. From within architecture and its periphery came several of the major critical studies which dealt with de-urbanization. Jane Jacob's 1961 *The Death and Life of Great American Cities* provided the definitive critique of high-Modernist urbanism and of its application to urban renewal. Her work was energized by her leadership in the West Village resistance in New York. Coupled with *Death and Life* is the 1963 study by Serge Chermayeff and Christopher Alexander, *Community and Privacy*, another defining work on the breakdown of propinquity in the new suburban urbanism. Coming out of the wasteland of the 1960s world of corporate discourse in American architecture, the book's powerful dissonance was significant.

As significant was the window that it opened on the emerging field of cyber-science, providing the first definitive work to reveal the potentials of integrating digital techniques within the design process. Alexander's subsequent 1964 text, *Notes on the Synthesis of Form*, further theorized this potential. The subtext in this work was to point toward necessity for a greater knowledge of the causal relationship between form and function: to push to new limits the old high-Modernist dialectic by deploying new tools. From other academic arenas came related messages: for example, Edward de Zurko's 1957 *Origins of Functionalist Theory*, which placed the "form follows function" dictum within a broad historical framework. Traditional formalists viewed such exploration of "design method" as heresy: the essence of American Beaux Arts pedagogy was still largely intact until '68.

By '68, the proliferation of behaviorist work tended to blur traditional boundaries between physical environment and social action; much of it directly or indirectly engaged with the evolution of cyber-theory during the previous two decades. The definitive antecedent was Ross Ashby's *Design for a Brain* of 1952, which paved the way for the many branches and nuances of operational philosophy including those related to architecture and urbanism. In this regard, notable is Richard Meier's 1962 book, *A Communications Theory of Urban Growth*, and the 1964 book edited by Melvin Webber called *Explorations into Urban Structure*, and especially his own essay, "Urban Place and the Non-Place Urban Realm." These texts raised contentious questions about the definition of physical form within behaviorist functional paradigms, and this work became especially maligned by traditional formalists. Indeed, it still is. The traditionalists attempted to uphold their design values under the guise of the urbanism of historicist collage or reductive high-Modernist tectonics. While it was important to keep certain things alive, they did not seek equilibrium between tendencies. Within architecture, behaviorism quickly entropied, relegating itself to organizations like the Environmental Design Research Association (EDRA) or the Design Methods Group.

Within the constellation of the new 1960s tendencies must be included the emerging group of urbanist architects who were looking at the functionalist impasse in terms of intermediate spatial languages between "form" and "function." Their work led most directly to the invention of "urban design." The most important work related to this tendency originated in Europe, principally from the Team Ten group, whose name was derived from the famous generational fracture at CIAM 10, precisely over the functionalist impasse. Team 10 thinking was projected internationally through the 1965 publication, *Team 10 Primer*, edited by Alison Smithson. It reached Columbia immediately, where it influenced an important constituency; perhaps as much a critique of the state and corporate usurpation of morality associated with high Modernism as a design pattern book (the pattern book phase began later with the 1960s revivalists).

If 1968 represented the end of a cycle, the memory of what it exposed to architects did not disappear immediately. National political expediency would reinforce certain of the positive governmental responses for a relatively short period. This was reflected in the activities of the academy. For example, the so-called advocacy work, which bypassed professional impotence through organization of community-run design consultancies, continued to flourish until the cuts of the second Nixon term. Students and faculty were at the core of this work, driven by such tactical texts as Paul Davidoff's 1965 "Advocacy and Pluralism in Planning." Advocacy was principally empowered by government funds, soon to be terminated when the perceived danger of such empowerment began to overshadow the expediency of maintaining appearances. Given this termination, activists comingling between the academy and the city quickly dried up, induced as well by internalized power struggles within both spheres. At Columbia, like many places, the acrimonious debates surrounding the functionalist impasse of the 1960s intensified and focused on the supposed dichotomies between spatial and social design. The architects felt compelled to defend their turf through retreat into aesthetic determinism, in alignment with the growing neoconservative political tide. Those defending the sanctity of social policy planning defended their turf through rejection of the relevance of spatial planning. No good came of this situation. Two non-interactive territories evolved in the guise of architecture and planning. The 1986 anti-apartheid protest was the last spontaneous collaboration between architecture and planning. Indeed, that was the true end of the cycle. It was also the last such activism in Avery Hall.

In the 1970s in New York, architectural debate shifted quickly, as did the larger political tides within the local and the national arenas. Reinforced by the Lindsay administration in place since 1966, and by the operational breakthroughs—for example, the New York State Urban Development Corporation—a period of design innovation did merge with activist realities for at least a few years after '68. The hardening ideological distance between the "spatial" and the "political," and the general retreat from the functionalist impasse, however, soon alienated the academicists. As for the activist realities, that legacy left reduced expectations. The guarded optimism of texts like Kenneth Frampton's 1973 "Twin Parks as Typology," which could still hold out for a humanized high Modernism, did not converge with the American urban realities. Proof lay in the early demise of Richard Meier's Twin Parks Northeast, which within a few years of its completion stood in partial ruin, only to be salvaged through "normalization" of its proto-Corbusian public spaces using extemporaneous fortification. The epicenter of debate in New York City shifted further downtown to the Institute for Architecture and Urban Studies founded in 1967. While the Institute moved debate quickly away from urban studies in any engaged sense, there was an early moment when it did foster an activist relationship to New York's urban reality, evidenced for example by the commitments expressed in its brochure of 1971, or its role in the architectural design for the Marcus Garvey Park Village, an Urban Development Corporation project in Brownsville in Brooklyn.

The fact is, the rich got richer, and the poor got poorer. It is also a fact that for New York, this condition has been spun into a success story. Beginning in the 1970s, the real problems New York City faced could be gilded over by texts such as Rem Koolhaas' 1978 *Delirious New York*, for whom, we thought, perhaps New York really was delirious. The density and propinquity which he celebrated was a manneristic, high-style "culture of congestion," focused on the period just before de-urbanization. His text converged with the most violent phase of the de-urbanization of New York: the period of incendiarism in the South Bronx and Central Brooklyn, urban renewal in its most "delirious" phase. This connection apparently escaped him. It logically follows that by 1996, his *The Generic City* turns from congestion to mega-urbanism, with meaningful assessment of the global takeover of mega-urbanism masked in wonder at the scale of the phenomenon, and with deployment of architectural paradigms which are more and more adapted from the 1960s, but less and less critically.

Finally, one view today would have it that the functional city is no longer spatial at all; that the spatial city is dead. Melvin Webber's 1964 speculation is now popularized as fact by Microsoft's Bill Gates in his 1996 *The Road Ahead*. He finds it expedient that the "spatial city is dead," which he argues in the most draconian terms. What he fails to mention, however, is that his own research and development is no longer originating in suburban garages; rather, it comes from the Silicon Alleys, and from the urban culture of density and propinquity. Question: Is this proof enough that in the long run, the virtual city can only reinforce the physical city? Will this help inform the dilemma as to why riots in LA rather than New York? We shall see.

1998 "SEVERAL CITIES"

"Several Cities and a Few things to be Said About Them," *Domus* 809 (November 1998), pp. 6-8.

The actual state of contemporary Euro-American urbanity, especially relative to cities of the 19th-century industrial era, is so disputed that any discussion of the possibilities for repairing the city can easily dissolve into dissonance. Comparative to the meaning "repair," "reparation" here holds the sense that a war has ensued for the past half-century relative to survival of the historical city. The distinction between repair, which implies thriving continuity, and reparation, which implies dystopic survival, is emblematic of the present-day ambivalence about the future of the city. If a truism is that we have achieved a "posturban" condition, it also follows that regarding the old urban centers, the truth can be stranger than fiction. The contradictions are what make the present period of urban evolution an interesting time to direct a post-graduate program in urban design. The academy probably reflects more pessimisms and contradictions about the city than does the marketplace. More so, the term "urban design" remains suspect: perhaps too much harboring the ideals of the 1960s and tacking the *savoir faire* of terms like "urbanism;" perhaps too challenging to the hegemony of "architecture" while also smelling a bit too much like "planning;" perhaps too engaged for the critical theorists. The historicist New Urbanism is hardly new, and not at all pluralistic. We have opted for "new urbanisms," and have moved from city to city: New York, of course, and Antwerp, Brussels, Detroit, and Caracas, to name several. We have unfolded a certain narrative, fragments in the definition of the urban condition at the close of the 20th century.

All protagonists would agree that older Western cities find themselves in a postindustrial era of development. However, the meaning of post-industrial is not so clear, nor is that of "development," in that both words refer to a known industrial past rather than an unknown future. What is obvious is that the post-industrial city is space consumptive in a different way than its predecessors. The vast industrial and rail areas of the 19th-century city lie marginalized while the outer periphery is usurped by a new generation of space-consumption with little or no connection between each. In this, the Brussels and Antwerp megalopolis is particularly interesting. Belgium developed the densest rail net in the world, which now is marginalized within large 19th-century urban rings, while an equally impressive late 20th-century highway infrastructure dominates the outer periphery, serving the new service industry and auto-suburbs.

Perhaps it is the same elsewhere, but the scale of the Belgian phenomenon is impressive—more "American" than America, especially when contrasted with what is left of the historic centers which remain crucial to national cultural identity. In Antwerp, the old shell survives, perceivable from the steps of the cathedral, the center of the capitalist world in Thomas More's 1516 *Utopia*—now tainted by the vacuity of the monofunctional tourist city. In the area of the Grand Place in Brussels, where tourist industry is everything, there is little difference between Gothic City and Disney City. Protagonists disagree on whether or not new "industry" is a matter of consumption or production: or even whether or not such distinctions can any longer hold.

Detroit remains the emblematic industrial city, which was destructed beyond fiction. The sheer scale of reclaimed open land is matched only by the scale of population shrinkage. At the center of Detroit, one could curate the world's first museum of abandoned skyscrapers. Detroit is definitively beyond repair in conventional terms, a demise which has been exacerbated by a severe racial dimension: with white flight to the suburbs via the automobiles created in the Motor City—and with the African Americans left behind. Detroit represents the most powerful affirmation of Guy Debord's hypothesis that the city of consumption must ultimately consume itself. Yet Detroit also puts in evidence that the domain of architecture and planning by tradition and pedagogy is also an industrial reliquary. There is no design culture for conceptualizing shrinkage rather than growth. One reflects that it may be better to let the ruins of the industrial age lie unattended until such time as there is sufficient knowledge to proceed.

But there is another side of contemporary Euro-American urbanity, which pertains to the post-industrial city which lacked 19th-century infrastructure in its origins: Caracas, for example, which can be said to be growing backwards into the 19th century. Until now, its primary formation has been based on automobile-related infrastructure, built as it was on an economy of petrodollars. Rather than highways, the rail infrastructure is lacking, which must now be inserted in a reversal of the normative 19th century process. Caracas as a city of the 21st century will build new 19th-century institutions: a new and first-time railroad station, a new and first-time wholesale market, a new and first-time national gallery. The highway infrastructure itself is transforming and absorbing into the densifying city. At the center of Caracas, the project of Carlos Gómez de Llarena has "normalized" the central highway spine into a "street" and a "park," which organizes certain of the new urban functions. At the same time, the traffic flow has been improved through "calming."

Caracas is still a developing city within a context of "real growth," in which the recent phenomenon of "designer urbanism" has held little interest. Designer urbanism has engaged the marketing of older industrial-era cities through promotion of projects by high-profile designers in the hope that they may become the target of international media, thereby enhancing possibilities relative to new investment. Antwerp tentatively started down this path in the 1950s through its "City and Water" organization, which focused attention on reuse of its old port and river and culminated in a project by Toyo Ito. But in Antwerp, not much happened as consequence, and the government changed. Nearby in Lille, there was some success with the inordinate noise created by Euralille and Rem Koolhaas—a short-term success; in Naples, it was less so with Kenzō Tange's "Centro Direzionale," which was only half-completed before it ground to a halt. The government also changed: now the Centro destiny is almost apocalyptic. Yet, it is to be surpassed by an even bigger project at Bagnoli. And so forth. In New York, Mayor Rudy Giuliani now wants his own such testimonial, not yet materialized, but presumably not yet another Guggenheim Museum. In any case, it looks like the "Bilbao phenomenon" may have peaked with Bilbao. And governments change.

Are these machinations indicative of a new power for cities, or of more and more marginalization? Relative to the European Community, there is a good argument that the removal of national borders will serve to strengthen urban entities: that the sublimation of the nation-state will reinforce the city-state. In the United States, however, there is no such structural change. The remaining urban political constituencies have become so dominated by the suburban majority that any shift in power can only come from economic strength or from insurrection. The two are interrelated. As the gap between rich and poor broadens, so does the possibility for insurrection. At the same time, the sources for an urban economy (as opposed to suburban) are tentative, especially relative to the emerging new global economies. In New York City, the relationship between the local economy and the stock market is brutally direct, as the crash of October 1987 demonstrated. Jobs and money disappeared overnight. It is too early to judge the effect of the market "adjustment" of August 1998. It is important to note, however, that the recent growth in prosperity of the city was fed by income from the city's investments more than by tax revenue. Even before August, there were dire warnings from inside the government about the consequences of over-dependence on this paper economy.

Some argue that in the face of globalization, old localized urban economies will continue to contract, making the traditional city less and less relevant; and that the city as spatial nexus is dead anyway. In the States, where the de-urbanist tendencies are most evolved, new thinking relative to the spatial city retains an aspect of cynicism and disbelief, which is reflected in the urban political infrastructure. Some time ago New York City managed to dismantle its once prestigious Urban Design Group. Obituaries for the spatial city can be compelling, especially when uttered by the likes of Microsoft Chairman Bill Gates, who in his book, *The Road Ahead*, argues that the cyber age eliminates the need for traditional urban spatial proximities. Gates' position makes certain sense in that he is in the business of selling software which is all about virtual rather than physical space. But the interesting thing is that Gates' products are highly dependent on the city: in New York the software industry of "Silicon Alley" is booming precisely because this milieu of urban propinquity and culture is required for research and development. Does the urban software workforce represent the last gasp of traditional urbanity? Will the Silicon Alleys ultimately help fulfill the prediction of the death of the spatial city? It is too early to know.

Out in Las Vegas the "New York-New York" Casino opened last year. It is a scenographic collage of Manhattan monuments knitted together in one structure. It arguably represents the final phase in the death of the spatial city: a virtual New York in the desert that can provide an urban experience without urbanism. On the other hand, it can also be seen as indicative of the "thriving continuity" of New York. In that respect, Las Vegas itself, the first city of the cybernetic age, the quintessential anti-spatial city, is now densifying and coalescing—without easy answers for the moment. Realities can be stranger than fiction.

1999 "DEADLOCK PLUS FIFTY"

Excerpted from "Deadlock Plus 50. On Public Housing in New York," with Michael Sheridan, *Harvard Design Magazine* (Summer 1999), pp. 4-9; republished in *Urban Planning Today*, ed. William S. Saunders, Minneapolis: University of Minnesota Press (2006), ch. 2.

The New York City Housing Authority (NYCHA) is by far the city's largest landlord, presiding over 180,000 apartments with at least 600,000 tenants; its 1997 budget was $1.7 billion. NYCHA occupies a central position within the socioeconomic framework of the city, and thus a grim outlook for public housing has dire implications for the entire city. The fate of New York's public housing remains tenuous, due partly to shifting federal policy and partly to shifting demographics. Today, 50 years after the Federal Housing Act of 1949, which set the standards for government housing, public housing in New York faces an uncertain future in which social and physical changes appear inevitable. Given the steady deterioration of low-income housing in New York over the past two decades and the exorbitant cost of new construction, NYCHA is now under enormous pressure to find alternative sources of revenue. At the same time, powerful political forces seek to maintain the status quo, however troubled.

Meanwhile, national housing priorities are evolving in ways not applicable to New York. Between 1995 and 1997, federal funding for the operation of public housing was reduced from $8 billion to $6 billion, and the annual contribution from the Department of Housing and Urban Development, which accounts for 90 percent of NYCHA's budget, fell from $400 million to $285 million. In New York, this reduction has made it increasingly difficult to maintain public housing. At the same time, federal policy has shifted: it is now focused on replacing high-rise projects with comparatively small-scale, low-rise development. In New York, however, this policy is proving impossible to implement. While the problems of the city's public housing have worsened, its population has changed, poverty has worsened, and social isolation has grown more pronounced. All the while, the city's physical environments have changed little. In many respects, today's housing dilemma recalls that of midcentury that prompted Lewis Mumford's 1950 assessment of the early progress of the large-scale NYCHA projects: "to correct a pathological condition, [the NYCHA] employed a pathological solution."[1]

Criticism of post-war public housing crescendoed in the late 1950s, when national architectural media became aggressively negative. By then the problems were obvious. Public housing had devolved to "low-cost" housing. Indeed, it was planned to be housing and nothing more: it included no traditional urbanism, not even retail, the provision of which was left to the private sector. Cost constraints made the high-rise "tower-in-the-park" the convenient model. Given various political taboos, the "park" was assumed to be the only option for site, or "landscape," development. New York was more heavily affected by high-rise construction than any other U.S. city. Already by 1957, of the 87,000 public housing apartments constructed in New York, approximately 45,000 (52 percent) were higher than eight stories. This critical mass established specific kinds of urban spatial typology and social management. By the 1990s, the proportion of high-rise towers was 64 percent (approximately 115,000 apartments out of 180,000).

In 1957, *Architectural Forum* published a series of articles, including Catherine Bauer's "The Dreary Deadlock of Public Housing," which was significant in many ways.[2] A prolific author, Bauer had already written a book, *Modern Housing* (1934), that had influenced national policy and design for two decades, and an important article, "Architectural Opportunities in Public Housing," published in *Architectural Record* in 1938.[3] Appearing at the beginning and end of this formative period for public housing, these publications contain an impressive if depressing indictment. In the 1930s, Bauer's primary models were the European socialist housing experiments of the 1920s and '30s. Government-sponsored housing was not built in the United States until the Great Depression. At the time, Bauer had no reason to suspect that "socialism" in America could so quickly degenerate into "pathology." Nor did she anticipate that the low-density suburban *Siedlungen* that she had admired in Europe (especially Germany) were not applicable models for the high-density "urban renewal" of American cities. In hindsight, Bauer's book was less a treatise on modern social housing than

1) Lewis Mumford, "The Skyline: The Gentle Art of Overcrowding," *The New Yorker* (May 20, 1950), p. 81.

2) Catherine Bauer, "The Dreary Deadlock of Public Housing," *Architectural Forum* (May 1957), pp. 140-142, 219, 221.

3) Catherine Bauer, "Architectural Opportunities in Public Housing," *Architectural Record* (January 1939), pp. 65-68.

a retrospective look at long-established, genteel European practices, and by 1957, Bauer did not like what she saw in the United States. She placed blame squarely on high-rise typologies and on the "institutionalization" produced by their scale, standardization, and social and physical solutions.

In the same 1957 issue of *Architectural Forum*, various writers suggested a number of now-familiar remedies for the problems of public housing: privatization, individual ownership, diversification of building types, localization of subsidies, community control, and subsidization of rents. But none acknowledged the uniquely dense New York context. For instance, although Bauer acknowledged that "New York is the one American city where apartment living also is most taken for granted," she was ambivalent about the implications of this fact. Throughout the 1950s, she advocated row-house typologies for public housing. In a 1952 article, she had criticized the "nationwide crop of behemoths."[4] And although she suggested that New York might conceivably be dismissed—"they have only themselves to blame"—she admitted that elevator buildings already accounted for two-thirds of national public housing production. The tendency to shrug off the problems of housing in New York, and to see New York in a kind of opposition to the rest of the country, has changed little over the decades—and therein lies one of the important reasons for the current public housing deadlock.

The 600,000 inhabitants of NYCHA housing are by now entrenched as New York City's "second city"—they comprise many of the city's residents who are classified as "very low income." For them, the escalating cost of housing is most burdensome. The median rent/income ratio for New Yorkers has risen from 19 percent in 1960 to more than 30 percent in the 1990s; thus, for inhabitants of the second city, NYCHA is an essential means of survival. Compared with other American cities, demand for public housing in New York is extremely high: 240,000 families are on the NYCHA waiting list. Strategies for de-densification that might work in other cities cannot work in New York. Public housing funds, which might be reduced in other cities due to decreasing demand, should in fact be increased in New York due to its increasing national share of families in need. Yet funds for New York have been reduced. This has led to deadlock. In this way, the second city, whose existence many prefer to ignore, is reinforced through economic and social disinvestment. Unlike most of the "first city," the second city has been unable to evolve into something better.

4) Catherine Bauer, "Clients for Housing: The Low-Income Tenant—Does He Want Supertenements?," *Progressive Architecture* (May 1952), pp. 61-64.

Its situation seems permanent, far beyond the institutionalization Bauer deplored. The poor in New York have become a self-perpetuating parallel city. Many NYCHA families are now third generation. More than 15,000 NYCHA residents work for NYCHA, living in extreme economic and social isolation. This isolation is manifested in the image of blocks of red-brick high-rise projects, clearly "places apart." The reintegration of these places into the rest of the city is the heart of the challenge to improve public housing in New York.

The past two decades have seen a widespread national reaction against high-rise public housing. In New York, however, the backlash has been muted, reflected mostly in relatively inexpensive strategies that do not displace existing apartments. Relatively little housing has been added—only 3,000 units in low-rise (three- to seven-story) buildings have been constructed since 1979—hardly enough to claim a typological change. During this same period, most of the apartments added to the NYCHA roster have been in older tenements rehabilitated through city receivership programs. Physical intervention in the housing towers has been limited: low fences added to the grounds, or more recently, panoptic electronic surveillance systems. Through all these changes, constants have been poverty, crime, and despair. Yet the residents, recognizing the chronic housing shortage and spurred by fear of displacement, seem determined to retain the status quo.

Recent efforts to redevelop NYCHA projects with Department of Housing and Urban Development (HUD) HOPE VI funding illustrate the special complexities of New York. Since 1993, HOPE VI has granted $1.5 billion for the rehabilitation of existing developments nationwide: the goal is to replace high-rise projects with low-density, mixed-income townhouse developments based on New Urbanist ideas. Intended to reduce the hard-core poverty and grittiness of public housing, this strategy is in danger of being seen as a "one-size-fits-all" remedy for a range of unwieldy problems. It is already obvious that it cannot answer one of the particular needs of New York, which is that density in the city's public housing actually should be increased. But not only do residents not want increased densities, but they also fear any substantial "improvements" that might result in gentrification by higher-income families.

In New York, the first HOPE VI grants in 1993 included $500,000 for rehabilitation work at Beach 41st Street Houses—four 13-story slabs in Southeast Queens. In 1995, $48 million in additional funds were granted for physical improvements and social services in the same development.

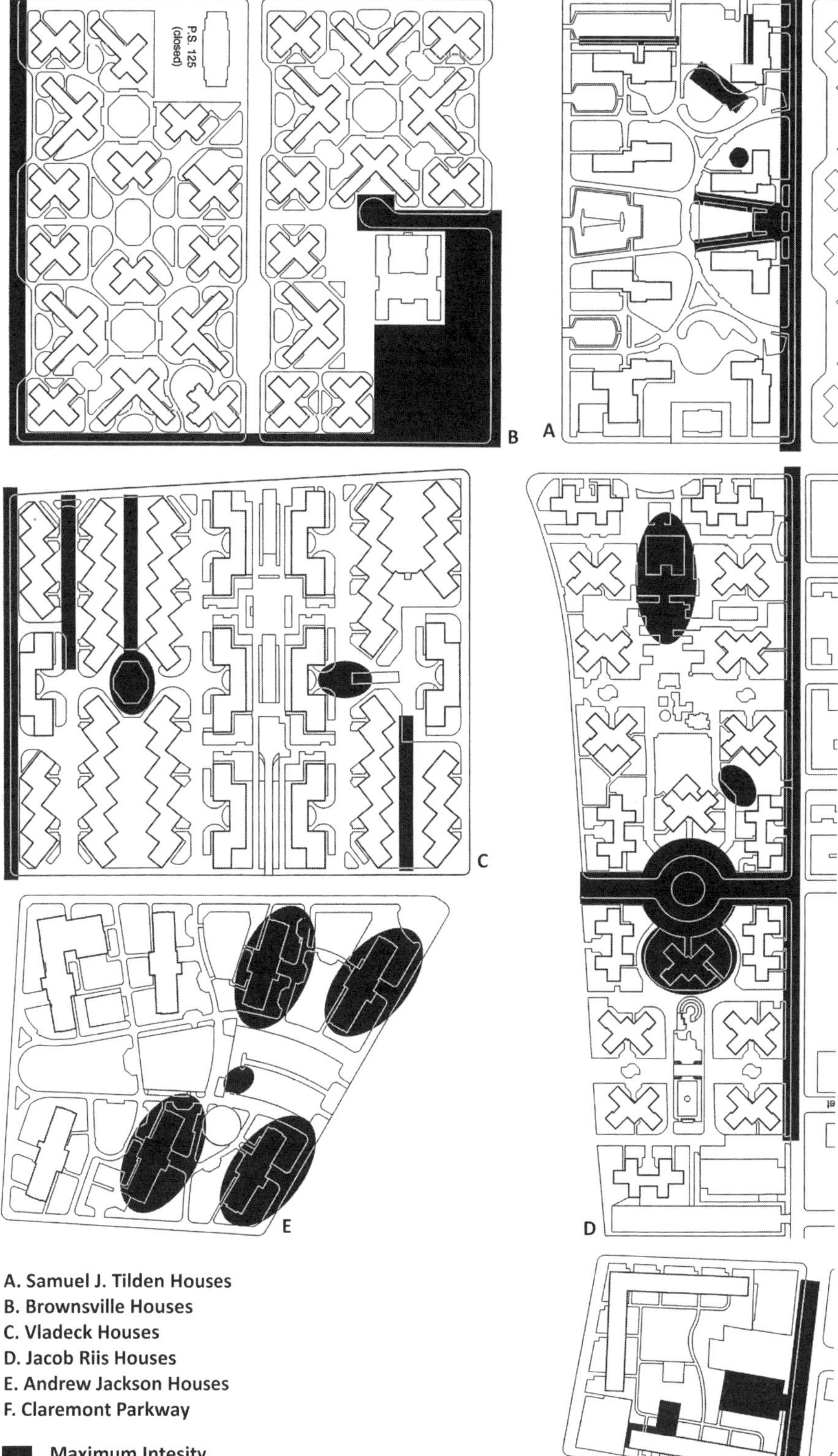

A. Samuel J. Tilden Houses
B. Brownsville Houses
C. Vladeck Houses
D. Jacob Riis Houses
E. Andrew Jackson Houses
F. Claremont Parkway

■ Maximum Intesity
Topographies of Fear NYCHA

PLATE N
"Topographies of Fear" New York, New York

1999. Study of "defensible space" strategies for the New York City Housing Authority. Columbia GSAPP Urban Design Research Group.

Research into the social characteristics of selected housing estates owned by the New York City Housing Authority (NYCHA) to determine site plan design modifications in addressing resident security concerns, building in part on the "defensible space" research of Oscar Newman at Columbia Graduate School of Architecture, Planning and Preservation (GSAPP) in the 1960s. Primary focus engaged in evaluating the effects of the "defensible space" strategies undertaken by NYCHA's Design Department over the previous 25 years, with a focus on six projects that represent a broad range of building types and contexts. Extensive tenant outreach affirmed that NYCHA applications of defensible space theory were too limited in scope and too uniform in application to produce significant, long-term changes in the development of environments. Of particular note are the spatial configurations of "fear" within the case studies. Options for addressing each of these diverse conditions engage both physical options and management policies.

1997. "Defensible Space Evaluated" research, GSAPP Urban Design Research Group under contract to NYCHA Service Agreement AE9600050. Richard Plunz, Principal Investigator; Michael Sheridan (MSAUD 1995), UDRG Project Director; NYCHA Project Manager, Michael Conard (MSAUD 1992); Project Team: Jeffrey Fagen, Tamara Dumonovsky Columbia School of Public Health; Ronald V. Clarke, Mercer L. Sullivan, Rutgers University School of Criminal Justice. Graphic representation: Audrey Dandenault (M.Arch 2022).

PUBLICATION: Urban Design Research Group, *Defensible Space Evaluated: Research Topics in Public Housing*, New York: New York City Housing Authority (1997); Richard Plunz and Michael Sheridan, "Deadlock Plus 50. On Public Housing in New York," *Harvard Design Magazine* (Summer 1999), pp. 4-9; republished in *Urban Planning Today*, ed. William S. Saunders, Minneapolis: University of Minnesota Press (2006), ch. 2. Also see Richard Plunz Papers, Department of Drawings & Archives, Avery Architectural and Fine Arts Library.

Two years later, after the residents refused to accept the redevelopment of 100 ground-level apartments into nonresidential uses and the relocation of families using Section 8 rent subsidies, HUD withdrew its HOPE VI money and started over again at the adjacent Edgemere and Arverne Houses, ten blocks away. In general, NYCHA has continued to pursue the economic integration of public housing projects into their communities as a means of fostering social stability and increased incomes. In 1997, NYCHA applied to HUD for a waiver from federal rent regulations at 16 of their 340 developments; NYCHA wanted to be able to accept more working families and to train and place residents in jobs in order to charge additional rent. But the application was cancelled after protests by tenant groups and their advocates, who feared that NYCHA would use the exemption to raise rents, evict families, and demolish or sell some developments

Despite such tenant resistance, the status quo cannot be maintained. Without a wider range of management policies and ownership options, fiscal shortages will become more severe, and physical and social conditions will deteriorate. Options for some degree of tenant participation in management or even ownership have been suggested for 30 years. Limited experimentation along these lines has successfully addressed the needs of some higher-income NYCHA residents. For example, in 1992, NYCHA purchased 30 vacant buildings, mostly five-story walk-ups, from the city and renovated them for sale as cooperative apartments. Approximately 4,000 applications were received for 730 apartments from residents of public housing and wait-listed families. That the buildings were in some of the more troubled parts of the South Bronx and Manhattan did not deter potential homeowners, who were attracted by (among other things) the prospect of being able to choose their neighbors.

The destruction of existing apartments and their replacement with fewer units are not a political option for NYCHA. The 240,000 families wait-listed for public housing and the extremely low vacancy rates mean that even limited demolition would be disastrous. Moreover, high construction costs and the scarcity of acceptable sites for replacement units make significant new construction impossible. By 1995, federal regulations required local housing authorities to locate new housing in mixed-income neighborhoods. But city-owned property is concentrated either in poor neighborhoods or in areas that are prohibitively expensive. Given this impasse, NYCHA was eventually permitted to divert the $230 million intended for new construction to the rehabilitation of plumbing, heating, and electrical systems in 22,624 existing units. This precedent points to an important reality: if little new construction is forthcoming and if public developments are to be economically integrated into their neighborhoods, then rehabilitating and transforming existing housing are the only option.

In the past, NYCHA has made limited attempts to upgrade its properties. In the early 1980s, the authority began a series of grounds security improvement projects, based on the "defensible space" theories of Oscar Newman. Unfortunately, the NYCHA work was based too literally on Newman's demonstration project at Clason Point Gardens, a fairly traditional development of two-story townhouses in the Northeast Bronx. There, within an almost suburban site plan, Newman used symbolic barriers to define front yards and tall fences to enclose backyards. The authority then applied symbolic barriers and seating areas to many of its developments, regardless of site plan or building type, but this resulted in the surreal juxtaposition of three-foot-high fences and 16-story buildings. A 1998 NYCHA study, headed by the authors of this essay, assessed a number of defensible space installations and found them ineffective.[5]

The residents' fears and management's hopes for the transformation of public housing both stem from the shaky assumption that a single formula can be applied everywhere and to the same degree. An overview of the evolution of U.S. public housing reveals that both fears and hopes are justified: in the 19th century, efforts to improve the dreadful conditions of 19th-century Manhattan tenements and contemporary trends in political and economic rationalism led to a monolithic response not only in New York but across the country. Much public housing in New York City and the nation has been predicated on approaches and policies thought applicable everywhere. But the variety and diversity of development locations and housing residents make this impractical.

The real question for the future of public housing in New York City is: What steps are necessary to transform these dismal and dangerous environments into communities in which residents can improve their lives? What seems likely is that new strategies of management and tenant participation will be needed for NYCHA properties and residents, including expanded terms of resident management and ownership. Attracting and retaining residents who

5) Columbia University Urban Design Research Group, *Defensible Space Evaluated: Research Topics in Public Housing*, New York: New York City Housing Authority (1997).

are employed and thus have some housing options may be the only way to prevent public housing from collapsing in crisis. A critical element in this struggle will be the transformation of the barren and ill-defined landscapes that surround high-rise apartment buildings: such spaces need to be well and clearly defined. And the "institutional" image of "tower-in-the-wasteland" must be addressed through the introduction of multiple scales and typologies. Given that the federal government now sees demolition as the solution to many of the problems of public housing, it seems hardly radical to explore how high-rise development might be rehabilitated physically and restructured socially and economically into viable components of the larger community.

The redesign of public housing is an enormous challenge. Neither self-conscious avant-gardism nor image-driven "retrogradism" will serve to create the physical and social structures necessary for resident accountability and security. What is needed instead is an enlightened and pragmatic approach that accepts the high-rise as a physical and economic fact and that develops the additional program and enclosure needed for security and comfort. After decades of trying to create large-scale residential environments from scratch, it is thoroughly clear that city-making is a cumulative process. A geologic reading of the city illustrates both the deficiencies of public housing as well as the necessarily cumulative nature of its transformation. To view these developments as finished and beyond redemption is to recapitulate the idealized and unrealistic approaches to urbanism by which these developments were conceived. These "object fields" represent arrested infrastructural urbanism, awaiting layers of addition and alteration. While traditional urban fabrics have tended toward maximum built volume, uniform building height, and equally distributed mass, the further development of the towers in the park should entail a continuous fabric with more topographic variation—peaks and valleys.

The superblock makes manifest the problems of institutional scale and undifferentiated open space. Originally developed as a tool by which urban planning and redevelopment could be practiced at a large—indeed transformative—scale, the superblock was all too successful. More than any other physical feature of public housing, superblocks isolate residents from the surrounding fabric. The reintroduction of streets into superblocks would enhance security and create the foundation for renewed physical and social structure. Lack of boundaries and of differentiated open space make superblocks threatening. The assumption of the early planners of public housing—that all exterior space should be public—created conditions that made social hegemony impossible. In addition to the reinsertion of street networks, the definition of exterior spaces, for instance, into semiprivate courtyards between buildings, buffer zones between buildings and streets, and private yards for ground-level apartments, can give both physical and social dimension to what are now frightening and impersonal spaces.

The low percentage of built-up areas in NYCHA high-rise developments has left many with excess open land. Some of this surplus, particularly along the street frontages, could eventually become valuable commercial property. Given that public sentiment, the booming economy, and court orders have all worked to curtail discriminatory lending practices, the redevelopment of commercial activity within public projects could be hastened by the construction of suitable low-rise strips. The sense of disconnection between high-rise buildings and their grounds was actually reinforced by the building design. The standardization of apartments had the odd result that an apartment on the first floor has no more access to outdoor space than one on the 10th floor. Much potential for rehabilitation lies within the buildings. The redesign of circulation cores, the expansion of apartments for extended families, and the addition of stairwells at the lower levels might be basic strategies. The creation of private yards for ground-level residents would further encourage the kind of low-rise fabric that would enhance social life within the developments.

Gates, fences, walls, and locks could serve to create barriers, physical as well as symbolic. Public circulation between street and building entry should be clearly defined, allowing residents to control and view access. Enclosing the perimeters of blocks to make yards with fences would also help to accentuate a positive of community: such places might be accessible only to those residents who overlook them or to residents of the entire building during certain hours. Although the idea of such differentiation among residents might seem shocking, most developments already have such differentiation: a de facto hierarchy, based on fear and criminal activity.

Research carried out over 20 years reinforces the need for integrated physical, social, and management initiatives in the transformation of public housing. Residents must be allowed, even compelled, to develop control over their environments. Central to this effort will be flexible management policies that help dispel the hostility that many residents feel toward the NYCHA. Such strategies might seem radical but imagine how radical our contemporary reality would have seemed in 1965: third generation tenantry, buildings controlled by criminals, the warehousing of the homeless, entire developments imploded at government expense. The unimaginable has become our history; we have come full circle to arrive again where we began: with isolated, albeit well-plumbed, ghettoes. It might be tempting to respond to such vast and complex pathologies with cynicism or hopelessness, but to ignore these challenges is tacitly to advocate further disintegration.

The degree to which current models of rehabilitation are impractical in New York underscores the need for multiple approaches to the deficiencies of public housing across the nation. To assume that a standardized program, favoring the destruction of viable buildings and the imposition of an urban monoculture, can be applied without regard for local circumstances has been a catastrophic mistake. Diverse conditions should engender diverse responses. While apartment ownership is a viable solution for many residents, for many others it is not. While transformation of the tower-in-the-park is appropriate in some cities, in many other cities it is not. The greatest danger is that simplistic, blanket "solutions" and "ideal" formulas will blind us to the greater pragmatic value of a range of solutions.

2001 "A GARDENER'S LOGIC"

Excerpted from "Beyond the Lake: A Gardiner's Logic," with Iñaki Echeverría, *Praxis* 2 (2001), pp. 88-91.

As a case study in the growing discourse on water and the future of urbanism, it is difficult to come up with a more forceful example than the Mexico City Metropolitan Region (MCmr) relative to the consequences of recent urban hyper-growth. Accordingly, a study of the MCmr can directly engage the revalidation of cities at the "mega"-scale as a model of social organization, and with the kinds of physical, economic, environmental, and cultural structures that will entail their well-being. The scale and complexity of the MCmr demonstrates that consideration of the "future of the urban" must venture beyond the conventions of present-day design methods and practice.[1]

Confrontation with the emergence of the megacity has brought about the re-apparition of large-scale planning projects, as exemplified by the Lakes Project. The proposal entails the reconstruction of a water body within the MCmr approximately 15 percent as large as the present-day city. In this regard, it emerges in opposition to a series of totalitarian visions that have caused the current situation of the MCmr. The polemical nature of the Lakes Project, inherent to the scale of the proposal, succeeds in activating discussion about the future of the region. However, limited by its reliance on nostalgic preconceptions about the city, the proposal offers a planning example that effectively exposes our collective inadequacy in conceptualizing the problem of the mega-condition.

The introduction to a publication of the Lakes Project, *La Ciudad y sus Lagos*[2], describes the impotency of the traditional masterplan to embrace

1) Luis Chias Becerril and Leonardo López Ruiz, "L'Insecurité á la ville de México;" José Hugo Hup, José Juan Zamorano Orozco, Teresa García Arizaga, and Oscar Salas García, "Anthropic Modifications to the Basin of Mexico Landscape;" Christof Parnrelter, "Peripheral Megacities in the Globalization: Mexico City, Bombay and Jakarta Compared;" in *Problems of Megacities: Social Inequalities, Environmental Risk and Urban Governance*, eds. Aguilar Guillermo and Irma Escamilla, México: Instituto de Geografía UNAM (1999).

2) Teodoro Gonzalez de Léon and Alberto Kalach, "Vuelta a la Ciudad Lacustre," *Quadri La Ciudad y sus Lagos,* Mexico: Editorial Clío (1998).

ZOCALO, MEXICO CITY MEXICO
04.01
SYMBOLIC CENTER
04.02
ZONAS POPULARES
04.03
HILLSIDE CONDITION
INTERSECTING LAYERS
N
1940
1950
1960
1970
1980

PLATE O
"Water Urbanisms" Mexico City, Mexico

1999. Mexico City ecology research. Columbia GSAPP urban design studio, Fall Semester.

Proposal for reinvention of Mexico City infrastructure based on the traditional water-based urbanism of Tenochtitlan, the historic Aztec city built as islands in Lake Texcoco. While little remains of the lake, it provokes speculation about ecologically motivated water-based infrastructure that can operate at multiple scales in both wet and dry seasons. Water collection infrastructure within the city integrated with public space as a collector of rainwater, catalyzes a formal, cultural, historic and ecological transformation of the physical landscape varying from one season to another. During the wet months of June, July, and August, open spaces transform into rain water collection sites which also function as non-potable water reserves. In heavy rains, run-off water is drained to larger reservoir areas such as Lake Xochimilco. In the dry season, stored water is pumped in the opposite direction to community open spaces and public institutions that additionally operate as localized water distribution sites. The most prominent receptor is the Zócalo plaza, which is the most important public space in the city. During the wet season, water collected from the Zócalo surface replenishes the aquifer and this process is reversed during the dry season.

1999. "Mexico City Water Urbanism" Proposal, GSAPP Urban Design Studio, Spring Semester. Faculty: Richard Plunz, with Moji Baratloo, Michael Conard (MSAUD 1992), Iñaki Echeverría (MSAUD 1998); Project shown: Phu Duong (MSAUD 1999), Liza Morales (MSAUD 1999), Paul Teng (MSAUD 1999). Graphic reconstruction: Lucy Navarro, M.Arch 2020). See Richard Plunz Papers, Department of Drawings & Archives, Avery Architectural and Fine Arts Library.

urban complexity in post-industrial cities of the 21st century, calling for comprehensive strategies which are open to change over time and capable of reacting to the discontinuous structure of today's cities. The question of water in the MCmr is infrastructural, where its transformation operates as an element in the reconceptualization of the codification of relationships between the city and its environment, its economic cultural context, its role in global imagery, and its future existence.

Yet, elsewhere in *La Ciudad y Sus Lagos*, it is categorically declared that for the MCmr, "the return to a Lake is not only a reality, but the ONLY possibility to warrant the future of our city." In this statement, the project's potential is perverted in failing to recognize the varied scale of the context and the complexity of the local ecological evolution, making it impossible to project beyond scenarios that are not simply determined by an apocalyptic present. A veil of incontestability eliminates the possibility to take ideas and discussion related to the future of the MCmr to a level that places in serious prospective the issue of attainable "futures." It patronizes the chances for the essence of its ecological issues to develop to reestablish a measured relation with water and the environment.

The rejection of water urbanism and a certain pathological relation with the Lakes prevailed during the Spanish Colonial era, in contrast to the symbiotic relation of Tenochtitlan, the earlier Aztec City, to its water environment. The Spanish colonizers' utopian predetermination of the New Spanish city plan was pervaded with nostalgia for the arid Kingdom of Castile and combined with a deep ignorance about cohabitation with water, transformed the valley's lakes into an enemy to be destroyed. In the popular psyche, Castilian obliteration of the water could transform it into a metaphor for revolution, independence, and liberty. Today, this conception still prevails. This deep cultural bias against water remains to this day, comparable to five centuries ago, with the prefiguration of a water image that is a fixed vision conceived under the logic of "before and after." Rationalized in the language of expertise, this conception risks eliminating the possibility of a populist critical position about the future(s) of the MCmr. In spite of the rhetoric about flexible urban structures and how to operate within them, the logic of the Lakes Project engages an outlook in which urbanism is simplified to the mega-scale while issues of urban complexity are avoided.

This logic, especially in terms of its implausible implementation strategies, is further enforced by the suggestion that forced or historical evolutions of the area, which have led to the current impasse of the MCmr, can be rectified by a monumental "corrective" action rather than transformed through an evolutionary strategy. Arriving at a credible implementation strategy would require acknowledging that the ecology of the MCmr has evolved to something without precedent. To acknowledge the irrevocably changed landscape it engages, planning and design for the city and region now must not only account for the MCmr proper, but also for the vast Mezquital Valley.[3] This is a conurbation comprising 83,000 hectares and accommodating approximately 500,000 inhabitants. This formerly poor and arid region has been transformed over the past 98 years into a prosperous oasis of green enterprise, fueled by the raw effluent of the MCmr. The Mezquital Valley has become an enormous "garden" extension of the MCmr, integrated with the urbanization proper. Thus, the whole of the MCmr, as an urban-ecological entity, far exceeds its metropolitan area of 19 million inhabitants.

The historic loss of Lake Texcoco engendered the gain of the Mezquital Valley. Conversely, the reconstruction of Lake Texcoco may not be undertaken without damaging the eco-enterprise of Mezquital Valley. So far, this issue has been dismissed, as it is *technically* possible to make current use of water in the Mezquital Valley more efficient (or at least this is argued in the Lakes Project proposal). But when one considers elements of the proposal—such as the sheer quantity of infrastructure to separate and treat drainage and rainwater, or moving an entire population to re-flood Lake Chalco—given Mexico City's immediate reality, the Project is not feasible in terms of either implementation or sustainability. More so, according to experts from the Instituto de Geografía UNAM, the natural tendency of Central Mexico as an entirety is to "dry up," and 50 percent of the Aztec's ancient lakes, or "dead sea," would have dried up at this point in history even if there had not been any further development in the Valley or neighboring regions.

To imagine that there can again be a "Lake" at the end of five centuries of ecological transformation is like fantasizing that the enormous oaks described in Pliny's *Natural History* can again be made to reappear in the Mediterranean. In Mexico City's ecology, as in the Mediterranean and elsewhere, a new era of "gardening" will have to build forward from what is, rather than backward to what was. The logic of the lake cannot be justified within the framework of a vast geography that has ceased to exist. This distinction is the difference

3) Humberto Romero Alvarez, "El Valle del Mezquital, México: A Case Study," in *Pollution Control: A Guide to Use of Water Quality Management Principles,* eds. Helmer Richard and Hespanhol Ivanildo, London: E & FN Spon (1997).

between a view of the ecological context of present-day Mexico City as an essentially sublimated ancient lake, and a vision that sees it as something entirely new. This is not to say that understanding the history of the Lake's removal is irrelevant. A long series of threshold increments must now be well understood in order to redirect the evolution of the past five centuries. This understanding points toward the fundamental value of reconstructing the process of removal of the lake as the most relevant historical model, but with the provision that the historiography of the lake removal cannot now be played in reverse.

Finally, we must acknowledge that the complexity of the megacity cannot be reduced to the question of geographical extension. The identity of a megacity, within the global theater, is economically and culturally determined. A planning proposal, such as that of the Lakes Project, requires a layer of information beyond hydraulics and geography, beyond the demonstration of its local financial and operative viability. It must integrate an operational viability for the MCmr within different scales and realms, as a global city and regional capital.

A sociocultural discussion concerning the imminent future of cities must be a part of the Mexico City discourse. Today, approximately 90 percent of Latin America's poor population inhabits urban centers. These centers may be considered cities, but most lack the services and the culture traditionally related to the city, putting in question the older urbanity, or even redefining completely the existing notion of "city." At the same time, the informal economic sector, in these urban centers, represents extensive potential in the form of micro and small enterprise (MSE). Although not considered legitimate by the enfranchised sector of the population, this parallel society (certainly far more than half of the MCmr population) will be the most vital component of whatever new city will emerge and must be central to any planning concerns.

Another focus should be on the production and consumption of culture in the future city. After the need for physical proximity has weakened as an economic concern, due to the development of telecommunications and regional systems of logistics, it will be increasingly crucial to explore ideas for the reconceptualization of the urban. In this regard, the future existence of cities may be more related to lifestyles than to economic imperatives as presently defined by industrialization. The economy of urban centers may revolve around the production of immaterial cultural goods, no longer beholden to transformation industries. This change will lend cities a new productive sense, generally implying creativity. A historical division between living and working, and between work and leisure, will be blurred or even erased. Traditional urban space, public and private, entertainment and education, may be reconfigured accordingly. In order to attract a new and productive international population, cities will need to foster appealing lifestyles and environments rather than traditional jobs. Clearly, in this scenario, the ideologies of Modernist urbanism, which date back to the first industrial revolution, will be not just obsolete but also anti-productive relative to the prosperity and well-being of future cities. Into this future the MCmr is well-positioned to move, but only if the cultural constraints of Modernism can be minimized and the relationship between the periphery, as an economic entity, and the center be strengthened.

An operational urban plan for the MCmr must be effective as a tool to restructure the city and the valley beyond a vision of natural landscape. Its logic should operate more as a "gardener's logic" where flux and forces are directed by design, policy, and planning, and results are open to speculation. Large-scale super-impositions framed by traditional master planning methods are not adequate to address the complexity of MCmr as a megacity. Urban propositions should be understood as ongoing investigations and should be evaluated across multiple future scenarios. Physical design decisions should be delayed allowing "form" to be informed and transformed continuously by new data gathered during the planning process. Strategies, results, and actions should be flexible to avoid sacrificing the urgent transformation of MCmr, due to the impossibility to develop any one particular idea.

A gardener's logic points away from the tradition of planning as reflected in the Lakes Project proposal, and toward open-ended planning. Within a model where the lack of a single facilitator, author, or authority is axiomatic, the architect or urbanist becomes a facilitator of communication within an interdisciplinary group of experts. The city is transformed into a landing site for the discussion and research of strategic local operations. If the architect provides an overarching "vision" it is not for immediate consumption or literal implementation but for the sake of discourse. More effectively, architects can broaden their participation by entering into engaged political action, as facilitators, developers, empowered politicians, and bureaucrats, in order to participate in more concrete bridging between visions and future realities.

2003 "SO SAYS..."

"So Says Richard Plunz," interview with Kristen Richards, *Oculus* 65 (Winter Issue 4, 2003-04), pp. 18-19.

Kristen Richards You have written about public housing in New York and elsewhere. Where is the greatest demographic need for housing in New York City physically and socially?

Richard Plunz I suppose this is terribly obvious, but the sector getting the least attention involves the lowest quarter of the population. Historically, public housing and various hybrid programs like Section 8 have covered this group. But today, these people are falling out of the picture. For example, consider "Public Housing," which is our oldest form of direct government intervention. There are at least 550,000 "official" tenants in New York City Housing Authority (NYCHA) housing alone, and a huge waiting list—but NYCHA is not in a position to build. Its activity has been relegated to management and piecemeal maintenance.

Certain other recent social housing programs are more or less related to what has been historically known as the "deserving poor" —people with jobs, one- or even two-income families. In this regard, the "big news" in the 1990s relative to social housing was "home ownership" programs designed to help lower-middle-income families to move up a notch or two, but these did very little for the people below this economic threshold.

KR With the Housing Authority building little, and the NYC Department of Housing Preservation and Development also limited by budgetary and other constraints, what is the future of publicly supported housing in the city?

RP There has to be an evolution back to a reasonable level of publicly supported housing production. This implies that adequate housing is a basic human right and a government responsibility, a position that may sound quaint and out-of-date. On this point, sooner or later we, as a society, will be forced to come back to a balanced system of housing production.

And in some respects, we slowly are. In the United States, after 60 years of devaluation of the city, there is a growing reaffirmation of "urbanism as a way of life," and in time, a new mandate for adequate urban housing is bound to be a part of this awakening. Urban centers are no longer easily discredited as living environments, for many reasons, including the question of resources. Let's just say that when the price of our gasoline reaches its true cost, things will change. That moment may come sooner than we might think. We cannot maintain dominance of global resources forever in order to sustain an "American way of life"—which is inherently unsustainable. As our global political and cultural assumptions catch up with us at home, the housing and urban implications will be staggering—and positive in my mind.

KR What are the implications for housing types?

RP The situation is not so easy to generalize. I am not sure one can always correlate a housing type with family income. For example, housing innovation that reflects the new definitions of family structures tends to move across the income spectrum. Yet, it is also true that, as demonstrated in the last half-century, high-rise housing may work for middle- and upper-incomes but presents demonstratable problems for lower incomes.

And relative to these venerable categories of "high," "middle," and "low" income, there now is more divergence than at any time in memory. This is true across the country, but especially in New York City. Manufacturing is gone, which for many people leaves only sub-salaries in service industries—the "McJobs" phenomenon.

In New York City, along with the growing divergence between income groups, for those on the bottom, there is a growing demand for housing together with a scaling back in housing production. One cannot help but wonder how long this can go on before there is a radical political manifestation around the housing question in New York.

KR How would you suggest that housing construction be significantly increased in New York City? How can it be financed?

RP Certainly, any increase in housing production for the lower-economic third will not happen without heightened local and national political commitment. The recent Giuliani and Bloomberg housing plans were political decoys and neither adequately conceptualized the problem. But at least they were again talking about housing!

Of course, there are more considerations than income. For example, much of the social housing built in New York City in the 1980s and '90s used densities far too low to support the infrastructure that was already in place. New York put a lot of effort into rebuilding housing on city-owned land left empty by the 1970s burnout but deployed low-density housing types. Now the city has little such land left. The rebuilding was a missed opportunity. Charlotte Gardens in the South Bronx was the most extreme example of land not put to the highest possible use—90 single-family houses in an area that formerly supported thousands of residents. There were plenty of alternative models to study. In the 1920s, Jackson Heights combined relatively high-density urban fabric with home ownership. This remains some of the best housing in the city. It had gardens. It was efficient and well-designed. You cannot say that about the Nehemiah housing of the 1980s and '90s—and there is no excuse.

KR Do your students at the Columbia University Graduate School of Architecture Planning and Preservation care about housing, or are they focused on other design studio subjects?

RP The Housing Studio at Columbia has been the backbone of the Master of Architecture program since I came here in the 1970s. Of course, things have changed. Back then it seemed important to study and understand history and typologies relative to housing design. By the mid-1980s, younger faculty interests shifted to other concerns under the loose rubric of housing "phenomenology." We are likely to move again toward typology, but more importantly, now is a period when we need to put the economic issues related to public/private financing for housing on the front burner.

Happily, urbanism is a reemerging subject within architecture. At Columbia, interest in urban design has grown enormously in the last 10 years. I am not sure we know exactly how to redefine urban design today but grappling with that question is part of the excitement. Urban design is a strategic operation, a political tool. It requires public debate. As an architect, you cannot convince the public to support a strategy if it is not presented in language that is accessible. Urban form-language is the province of architects. Urban design is expanding the relevance of architects.

KR What do you consider as some of the major issues facing the city that have urban design implications?

RP New York has experienced a long period of prominence as a global capital. Yet there has also been a long, dry period in terms of developing physical infrastructure compared to other modern global capitals. There have not been any major infrastructure projects here since the 1950s and '60s road building, with the attempt at a new rail link to JFK Airport notwithstanding. (Compared to airport links in other global capitals, it is pretty deficient.) The same can be said for our attempts to deal with sanitation needs. Infrastructure is extremely expensive and long-term, and the allocation of resources is creating debate and a lot of second-guessing. The debates surrounding the rebuilding of Lower Manhattan bear this out.

We are at a moment of either renewing New York's role as a global economic engine, or simply hoping that it can just hold its own. For renewal, we need large-scale public investments strategically placed. And we need to protect existing infrastructure as an irreplaceable resource. The last rail yard in Manhattan went the way of Trump's condos. Now the politicians are starting to catch up but from behind! There is talk again about the Second Avenue Subway. Mayor Giuliani did try to revive plans for the freight tunnel to Brooklyn that has been proposed for about 80 years. But right now, and perhaps forever, that kind of investment is prohibitive. We could not afford to give away our freight capacity. We have eradicated a lot of irreplaceable stuff, which we may well need again. Throughout history, the science of city building has had a way of amplifying the deficiency of short-term strategic decisions through their long-term effects. Cities grow and decline. The handwriting is on the wall.

KR As a teacher, you have influenced at least three decades of students, including many now in practice. What satisfaction do you get, if any, from what they build?

RP When I came to Columbia, it was a very different place. The academy was coming out of the 1960s, and out of social programs that helped a sizeable number of students who otherwise could not have afforded an elite private university. They were bright, interested in making a difference, vocal, and opinionated. Their presence made a big difference. It was a very exciting, nitty-gritty time. Students had spirit and they had a positive drive which included questioning what mainstream architecture was all about.

That generation's concerns eclipsed as economic support decreased and costs rose. We moved into the so-called "narcissistic phase," with homogenous, relatively well-off students who could afford Columbia. In the mid-1980s through the 1990s, glamour and style overly dominated, driven and reflected in trendy print and new media. But today, a third generation is moving in another direction. "Design" is not their only reason for being. Students are interested in strategic urban mechanisms—how cities function relative to economics, ecology, and information technology. Perhaps they are again becoming political animals in the best "public good" sense.

KR Any regrets about not having designed more housing yourself?

RP Yes, of course. But a bigger regret is that over the years, more of my students have not had the opportunity to design more housing. The real pity is that we have had two generations of students with rather limited opportunities within the professional world of architecture. Some of the most gifted left to enter other fields. The good news is that their training allowed them to do so. By this I refer to design studio pedagogy, which is a unique and very significant form of critical inquiry, and useful in all aspects of environmental problem-solving.

2007 "PEDAGOGY AND URBANISM"

"Interview by Jia Mei and Ziyu Zhuang," *Inter-Views: Trends of the Top Architecture and Urbanism Programs in Europe and North America*, ed. Fei Wang and Junfeng Ding, Beijing: China Architecture and Building Press (2010), pp. 112-121.

Jia Mei As the director of the Master of Science in Architecture and Urban Design program, we are interested in your definition of the program in relation to its name. Could you briefly introduce the program and its curriculum?

Richard Plunz Actually, I had nothing to do with the name—but it does accurately reflect the reality that it is an "urban design" program principally for architectural designers. Of course, one can have other definitions of the realm of urban design—for example, urban design for engineers, for ecologists, for lawyers, for urban policy wonks, and the like. The goal of our program is to expand the traditional realm of architectural pedagogy to urbanism while retaining the great relevance of professional architectural training. The curriculum is an integrated and highly collaborative design studio sequence correlated with classroom coursework. It is directly engaged with developmental realities facing New York and other global cities.

Ziyu Zhuang Our experience of the degree is that of a very clear and skill-based curriculum that allows students to develop an expertise for adaptable practices in different urban schemes. How would you respond to criticism on the repetitive nature of three "similar" sequenced design studios and a potential lack of flexibility in the program's organization?

RP Three semesters is a very short curriculum for the breadth of material that we try to cover. I am very skeptical about this idea of "flexibility." Of course, the Urban Design (UD) program is not for everyone, and there are other options. At Columbia, students can opt for the Advanced Architectural Design (AAD) program, and pick urban studios by lottery, with the intent to somehow extend their undergraduate education. At any rate, I totally disagree that the three semesters are too similar in terms of content. They are quite different, although there is the overall goal of coherence within the sequence.

Maybe it would not hurt to do the "similar designs" four or five or six times—until one becomes really accomplished? Or maybe for the rest of your life? Someone has said that the novelist really keeps writing the same book for a lifetime—no matter how many different books they write. There is value in growing through the cyclical rediscovery of a design exercise.

ZZ We notice a high proportion of our professors are trained as landscape architects, as well as a great number of students entering the program with a background in landscape design. With the absence of an explicit landscape program at the Graduate School of Architecture, Planning and Preservation (GSAPP), is there an intention to lead UD in closer association with landscape architecture? How would you differentiate or associate the two in "style"?

RP We have had landscape architects as students in prior years, so this is nothing new. For some time, we have had landscape architects among each semester's faculty, quite simply because the field of landscape architecture is "urbanizing," and it is far more relevant to urban design now than it once was. And therefore, in this sense, the UD program has moved closer to "landscape design." If we speak of a landscape design style: "style" is a term that doesn't much interest me—so much so that I don't really know what it could even mean. But certainly, landscape design considerations can bring additional criteria to bear on urban design projects.

JM How would you situate the program within the GSAPP's broader academic environment? The school is often praised for its strong use of digital tools and rigorously theoretical research: can you speak to these characteristics as they apply to the UD studio?

RP The Urban Design program considerably expands the realm of pedagogy and discourse within the GSAPP. It represents a clear alternative to the other programs in general, and to the AAD and Urban Planning (UP) programs in particular. Being situated as it is, in the middle of everything else that goes on here, UD students have a certain luxury of maximum exposure, and of the possibility of taking elective courses of almost infinite variety. As you know, our studios enjoy the same considerable digital resources as all other studios. Of course, we may deploy them in diverse ways from some "architecture" studios, but so what? And the digital resources provide a fundamental base for the Urban Design studio sequence, starting from your first day of class.

JM As you direct the Urban Design program, you simultaneously teach an architecture studio available to students of the Master of Architecture and Master of Science in Advanced Architectural Design (AAD) programs. Could you speak to how your approach to each possibly differs or overlaps?

RP I teach an architecture studio in the Architecture and AAD programs. The studio I taught last fall involved my own particular interests as an architect, as do those taught by others of the architecture faculty. My studio was the fourth that I have done in collaboration with the School of Engineering. Engineering students were involved, having a positive effect on the studio emphasis having to do with public space, urban micro-infrastructure, urban nature, and public health. Of course, some of these issues overlap with my Urban Design studio, but that's entirely normal.

ZZ You previously held the role of Chairman of the Division of Architecture, and 14 years ago took charge of the Urban Design program direction, in addition to your established and ongoing research on questions of housing. How have these shifts in roles influenced your overarching pedagogical scheme? Have intersections and distinctions between architecture and urban design changed under these different title frameworks?

RP Back in 1992, the presence of the UD program in the school had pretty much evaporated, so the then Dean, Bernard Tschumi, asked me to reinvent the program. And that's what we did—with a very dedicated faculty team. Of course, I was always interested in urbanism and housing, so I guess I was a logical choice to take this on. But I am interested in many things, and certainly, I have encouraged the evolution of the program emphasis since 1992. That is the way it must be, especially for a program that is collaborative—where ideas come from a collective (students *and* faculty), rather than from a single individual.

ZZ In your studio course, you have guided students to focus on smaller scaled interventions and their meanings and applications, without sole reliance on the quality of graphic representation. What kind of set standards and criteria do you use for what you define as "good", or rather "successful", urban and architectural design?

RP Yes, this is the "architecture vs. urban design" thing, I don't believe a bit of it. It's "The Scale Canard" that I wrote about some time ago.[1] Scale is always

1) "The Scale Canard," *Daidalos* 61 (September 1996).

independent of "urbanism," and as you know, I sometimes have said that a park bench can be urban design—meaning that the question is not one of scale but of complexity, of inclusiveness, of considerations of context at all scales. And one mandate of the UD program is to make the sensibility of this argument apparent to designers, such that they can handle urban operations with more skill than normative architects. Because urban design is fundamentally a public art, this expanded skill set is extremely important. And of course, "graphic quality" is extremely important, especially for this public interface. I am as interested in graphic quality (read aesthetics) as the next architect, and maybe more so. But I am not interested in projects masquerading as urban design without the public legibility that our particular craft entails.

ZZ The proportion of Chinese students (from either Mainland China, Hong Kong, or Taiwan) enrolled in the UD program seems comparatively higher than other programs in the university. Chinese urban centers have become a popular source of research among students in recent years, but this is not reflected in the offered UD studios. Could you explain the reasons behind this dissonance?

RP Sure, there is an increased number of Chinese students now—and more students from India and elsewhere. This is normal. China is developing economically and urbanizing enormously. Compared to 10 years ago—even five years ago—there is much more money in China for studying abroad. The interest in studying urban design in New York City should be related to understanding a particular approach to the discipline, and to interpreting it critically for application in China or elsewhere. Let's just say that, if there appears the right opportunity to do a studio in China, great! And we can learn from China. It is true that global cities everywhere have much to teach each other. But New York is our primary laboratory, and that is appropriate for the aims of the program.

ZZ Engagement with "informal housing" appears to be recurring throughout different UD studios and courses. How would you qualify this informality? As your research activities span different environments in a variety of countries on different continents, what sorts of social, economic, or political factors would you identify as most critically impacting housing?

RP "Informal housing" can have many definitions, but I think the most basic has to do with the economics of housing production. "Informal" is obviously outside of the "formal," and outside of the established and enforced official banking channels and building regulations. As I have often said, the informal phenomenon does not imply marginality. In many developing economies, it is the principal mode of housing production and can be considered illegitimate only with respect to the formal sector. And so, of course, if we do a studio in a developing economy, such as Guayaquil this past semester, it would be irresponsible to ignore the informal—it is the largest part of the production of the built environment. And we can learn much from this kind of engagement, including the potential of alternate design languages—alternatives to the mediocrities and dysfunctionalities of "official" design. I think everyone in your class became enormously interested in the efforts of the urban poor in Ecuador to fashion their own environments and in the ultimate success of these efforts, including the housing—informal as it is. Of course, this process produces problems, in particular at the larger scale of inappropriate growth, with attendant ecological conflicts and the like. But as designers, if only we could have the humility to recognize and enhance the enormous energy and know-how coming from the informal. It is a discussion that has been on the table for a half-century or more—but informal urbanization goes on, basically without us.

2010 "LANDSCAPE IN A NEW KEY"

Excerpted from "The Design Equation: Landscape in a New Key," *Landscape Architecture China 13*, no. 5 (2010), pp. 37-45.

In certain ways, current times remind us of the formative period more than five decades ago, when just like today, urban phenomena dominated a large piece of the design profession's discourse. At that time, the digital revolution was still in its incipient period, while engaging with what remains some of the most important theoretical work related to the ongoing information revolution: Ross Ashby's *Design for a Brain* (1952), Stafford Beer's *Cybernetics and Management* (1959), Norbert Weiner's *Cybernetics* (1948), Anatol Rapoport's *Operational Philosophy* (1953), among many others. At that same moment, the challenge of global urbanization and housing production also gave rise to important theoretical antecedents that are extremely relevant to our present period: Jean Gottmann's *Megalopolis* (1961), Bernard Rudofsky's *Architecture Without Architects* (1964), Charles Abrams' *The City is the Frontier* (1965), John F. C. Turner's pioneering work on squatter settlements published in *Architectural Design* (1963-68), among many others. Simultaneously, the changing global ecological condition was first measured with alarming immediacy, and in hindsight, with remarkable predictive accuracy, perhaps most comprehensively by those associated with the Club of Rome, whose intellectual capital has seen no equivalent in the intervening decades.[1]

For urban interventions, new categories augmented the distinctions between "architecture" and "engineering": "urban design" and "environmental design" reconfigured older concepts of what design expertise could entail. With these new categories came new notions of the possibilities of design language necessitated by the new urban landscape. Perhaps Susanne Langer

This essay reconfigures two earlier essays by the author: "The Design Equation," ed. by Richard Plunz and Maria Paola Sutto, *Urban Climate Change Crossroads*, Farnham, Surrey, UK: Ashgate Publishing Limited (2009); and "Re-centering Around Climate," *Domus* 930 (November 2009).

1) See Donella H. Meadows et al., *The Limits to Growth: A Report from Rome Club's Project on the Predicament of Mankind*, New York: Universe Books (1972).

articulated this new condition best in her *Philosophy in a New Key* (1942), especially relative to the expanding realm of visual communication as an analytic tool relative to the experiential world. In the years since, perhaps no other of the traditional design disciplines has transformed so thoroughly as "landscape architecture," now intimately tied to the new urban imperatives through the pervasive rubric of "landscape urbanism." Beginning with the pioneering work of Ian McHarg, *Design with Nature* (1969), landscape architecture became the primary bridging discipline between design and the natural sciences, and for the urban realm, this text has become a primary force for innovation in urban design operations. For the overriding issue of urban adaptation to evolving parameters of climate change, the question of urban "landscape in a new key" is a convenient starting point toward understanding remediation.

It is common to point out that our latest phase of global urbanization represents a fundamentally new phenomenon of scale, comprising the new mega-cities of the "developing world." For example, more than 100 cities in China have grown to over one million population each over the last decade or so. It is also common to point to the strain on global resources that this new urbanization entails. We are speaking here of the association of basic resources—water, energy, and material resources—with lifestyle changes. Pressure for growth has not been limited to new cities. It also engages the old. An important dialogue is yet to happen between "developed" and "developing." Recentering older cities as positive models for the future is imperative. However, the old mega-cities prove insufficient as models in the face of new urban challenges—especially related to ecology and mega-issues like global warming.

On the question of urbanization and global warming, experts raise even more questions today than even only 14 months ago, when in February 2008 the Urban Climate Change Crossroads forum was held in Rome.[2] Wishful thinking has since surfaced that both urbanization and global warming may be somehow slowed by the recent worldwide economic turmoil. Such is unlikely to be the case. Indeed, barely a year after the Rome forum, Lord Nicholas Stern, whose 2006 report was cited by so many of us, advised that the

2) The forum, "Urban Climate Change at the Crossroads," was held in Rome (February 4-5, 2008), organized by the Camera di Commercio di Roma, the Fondazione Adriano Olivetti, and the Urban Design Lab of the Earth Institute at Columbia University. It addressed climate change issues related to urban adaptation inclusive of both natural and social science considerations.

situation was already more serious even than previously thought, suggesting that the effects of global warming are coming faster than predicted even only several years ago. He has since made further adjustments in anticipation of the Copenhagen Climate Change Conference in December of 2009. Like the warming, there is no evidence that urbanization will abate. It may intensify as our global insecurities grow. For instance, the resettlement of climate refugees may serve to further focalize the world's cities. Climate change and GDP are interrelated such that the so-called "developed" world will not be exempt. In the United States, the new urban wave is already nascent as the economic and psychological advantages of suburban lifestyle are eroding. Add to this the climate equation, already evidenced in the resettlement from New Orleans to other cities, and we begin to sense the complexity of our shared urban futures.

Within the realm of the developed world, we might celebrate that people are returning to cities. However, the kind of city they return to is a crucial issue and an important component of the recentering question. For example, the infrastructure of older cities is environmentally substandard and impossible to upgrade if one follows normative thinking—such that there can never be adequate water and energy delivery, adequate sanitary systems, adequate waste handling, and so on. All of these basics require rethinking assumptions of scale, efficiency, and sustainability. The mega-scale infrastructural approaches of the industrial era no longer function. Infrastructural innovation must include the micro-scale. Older industrial-era cities must reinvent their economies, and this process relates directly to the reinvention of their infrastructures around new sustainability criteria.

In the United States, our 20th-century cycle of urban dispersal is finished. We are entering a new era of consolidation for which simple densification provides only the beginning of an explication. Recentering must be associated with spatial and social qualities, spearheaded by equity issues. An aspect of recentering involves sociological and cultural phenomena and a psychological dimension as basic as urban security on many levels. In the new era of direct competition between cities, these realms of consideration will be increasingly important. Climate science is social science. Climate and environmental justice considerations are directly connected to the development of social capital. Cities that attract social capital will simultaneously be far more likely to achieve success through new enterprise and an expanded economic base—particularly knowledge-based urban economies—and realize adaptation strategies for global warming. The making of urban competitive distinctions starts here. If continuing urbanization and global warming are the future, urban competition and climate will be a fundamental amalgamation to the recentering of the 21st century.

Let us consider the work of the British economist, Ezra Mishan, who was associated with the Club of Rome—and who still provides a relevant critical perspective on the culture of consumption. Especially useful is his "Mishan Model," published in *The Costs of Economic Growth* (1967), that effectively demonstrates the limits of automobile culture. Mishan's crucial judgment was that, even after public consensus would one day conclude that less or no automobiles are socially preferable to transport dysfunction, the system will not have built-in controls such that fewer automobiles can ever be obtained without extraordinary intervention external to the transport sector. By using the automobile as a metaphor for our broader global growth, we can begin to understand the enormity of the questions surrounding global environmental change today—and that the growth of global consumption and environmental degradation is not easily reversed without unprecedented global intervention.

Mishan provided a paradigm for the "manifest destiny" of the so-called American Century, as a global power has played itself out. Until very recently, in so many sectors, American hegemony was expected to govern the planetary trajectory. In the run-up to the U.S. invasion of Iraq in 2004, President George W. Bush used the argument that there must be "... no holding back, no compromise, no hesitation" in protecting the "American way of life."[3] But the evidence is well in place that the American way of life is itself unsustainable. Even in disregarding the futility of the war itself, the connection of the culture of consumption in the United States to the growing depletion of the world's oil reserves, its crucial life support, means that the American way of life enters an excruciatingly difficult period. This is arguably ultimately for the better. In absolute terms, within recorded history, there is no precedent on a global scale for the environmental interventions that now unfold. However, in terms of relative scale—of human response—other very interesting questions arise altogether. We are not alone in history and can find solidarity in powerful precedents.

Understanding the question of adaptation engages a huge historical dimension. Arguably, environmental adaptation has been a "normal" constant

3) President George W. Bush and British Prime Minister Tony Blair, remarks at The Cross Hall (November 20, 2003), transcript, the White House, Office of the Press Secretary <http://www.whitehouse.gov/news/releases/2003/01/20030131-23.html>.

condition of human history but appears anathema to modern design culture.[4] If we simply do not look back, relative to this history, and especially to ecology, is it possible that we have arrived to a "post-historical period," where the easiness of past is no longer so resonant? The brilliance of Bill McKibben's *The End of Nature* (1989) was in articulating precisely this point more than a decade ago.

The gamble for ecological survival has always been reliant on technology and design—and when the technological limits are obvious, design adaptation must follow. When design adaptation became inadequate, humankind moved on. Such a design imperative emerged with Hurricane Katrina in New Orleans. New York City now faces a similar fateful moment with hurricanes and sea level rise. As does Bangkok, sinking as the sea rises. Quito, losing its water supply as the glaciers melt (15 years out). And so on. We have assuredly arrived at the issue of "limits"—rendering questions anticipated by the Club of Rome immediate.

How urban adaptation occurs goes beyond building seawalls, moving from flood plains, inventing more robust infrastructures, and the like. A part of our consideration at the scale of urbanism is the changing nature of urban enterprise itself—of industry. Urban climate change adaptation involves urban economies—not just global, but also local; new forms of production; and specifically, new urban industry that can integrate with the adaptation process itself. This trajectory engages what has been popularly described as a new field of "restoration ecology" and is corollary with degraded urban contexts—and therefore has the potential to generate new urban production.

In cities, the restoration economy is increasingly critical, as restoration science moves from built fabric to the urban "natural environment". This follows the logic that degraded urban ecosystems may provide more economic opportunities than detriments.[5] Involved are emerging new forms of "natural" resources. The concept of nature as "accumulation strategy" is expanding to include the redefinition of nature itself. Degraded and consumed

4) Within the field of archeology, there has been very interesting new work correlating built form and climatological science. For example, see Eberhard Zangger, *The Future of the Past. Archeology in the 21st Century*, London: Phoenix (2002).

5) The restoration economy concept is well-summarized in Storm Cunningham, *The Restoration Economy: The Greatest New Growth Frontier,* San Francisco: Berrett-Koehler Publishers, Inc. (2002). The economics of the new eco-enterprise is well analyzed in Herman E. Daley and Joshua Farley, *Ecological Economics: Principles and Application*, Washington DC: Island Press (2004).

environments are no longer seen as a liability, but rather as a powerful new frontier of capital accumulation—such that "nature is increasing if selectively replicated as its own marketplace."[6] The social and monetary costs and benefits must factor this expanded arena of considerations, and this economic adaptation must go hand in hand with physical adaptation within climate strategies.

Embedded in the concept of the new urban production is a critique of our inherited premises of "economic growth." The old models rely on the assumptions of always-expanding material consumption fueled by always-growing economies. Characteristic of these models is also a separation of economics from ecology, with economists ignoring natural contexts, and ecologists ignoring human contexts—a formulation that no longer guarantees human progress. Urban economies that thrive in our new era will have to function within a second modernity, antithetical of the first that rejects the "canonical assumptions" of insatiable wants and infinite resources leading to supposed "growth forever."[7] The question of a new beginning, of climate change as a positive economic force, renders a possible positive prognosis. As the German sociologist Ulrich Beck argues, now is a moment of a "second modernity," which is "being born within the interstices of the first modernity, most of all within its cities..."[8]

When science interacts with the city, design is an essential stimulant. Geo-environmental analysis aside, the primary language for urban intervention has entailed "design," deployed as a catalytic urban tool and an effective means of visualizing the complexities of the intervention strategies for public discourse that urban design research must evoke.[9] The huge question is whether the design fields are at all adequately equipped to manage the adaptation problems: Ulrich Beck's "glocalization" challenge, the new

6) On the historical shift in environmental capitalism see also: Leo Paniteh and Colin Leys, *Coming to Terms with Nature: Socialist Register 2007*, London: The Merlin Press (2006). Of particular interest is the essay by Neil Smith, "Nature Accumulation Strategy," pp. 16-36.

7) On "canonical assumptions," see Daley and Farley, op. cit., pp. xxi-xxii.

8) Ulrich Beck and Johannes Willms, *Conversations with Ulrich Beck*, Cambridge: Polity Press (2004), pp. 39, 183.

9) Serge Chermayeff first defined the concept of "design as catalyst" in reference to urban and environmental design. See *Design and the Public Good. Selected Writings, 1930-1980 by Serge Chermayeff*, ed. Richard Plunz, Cambridge: The MIT Press (1982), pp. 289-295.

technological realities, the general post-historical context. Certainly, the context for design activity is changing rapidly, but Western design culture has evolved over the past four or five centuries, such that appearances aside, a change in trajectory on the scale of the ecological change that we now face will be challenging to say the least.

It is especially during the past 150 years or so that our present professional limitations have crystallized: with the separation of architecture from engineering; the evolution of isolated design discourse and pedagogy; with artificial distinctions between the design of buildings, urbanism, landscape, interiors, products, and the like. These old problem sets are now obsolescent, with redundancies in terms of intellectual and operational outlook. Today, especially for environmental challenges related to global development and sustainability, and for questions of adaptation by design, there is a growing challenge to these institutionalized categories. Design is intimately connected to both the ecological and political science realms—and ultimately, to the question of power—and its abuse. Yet the world of design culture has always resisted forthright admission of this reality—and for the "design equation" within the climate change challenge, this denial is complicit to the incapacity of the profession to deal with the environmental challenges that climate change intensifies.

For decades, architecture had considered itself the "mother" activity for the design of the built environment—even as it became more and more marginalized. This trend has intensified with the present wave of global urbanization. The field has always accounted for a small percentage of the built environment, but in the new scale of global urbanization, it is minuscule. High architectural discourse has become more and more restricted to the world of high fashion, to the exclusion of the other some 99 percent of buildings. The problem is that high fashion is emblematic of the "mainstream" values of design culture—and manifestos will not achieve a new legitimacy for design. There is a need for new fundamental design knowledge.

While the demand for built environment expertise is growing, the building industry worldwide is the most extraordinarily wasteful and destructive of all human enterprises, placing it at the epicenter of any adaptation strategy. Certainly, the design marketplace itself is adapting to the new global context, including academia; however, it is quite possible that there is far more interest in design culture from the outside looking in, than vice versa. As the natural sciences "urbanize," as they certainly are in our present wave of globalization, they are finding that urban science gets complicated, principally through the necessity for political engagement. Simply stated, climate science is all-encompassing: it too is urbanizing.

It is fortunate that new realities coerce science and design into new relationships. The kind of creative process inherent to design methodologies, for so long anathema to the scientific "method," is suddenly gaining notice and some credibility from the science side. The problem, however, is reciprocity—and whether the superficial hermeticism that has come to characterize design discourse is able to meet this challenge. No one, however, can deny that this is an interesting catalytic moment. While the aesthete side of design culture is attempting to hold its own as an offshoot of the fashion industry, the cracks in this position are widening. There is an evolving new academic amalgam involving business, science, and design deliberately blurred in response to new problem sets and scientific boundaries.

The momentum for this approach, at least in the United States, is quickly strengthening around the global warming phenomenon. Nevertheless, our centers of learning will have to wake up to realities beyond the attractions of new business models. In spite of new visualization and fabrication tools, designers will have to acknowledge the reality that design culture seems to have regressed from where it was in the 1960s—on the applications side of things, at least in terms of exploring a sustainable new "world model." Design culture needs to trace the same ground as the natural sciences have already covered during the last four decades—and more. Indeed, the urban "landscape" is shifting.

2013
"CITY OF HEALTH"

From "Introduction," in *Re-envisioning Health in Kumasi: Spatial Strategies*, New York: Urban Design Lab, Columbia University Earth Institute, 2013.

> *The transition from the industrial society to the post-industrial society is being processed in the so-called "developed" world. Simultaneously, the largest part of humanity is undergoing several progressive phases of industrialization. In the "First World," linear, historical thought, which is founded on texts, is being challenged by thinking that is structured by post-textural codes, such as that of technical images. In the "Third World," efforts are being made to increase adult literacy… Current times are marked by the discrepancy between the established social forms, thought structures, and levels of consciousness.*[1]

Although written several decades ago, Flusser's "discrepancy" still holds. In this regard, our work may well raise more issues than it resolves, but it does point toward urban development alternatives to the normative practice of the past several decades. Let's think of it as "diagnostics" that help to illuminate the fact that our present wave of global urbanization simply has not behaved according to normative models associated with the recent experience in the so-called "developed" world.

Of course, in recent years the global discrepancies between categories of development have contributed to profuse frustrations. Perhaps the most universal has been the unattainability of the Millennium Development Goals (MDG) that have been part and parcel of global development metrics as envisioned by the United Nations since 2000. As of 2010, these 21 targets and 60 indicators have been largely unmet; and at best can be seen as symbolic objectives that might encourage developmental progress and donor support; but not as attainable practical outcomes. Even within this positivistic interpretation of MDG strategy lurks the contradiction of attempting to achieve credibility through failure, with critics pointing to a certain futility of

1) Vilém Flusser, *Post-History*, Minneapolis: Univocal (2013). Originally published as *Pós-História: Vinte Instantâneos e um Modo de Usar*, Brazil: Duas Cidades (1983).

the whole exercise.[2] There are diverse views on this question,[3] but certainly, the difficulties associated with our present global hyper-urbanization lend support to the need for new strategies. In general, even the universally deployed Gross Domestic Product (GDP) as a measure of national progress has severe limitations especially as applied to contemporary developing economies. The emergence of alternative indicators such as the Global Progress Indicator (GPI) gives evidence of the shortcomings.[4] There is even some question as to the relevance of positive growth of GDP at all; especially when other metrics such as GPI are simultaneously in negative territory.

Today, it is urbanization that is driving both GDP as an indicator of global progress; and the more comprehensive attempts such as GPI, or even other "happiness" metrics. While global urbanization is unprecedented in scale, comprehensive metrics capable of measuring its progress are not easy to come by, especially for the problem of the spatial city. Our basic dilemma is that urbanization operations that have evolved in the developed world are substantially estranged from those presently deployed within the developing world to the extent that the former appears to be largely irrelevant. For example, it is futile to think that a city like Kumasi, which in 30 years has roughly doubled its population, can follow the same conventions of planning that prevail in cities of roughly the same size like Atlanta or Philadelphia. Kumasi's economic circumstances are absolutely different, starting with an informal sector growth in Kumasi that dominates all else, variously estimated at over 75 percent of the local workforce.[5] This urbanization absolutely entails differing processes and metrics than the whole of our professional knowledge has given us over the past two centuries. Yet these models tend to dominate, either directly or indirectly, global development strategies.

In most of today's developing world, the resources to implement developed-world strategies are simply not available, even with the benevolence of international donors and the like. For better or worse, services must be

2) Richard Manning, "The Impact and Design of the MDGs: Some Reflections," *IDS Bulletin* 41, no. 1 (January 2010).

3) Jeffrey D. Sachs, "From Millennium Development Goals to Sustainable Development Goals," *The Lancet* 379 (June 9, 2012), < https://doi.org/10.1016/S0140-6736(12)60685-0>.

4) Ida Kubiszewski et al., "Beyond GDP: Measuring and achieving global genuine progress," *Ecological Economics* 93 (2013), 57-68.

5) Sam Afrane and George Ahiable, "The Informal Economy and Microfinance in Kumasi," in *The Fate of the Tree. Planning and Managing the Development of Kumasi, Ghana*, eds. Kwasi Kwafo Adarkwa and Johan Post, Accra: Woeli Publishing Services (2001), ch. 7.

provided as retrofit to urbanization—perhaps at best, as microscale nodal strategies for new development. In Accra, for example, in the 1980s, the dream of implementing a single large sewage system was fraught with failure even after the centralized Jamestown treatment plant was built with donor support. It could not be maintained; and the feeder system was too limited. In Accra, other "top-down" initiatives like a centralized waste-to-energy facility have been met with similar stalemates; and point toward alternative "bottom-up" strategies.[6]

Urban design in all our worlds is inherently connected to indeterminacy as it relates to economic possibilities and to evolutionary strategies. Formalist ideologies and static implementations largely dominate normative urban design practice in the developed world. Difficulties with transferring this practice to the developing world are compounded by the lack of relevance of these conventions, and more importantly, by the lack of alternative knowledge that can be operational in developing economies, in spite of the enormous demand.

The above is especially true for urban infrastructure. Today it is not possible to implement the same kind of large singular moves that dominated the development of cities in the industrializing 19th and 20th centuries in Europe and North America, such as large-scale, universalized networks for advanced services and highly rationalized physical infrastructure. For the case of the urbanizing area of Asokore Mampong, in Kumasi, a localized strategy of highly nodal infrastructure that can provide basic services and direct the densification around such nodes seems particularly pertinent.[7]

It appears that development in both Accra and Kumasi has outpaced top-down strategies and as such, affords the option of "leap-frogging" old top-down development models completely even as their advocacy continues to proliferate from some interests. For example, on the table in Kumasi remains the elusive notion of completing a "ring road" that would undoubtedly be symbolic of capacity for infrastructural advancement but also, if realized, would attenuate sprawl to no good end while serving very limited functional need.

6) A Columbia Urban Design Studio in 2011 researched similar strategies. See *Urban Development in Accra, Ghana: An Implementation Toolkit*, New York: Urban Design Lab Earth Institute, Columbia University (2011).

7) A Columbia University Urban Design Studio in 2012 researched similar strategies. See *Re-cultivating the Garden City of Kumasi*, New York: Urban Design Lab Earth Institute, Columbia University (2012).

In many ways, the economic impracticality of the Kumasi ring road proposal has presented an opportunity to review the entire question of mobility. In any event, by contrast for both cities, our work has explored the efficacy of bottom-up. This entails the option of many small infrastructural moves rather than singular large ones. Essential to this consideration is repetitive operations—and the understanding that large scale is also small scale. Repetitive small units accumulate to accomplish large-impact infrastructural moves.

When reflecting on the question of enhancing mobility in Kumasi, it seemed more logical to suggest building on the existing systems rather than proposing huge schemes with no possibility of practical implementation. In this regard we found the existing informal transit deploying the *tro-tro* to be of immense interest. And from this consideration, the invention of the *tro-tro* mass transit project evolved as a system that can vastly improve the efficiency of the existing informal system that already moves several hundred thousand persons per day via privately owned vans and mini-buses. It is clear that this existing system will remain in place for many years, such that investment in its efficacy is an immediate priority. Positive results are attainable with minimum investment compared to normative mass transit options, such as bus rapid transit or fantasies such as light rail or subway that even developed urban economies can ill afford, including New York.

Interestingly, much is now shared between the so-called developed and undeveloped worlds around infrastructure challenges, as 19th-century conceptions begin to obsolesce globally. For example, New York City shares certain sewage problems with both Accra and Kumasi. In New York, with every rainfall of one-quarter inch or more, untreated sewage is dumped into the Hudson and East Rivers due to an obsolete combined grey and black water system and the incapacity of the centralized plants to treat both during rainfall. New York can no longer afford the huge infrastructural investments made in the 19th century: in this case, a two-pipe system to separate the rain and wastewater. The only realistic option is to intercept the rainwater with a predominently bottom-up approach entailing hundreds of depots. And with this, New York arrives at a similar approach to Kumasi, for example, where a predominently top-down approach is also not feasible. In Kumasi, for basic water and sanitation infrastructure, the huge urbanization of the past 20 years will have to be retrofitted in a multi-nodal system, to be developed in small increments that are highly additive, and in this lies the clues for the spatial distribution of further densification within the existing fabric, and for the new urban extensions.

The same issues exist for the question of sustaining micro-enterprise, which is absolutely essential to the informal sector, without which 75 percent of the city's economy becomes dysfunctional. In Kumasi, for the case of Fante New Town, this informal sector, apart from all else, is providing a substantial portion of the city's food infrastructure. It is the vibrant center for breadstuff and other goods. It also has much of the pre-modern legacy of the built fabric of the city, including the traditional compounds for baking juxtaposed with attractive colonial-era structures. Both should not be lost as they can be crucial to the future economic development of the city. For this reason, it is important to develop a strategy of resistance to the likely destructive forces of new development due to the centrality of location and the perceived opportunities for the emerging formal sector. A complex strategy of allowing change while micro-managing protection entails insisting on the efficacy of the area and reinforcing its boundaries.

Perhaps the most inclusive issue entailing all of the above and more is the question of urban health. Health is mobility: food systems; water and sanitation; and access to health services. Localized hospitals put in context all of these considerations. They direct global health services toward the improvement of local services. They connect into the improved regional transit to better integrate disparate facilities. They tie into local enterprise by jump-starting homeopathic production. They connect to a globalizing economy of health tourism. They question the very definition of "hospital" in the 21st century. In this synthesis is illustrated the potentials for interconnectedness within the infrastructure of the future: rainwater is also cultivation is also health is also mobility is also livelihood and vice versa.

In some of this, there is nothing new—just lessons that we have forgotten. In some ways, we are at a decisive frontier of new urban knowledge. Benjamin Ward Richardson's famous treatise on *Hygeia, a City of Health* (1875) was a holistic definition of the ideal industrial city. Of course, the "industrial city" no longer takes the same form anywhere. We are all "post-industrial." Still, the intentions embedded in *Hygeia* can be translated to "Kumasi, a City of Health" 140 years later, as Kumasi leapfrogs that moment for our present. We all have much to learn, and Kumasi gives us answers.

2018 “CROWDSOURCING INFRASTRUCTURE”

Interview with Eve Glasberg, “5 Questions: Richard Plunz on Crowdsourcing Urban Design with Twitter,” *Columbia News* (March 2, 2018), <http://news.columbia.edu/content/5-Questions-Richard-Plunz-on-Crowdsourcing-Urban-Design-with-Twitter>.

Eve Glasberg During a storm, several thousand swales (low-lying channels that are shallower than a ditch) across New York City collect rainwater runoff and keep it from flooding the sewers. While working on an app to help monitor this system, Richard Plunz and his colleagues at the Earth Institute’s Urban Design Lab found that community involvement would be just as critical to its success as technology. “The only practical way to monitor these sites is via social media, allowing people in the neighborhood to report on the status of green infrastructure,” said Plunz, whose team collaborates on a broad range of multidisciplinary research projects, including investigations of new ecological realities facing cities, next-generation economic development and the intensifying effects of climate change. Now, he and his colleagues are studying how this crowdsourcing approach might apply to the entire field of urban design. Their project combines mapping techniques with Twitter usage data to gain a real-time understanding of how people occupy public space.

Richard Plunz Social media provides the first tool for gauging how areas with high-density tweets, such as parks, tourist attractions, and transit hubs are actually used. “Over time, we anticipate that social media will help us to produce a new generation of urban design and planning tools that address how to make these spaces more environmentally and socially resilient.

EG What have you learned from analyzing Twitter use in public parks?

RP We have been able to confirm the efficacy of real-time geospatial tracking of information, which is already an important breakthrough in terms of urban design. What we did not anticipate was the potential for understanding sentiment regarding urban settings and in response to real-time tracking, especially in affirming the accuracy of Twitter data relative to specific events and conditions. We have also considered the potential for predictions related

PLATE P
"Twitter Hotspots" Manhattan, New York

2017-2022. Crowd-sourced infrastructure research. Columbia University Earth Institute Urban Design Lab.

Research into use of crowd-sourced geolocated data as an indicator of movement dynamics and public space usage in New York City. Geolocated Twitter densities were mapped and correlated with various considerations from physical infrastructure to cognitive properties. "Hot spots" were closely associated with mass transit usage, especially with subway access points. The efficacy of real-time geospatial tracking of information pointed to an important breakthrough as an urban design tool. Because Twitter data is 24/7 and a conscious stream in continuum, it provides a collective picture of social responses to particular situations and contexts and becomes a fluid tool for future planning, as opposed to a static system focused on specific issues at specific times. Because Twitter is fundamentally cognitive in nature, the project evolved into the deployment of sentiment analytics to advance the understanding of park usage as an element of well-being. Such cognitive mapping of urban environments entails a mental decoding of information that has been a preoccupation for centuries as a metaphysical construct, now evolved into an operational tool. Later iterations explored sentiment related to the COVID-19 pandemic.

2017. "Manhattan Twitter Hotspots" Research, Earth Institute Urban Design Lab. Richard Plunz, Principal Investigator; Project Team: Amy Motzny, Laura Uguccioni, Maria Paola Sutto.

PUBLICATION: "Twitter Sentiment in New York City Parks as measure of well-being," with Yijia Zhou, Maria Isabel Carrasco Vintimilla, Kathleen McKeown, Tao Yu, Laura Uguccioni, and Maria Paola Sutto, *Landscape and Urban Planning* 189 (2019), pp. 235-246. Also see Richard Plunz Papers, Department of Drawings & Archives, Avery Architectural and Fine Arts Library.

to people and events. For example, in our work on the High Line, we can distinguish between New York residents and tourists. We can anticipate hours before an event that it could be oversubscribed and therefore require special precautions relative to security and logistics.

EG What made you choose Bryant Park, Washington Square Park, and the High Line?

RP These particular parks are representative of three different ways that public space is used. Bryant Park has the most potential for Twitter-based analytics, given its heavy usage, especially on weekday lunchtimes. Washington Square Park has a much greater full-time occupancy, which gives a more expansive view of its use. The High Line's long trajectory and large percentage of tourists provide yet another reading and perspective on the relationship between a park and its people. We are researching the effectiveness of Twitter in helping to understand these different characteristics in real time and the possibilities for correlating them with many variables, including weather patterns and social events.

EG What can Twitter tell us that surveys can't?

RP Twitter data is 24/7 and in a continuum, a conscious stream, a collective picture of social responses to particular situations and contexts. It provides a tool for future planning as opposed to a system focused on specific issues at specific times. It is fundamentally cognitive in nature and, therefore, represents a huge advance in our comprehension of how we interact with our environment and vice versa.

EG What are the practical applications?

RP There is real-time monitoring of public space density-of-use patterns and even usage prediction related to specific public events. It's also possible to use Twitter density and sentiment as a tool for long-term design considerations. This can include, at different scales, the redesign of public parks—adding more grass and trees, for example, or new activity areas, or figuring out if nearby buildings or construction are having a negative impact on vegetation. Is a park being overused? Or are users dissatisfied and, if so, why? How can a park be more effective and have more social benefits? The next 10 years will be huge in reaching a new understanding of every aspect of our built environment via social media data.

EG What are the limitations of this approach? Where would you like to see it go?

RP Perhaps the biggest limitation now is the uneven distribution of Twitter usage throughout the city. In our study, we ended up focusing on lower Manhattan, in part because there is sufficient Twitter data for these areas. Central Park had to be eliminated because the Twitter-density patterns are so dispersed. We anticipate that this problem will disappear as the use of Twitter-like social media grows. That will be the moment when techniques like ours become everyday practice, opening a new window into urban cognition. The cognitive mapping of urban environments entails a mental decoding of information. It has been a preoccupation for centuries, but more as a metaphysical construct. As precedent to our work, there have been iconic studies; from Italian architect Giambattista Nolli's 1748 plan of Rome, to Baudelaire's 1847 *flâneur*—who walks the city in order to experience it—to urban planner Kevin Lynch's *The Image of the City* analytics of the 1950s. We are moving from urban cognition as a primarily literary and conceptual tool into the realm of it becoming an operational tool for spatial design. This is a new moment for an ages-old preoccupation.

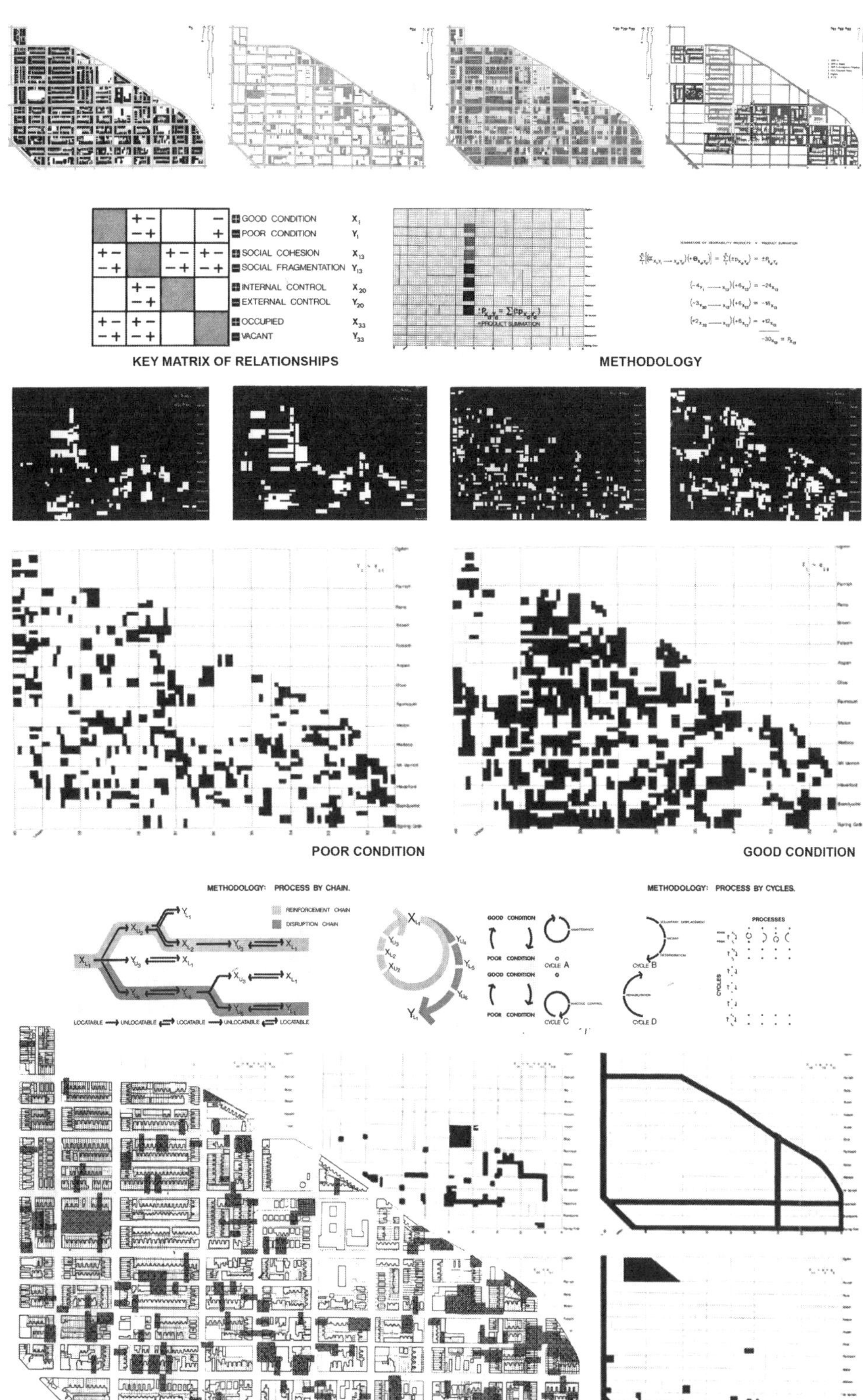
GOOD CONDITION X_1
POOR CONDITION Y_1
SOCIAL COHESION X_{13}
SOCIAL FRAGMENTATION Y_{13}
INTERNAL CONTROL X_{20}
EXTERNAL CONTROL Y_{20}
OCCUPIED X_{33}
VACANT Y_{33}
KEY MATRIX OF RELATIONSHIPS
METHODOLOGY
POOR CONDITION
GOOD CONDITION
METHODOLOGY: PROCESS BY CHAIN.
REINFORCEMENT CHAIN
DISRUPTION CHAIN
LOCATABLE UNLOCATABLE LOCATABLE UNLOCATABLE LOCATABLE
METHODOLOGY: PROCESS BY CYCLES.
GOOD CONDITION
POOR CONDITION
CYCLE A
CYCLE B
CYCLE C
CYCLE D
PROCESSES
CYCLES
INFILL HOUSING LOCATIONS

PLATE Q
"Digital Sedimentation" Philadelphia, Pennsylvania

1969-1970. Agent-based mapping, Mantua community, Philadelphia. Pennsylvania State University architecture studios.

Development of an agent-based digital model of urban dynamics within the Mantua neighborhood in Philadelphia, a community with severe poverty and social dysfunction. Field research entailed a year of residence on site and collaboration with the Mantua Community Planners, a "Project Area Committee" formed with the support of the Omnibus Housing Act of 1960 to engage urban communities in making decisions regarding design and construction. A second year entailed university-based analysis of the field documentation in collaboration with the United States Public Health Service. Algorithms were developed to assist in the interpretation of the physical and social transformation. A digital model of change processes was developed as a planning tool. While digitalization was made by hand, it anticipated the deployment of computer software that one day could bring the model to full interactive capacity. The model was tested to determine optimal sites for prototype infill housing design studies.

1969. "Mantua Model Maps and Algorithms," Mantua Design Studio Workshop in collaboration Mantua Community Planners and the United States Public Health Service. Faculty: Richard Plunz; Students: John Cowder, Allen Neyman, Robert Pistilli, Lee Strickland, with Charles Baker, Tiko Campbell, Steven Lomicka, Gary Smalls; Edward Jakmauh, United States Public Health Service. Graphic representation: Maria Isabel Carrasco (MSAUD 2017), Lucy Navarro (M.Arch 2020), Nelson de Jesus Ubri (M.Arch, MRED 2021).

PUBLICATION: *Mantua Primer: Toward a Program for Environmental Change*, ed. Richard Plunz, United States Health Services Research Branch, Publication Planning 1, University Park: Department of Architecture, Pennsylvania State University (1970). Also see Richard Plunz Papers Archive, Department of Drawings & Archives, Avery Architecture and Fine Arts Library; Plunz Mantua Collection, Temple University Special Collections Research Center, Philadelphia.

2020 "REALIGNING PROPINQUITY"

"Reflections On Leuven as Martyred City and the Realignment of Propinquity," *Revival After the Great War: Rebuild, Remember, Repair, Reform*, eds. Luc Verpoestet et al., Leuven, Belgium: Leuven University Press, 2020, pp. 55-63.

I find it intriguing to return once again to Leuven and to the Katholieke Universiteit, to reflect on the significance of the events here of a century ago that are still with us today in one form or another. We are meeting in the place of the former university library, rebuilt after the war but that no longer operates as a library. I ask your indulgence in reading the following account from 1914 of the fate of a professor at Leuven who would have, on a regular basis, passed through the Oude Markt and the university library, before its destruction on August 25, 1914.

> *I am the son of a Louvain Professor. I met at Furnes [Veurne], whilst I was with the army, a man who was a refugee from Louvain… He came to give me information as to the happenings at my father's house, of which he had been left in charge. He told me that when the Germans arrived at Louvain, they took possession of my father's house and completely looted it, taking away all portable articles of value and destroying the furniture and other contents. That they stabled horses in the drawing room. That they destroyed, tore up, and threw into the street my father's manuscripts and books (which were very numerous) and completely wrecked his library and its contents. That finally the Germans burnt the house together with all others in the neighbourhood. The Germans also destroyed the manuscript of an important work of my late father which was in the hands of a printer.*[1]

Apart from the above transgressions, the professor's lifeworld in Leuven was definitively erased with the burning of the university library and its

1) Committee on Alleged German Outrages, *Report of the Committee on Alleged German Outrages Presented to Parliament by Command of His Majesty*, London: H.M. Stationery Off., Eyre and Spottiswoode, Ltd., printers (1915), p. 107. Leuven professor Léon Noël describes the events of August 26 in *Louvain, 891-1914,* Oxford: Clarendon Press (1915), pp. 203-241.

300,000 books and manuscripts dating back centuries. Leuven was said to be "martyred."[2] Although the sacking of Leuven remains unspeakable today, similar atrocities have since been perpetuated elsewhere in the world. Let's reflect for a moment on our own academic worlds and imagine ourselves in the place of those Leuven faculty in 1918 during their deliberations on rebuilding. I can imagine that we might be tempted to put everything back. There was the capacity to do so a century ago. Yet rebuilding went beyond "restoration," such that today Leuven remains an important precedent for understanding the options for urbanism that have been lost in the normative urban planning protocols of the remainder of the 20th century.

On the Western Front, the logistics of destruction and reconstruction were immense, even by today's norms. In Belgium and France, by one estimate, 3,430,000 hectares of land were destroyed and in Belgium alone, 242 municipalities had to undergo reconstruction.[3] In Leuven, by various accounts, 1,081 houses and some 2,000 buildings overall were completely destroyed, with extensive partial damage to others; 25 to 30 percent of the city terrain was "scorched earth."[4] In Belgium, by various estimates, up to two million people became refugees: one-third of Belgium's population at that time. At least half a million refugees remained in France and the UK until well after the war, and of course, many from Leuven would have remained displaced for some period given the devastation.[5] Surely the Belgian displacements of

2) There was considerable contemporary reportage related to the sack of Leuven, including the work by the *Committee on Alleged German Outrages*. Also useful has been Richard Harding Davis, *With the Allies*, New York: Charles Scribner's Sons (1914). Another useful contemporary account is given in Léon Noël, op. cit. The characterization of Leuven among "martyred" cities in Flanders appears early on in the account of Albert Fuglister, *Louvain, Ville Martyre*, Paris: Éditions Delandre (1916).

3) Figures referenced in Dries Claeys, "World War I and the Reconstruction of the Countryside in Belgium and France: A Historiographical Essay," *Agricultural History Review* 65, no. 1 (January 2017), pp. 108-129. A comprehensive survey of the war damage is given in Hugh Clout, "The Intensity of Devastation," *After the Ruins: Restoring the Countryside of Northern France after the Great War*, Exeter: University of Exeter Press (1996), pp. 19-52.

4) Among the sources for destruction logistics in Leuven are Marcel Smets, "The Reconstruction of Leuven after the Events of 1914," overprint, Cities in Development 19th-20th Centuries, 10th International Colloquium, Spa, Belgium (September 2-5, 1980); and John Horne and Alan Kramer, *German Atrocities, 1914: A History of Denial,* New Haven: Yale University Press (2001), p. 40.

5) Larry Zuckerman, *The Rape of Belgium: The Untold Story of World War I*, New York: New York University Press (2004), p. 85. The scattering of the Katholieke Universiteit Leuven faculty is described in Mark Derez, "The Flames of Louvain: The War Experience of an Academic Community," in *Facing Armageddon: The First World War Experienced*, ed. Hugh Cecil and Peter H. Liddle, London: Cooper (1996), pp. 617-629.

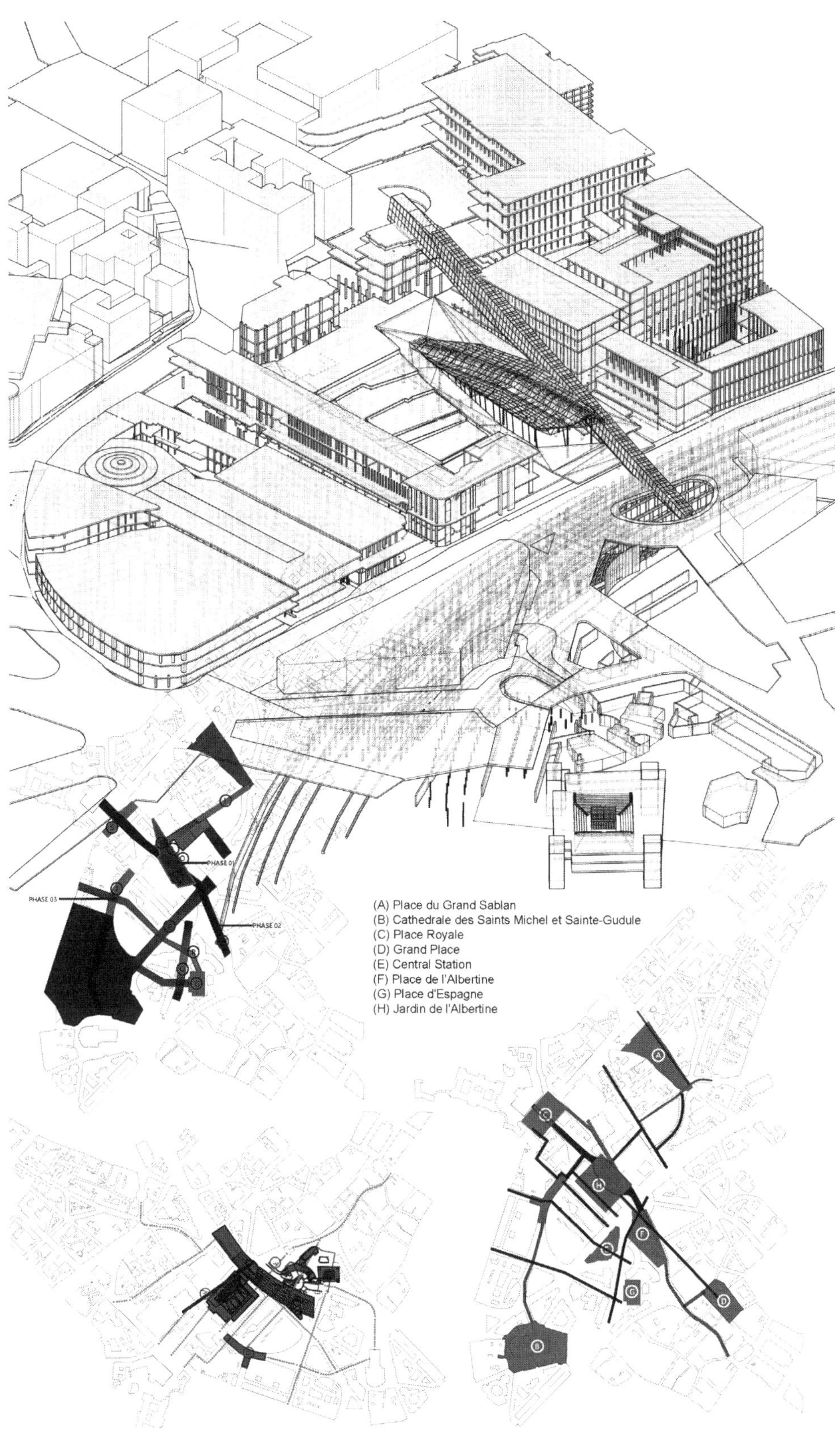
PHASE 01
PHASE 03
PHASE 02
(A) Place du Grand Sablan
(B) Cathedrale des Saints Michel et Sainte-Gudule
(C) Place Royale
(D) Grand Place
(E) Central Station
(F) Place de l'Albertine
(G) Place d'Espagne
(H) Jardin de l'Albertine

PLATE R

“Beyond Archeology” Brussels, Belgium

2000. Invited proposal for Mont des Arts redevelopment, Brussels 2000 European Culture Capital. Design + Urbanism LLC, New York design team.

Proposal for integration of the Mont des Arts in Brussels as a localized and defensive strategy to recapture the centrality of the site within the life of the city. The contextual hinterland is roughly the area of the old quarter of La Putterie, from the Place du Grand Sablon (A) at the south; to the Cathédrale des Saints Michel et Gudule (B) at the north; the Place Royale (C) at the east; and the Grand Place (D) at the west. Within this constellation is the Central Station (E), the Place de l’Albertine (F), and the Place d’Espagne (G). The Jardin de l’Albertine (H) is reinforced as the epicenter of the area. Important to this recentering is the recognition of the several sublimated historical layers within the site, excavated as a new linear sectional transect and proposed as a Museum of the City of Brussels. The archeological excavation of the Palais de Charles Quint in the Place Royale is re-roofed in glass, exposing the urban remains to the city above. This “City of Glass” encourages diverse readings of the subterranean city. During the day, sunlight penetrates the lower urban world. At night, the opposite holds, with the subterranean world illuminating the public spaces.

2000. “De-Masking Mont des Arts,” Invited Project for Brussels 2000 European Culture Capital. Design + Urbanism, LLC, New York; Richard Plunz and Viren Brahmbhatt, Partners-in-Charge; Tim Macfarlane, Structural Consultant, Dewhurst Macfarlane and Partners, New York; Design Team: Mark Ackerson (MSAUD 2000), Maja Vidakovic (MSAUD 2000), Melanie Taylor (M.Arch 2000), Anna Pew, Earl Jackson (MSAUD 2000), Bill Kenworthy (MSAUD 2000), Bijou Chirathalattu, with Tanya Villebrandt, Akihiro Aoki, Katherine Takahara, Liana Cassel, Gary Stoltz (M.Arch 2001).

PUBLICATION: Richard Plunz and Viren Brahmbhatt, “De-Masking the Mont des Arts. Panorama Populaire,” *Vacant City: Brussels Mont des Arts Reconsidered*, ed. Bruno De Meulder, Rotterdam: NAI Publishers (2000), pp. 306-313. Also see Richard Plunz Papers, Department of Drawings & Archives, Avery Architectural and Fine Arts Library.

World War I were unprecedented in early 20th-century Western Europe. Today, however, these numbers pale in comparison to the escalating wartime and climate migrations well underway.

In the Spring of 1979, Professor Marcel Smets and I were walking through the Oude Markt in Leuven. I knew almost nothing of the Belgian reconstruction, and I suggested that it should be properly studied as an important moment in the annals of 20th-century urbanism. Several years later, Smets published his pioneering study, *Resurgam*,[6] as a companion to the 1985 exhibition in Brussels. *Resurgam* further piqued my interest. It seemed that the unprecedented scale of rebuilding could be understood as consciously "Modernist urbanism." Any other day, I might have dismissed the Oude Markt as a picturesque but superficial scenography. But on that day in 1979, I was instead tempted to understand the rebuilt Leuven as a unique modern urban artifact made in parallel to other, radically new urban strategies that were unfolding in the early 20th century. I speculated that what I saw could be understood as an intentionally "modern" project; not just a historical reproduction and not just an inherited 19th-century practice. I found it odd that the rebuilding did not occupy an important place in the context of the evolution of the cannons of Modernism and regionalism. The scale of the operation alone would make it a "modern" initiative.

Marcel Smets' contribution was precisely to raise questions related to our accepted cannons of 19th and early 20th-century Modernist urbanism and to ask why this moment of learning and practice in Flanders and Leuven has been so ignored; and conversely, to ask why the emerging and radically new "Modernist" tendencies in urbanism were absent in the rebuilding. As a student, I had studied the radical approaches to urbanism elsewhere, concurrent with the Belgian reconstruction. There were the *Villes-Tours* of Auguste Perret and the Radiant City of Le Corbusier. There was the immense Russian constructivist-era urbanization. There was the beginning of the American de-urbanist movement that transformed the United States over the next half century or more. And there was the American resistance to de-urbanism; the affirmation of 19th-century "urbanism as a way of life," to use Louis Wirth's phrase. But excluded was the largest single urban initiative in Europe in the 1920s.

One can suggest that the rebuilding of Leuven was testament to complex motivations far beyond a simple reincarnation of the 19th-century ideals of

6) *Resurgam: la reconstruction en Belgique après 1914,* ed. Marcel Smets (March 27-June 30, 1985), Crédit communal et Centre d'histoire urbaine, Leuven (1985), passage 44.

Camillo Sitte, Josef Stübben, Charles Buls, or the nationalistic tendencies of the German protagonists.[7] The Belgian reconstruction did engage a certain *realpolitik*, including the German attempt at post-war occupation and interference with post-war planning.[8] Yet already in 1914, there were Belgian urban alternatives that anticipated the Modernist German *Zeilenbau* planning that came into common practice only after the end of the 1920s. For example, in 1914, the completion of Émile Hellemans' housing in the Marollen in Brussels considerably predated the *Zeilenbau* formulas. It was Bruno De Meulder's research as a graduate student at Leuven in 1983 that first made me aware of the precedent of Cité Hellemans in identifying alternative Modernist cannons.[9] Although such alternatives were surely well-known, Leuven represented a conscious resistance to this emerging "Modernist" urbanism that has since exhibited so many signs of failure throughout the world. In some sense, the rebuilding leap-frogged what was to evolve later on in the 20th century. An important question is: why this gap? And what can be some of the causes for eschewing the new Modernist tendencies? One can understand that Hellemans' Marollen would have been considered too radical for the reconstruction effort in Leuven; and too that the realization of the emerging orthodox ideals for an urban Modern Movement were not yet fully operable. Instead, for Leuven, one can suggest that there was a desire for historical continuity in the aftermath of the war with an unprecedented scale of destruction. And this continuity can be related to revaluing the propinquity of the medieval Leuven, in opposition to the potentially alienating effects of the new urban tendencies.

Given the immense devastation in Leuven, one can hardly conceive of a rebuilding strategy that would not reaffirm historic propinquity as an antidote. Leuven could only be retrieved by deploying a spatial fabric constrained

7) A useful summary of this dynamic is provided in Wolfgang Cortjaens, "'The German Way of Making Better Cities:' German Reconstruction Plans for Belgium during the First World War," *Living with History, 1914-1964: Rebuilding Europe after the First and Second World Wars and the Role of Heritage Preservation,* ed. Nicholas Bullock and Luc Verpoest, Leuven: Leuven University Press (2011), pp. 44-59.

8) Johan Van den Mooter, "German Reconstruction in Belgium during World War I: A Regional Experiment," in *Regionalism and Modernity: Architecture in Western Europe, 1914-1940*, ed. Leen Meganck, Linda Van Santvoort and Jan De Maeyer, Leuven: Leuven University Press (2013), pp. 49-73. A summary of Leuven refugee dispersal is given in Mark Derez, "The Flames of Louvain: The War Experience of an Academic Community," pp. 617-629.

9) Bruno De Meulder, *Galerijwoningen te Brussel. Proeve van een historisch-typologische analyse van de sociale meergezinswoningbouw in de Brusselse agglomeratie 1870-1914*, Masters diss., Faculty of Architecture Katholieke Universiteit Leuven (1983).

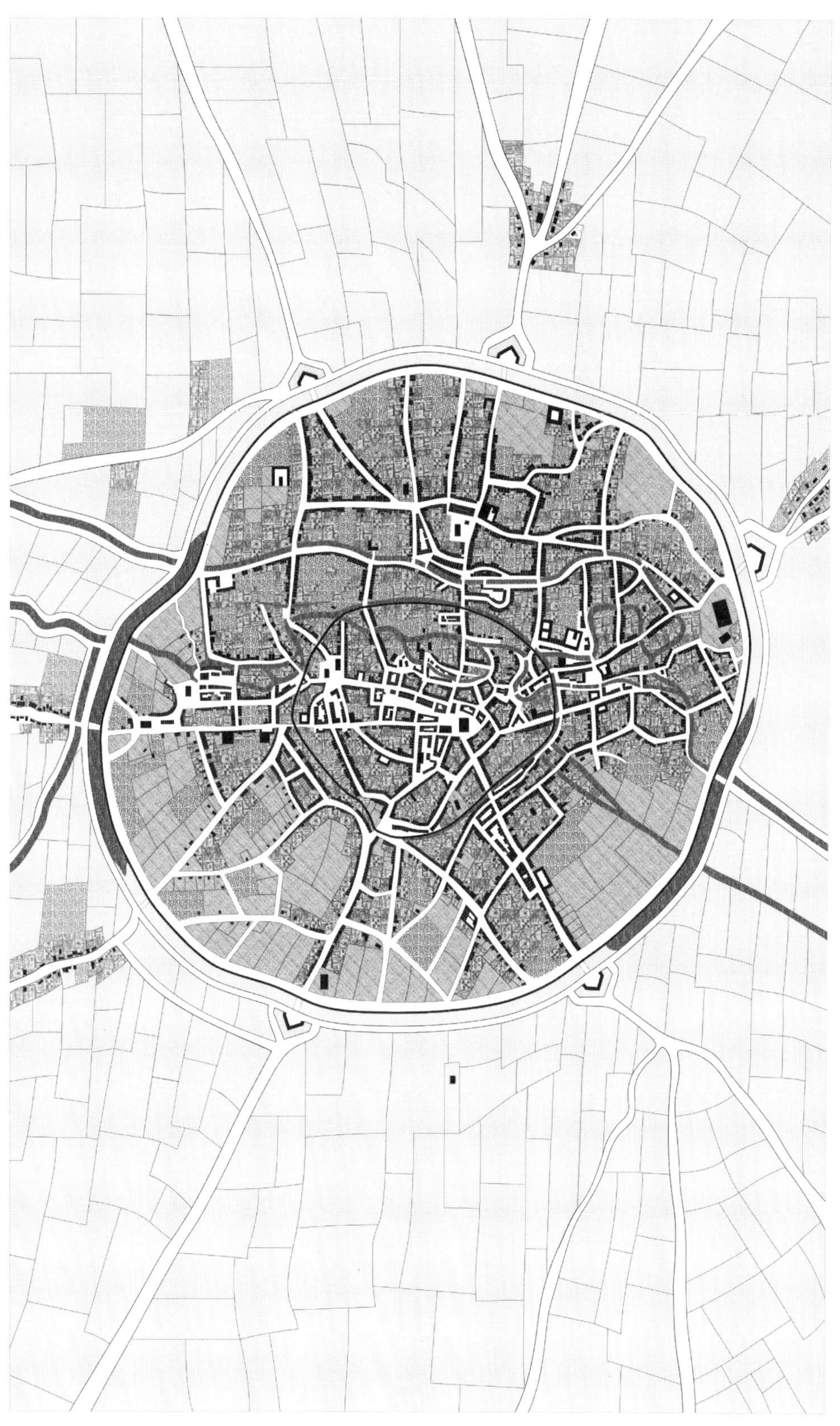

PLATE S
"Medieval Encystment" Leuven, Belgium

2020. Research into metempsychosis of medieval urbanism, Leuven, Belgium.

Research into rebuilding Leuven after WWI, within the context of the Belgian reconstruction, the largest urban project of the 20th century to that time. The rebuilding of Leuven can be understood as the antithesis to the emerging 20th-century urban Modernist cannons. Examination of the van Loon plan of 1649 reveals dense social propinquity in proximate rings of non-Cartesian "unself-conscious" geometries that grew gradually in response to local contingencies. Medieval Leuven effectively represents Eero Saarinen's analogue of the city as human muscle, in contrast to modern rapid extension deploying large-scale geometric systems inherent to "master planning." For the Leuven reconstruction, the metempsychosis of the previous medieval geometric order became the device for rebuilding. It can be understood in the context of the complex spatial hierarchies of collective human needs of centuries prior. This analysis interrogates the premise of deploying "urban encystment" as an operational tool for spatial ordering in present-day cities.

2020. "Leuven Van Loon Transformation." Faculty: Richard Plunz, with Andres Julian Alvarez Davila (M.Arch, MSHP 2022).

PUBLICATION: Richard Plunz, "Reflections on Leuven as Martyred City and the Realignment of Propinquity," *Revival After the Great War: Rebuild, Remember, Repair, Reform*, eds. Luc Verpoest et al., Leuven: Leuven University Press (2020), pp. 55-63.

by the demands of survival of social class and culture. Seen from today's perspective, the rebuilt Leuven anticipated a new urbanism inclusive of a cohesive social vision that had its origins in its medieval core. The emerging urban Modern Movement was already obsolete by the time of its massive global implementation in the aftermath of World War II. Ironically, the urban scourges that had nurtured the "sun, space, and green" of Le Corbusier's Radiant City were already being ameliorated as modern medicine superseded hygienic design arguments against the propinquity of the historic city.[10] Given this consideration, one might postulate that the rebuilt Leuven was prescient of the next Modernist city of the 21st century, rather than the other contemporary visions of the 1920s.

A legacy of the rebuilding in Flanders is the curious story of Renaat Braem, who prominently pioneered the new urban Modern Movement with a more measured variant for Antwerp, in contrast to Le Corbusier's West Bank plan.[11] As a child, he would have witnessed the destruction of Flanders firsthand; and he would have witnessed the reconstruction of the Flemish towns personally, as well. Those citizens depicted in Braem's Linear City proposal for Antwerp were denizens of an entirely new postindustrial world. They were the modern people of leisure in an environment devoid of the regimes of 19th-century labor, who would have the time to frolic in the "sun, space, and green," and they rejected the propinquity of the historic Flemish towns. In time, this new urban world became more dystopian than the old in many cities around the world. Yet, in the post-World War I era, it surely was an engaging vision and effective socioeconomic instrument, as much for Flanders as for Manhattan by the 1930s. The Radiant City and the *Zeilenbau* would continue to dominate much city design practice for the next half-century, including the massive public housing that has been among my long-term preoccupations in New York City. By the 1950s in New York, however, we had arrived at a definitive impasse resulting in the "dreary deadlock of public housing" that perhaps more than any other urban design option, cast a pall over the city.[12]

10) F. B. Smith, *The Retreat of Tuberculosis, 1850-1950,* New York: Croom Helm (1988). The obsolescence of modern "green" urbanism as tuberculosis antidote has been variously discussed in urban ecosystem literature. See Robert I. McDonald, Peter J. Marcotullio and Burak Güneralp, "Urban Governance of Biodiversity and Ecosystem Services," in *Urbanization, Biodiversity and Ecosystem Services: Challenges and Opportunities*, ed. Cathy Wilkinson et al., Dordrecht: Springer (2013), pp. 539-587.

11) Francis Strauven, *René Braem: Les Aventures Dialectiques d'un Moderniste Flamand*, Brussels: Archives d'Architecture Moderne (1985), pp. 119-124.

12) See Richard Plunz with Michael Sheridan, "Deadlock Plus 50: On Public Housing in New York," *Harvard Design Magazine* no. 8 (Summer 1999), pp. 4-9. Republished in William S. Saunders, ed., *Urban Planning Today*, Minneapolis: University of Minnesota Press (2006), pp. 14-23.

So, apart from all else, my reflections are related to my particular interests that engage the realignment ideals of propinquity, of community, of space, and of place. Such were at the origins of medieval Leuven, and they are the ideals that lay at its recreation in the aftermath of World War I. While for sure reconstruction changed the old social fabric, seemingly what was retained was the urban crucible—the container, put back as a celebration of Flemish urban culture and as defiance of the attempt at its annihilation. As crucible, Leuven has been very important to my own formation, and I include the group of faculty colleagues with whom I have shared ideas over many years. We have all been subliminally connected to the ideal of propinquity, both spatial and intellectual. I believe that this condition continues to affect this place in ways large and small, mainly unspoken, in the ether as much as in the stones. Such is the strength of this place. Yet back in 1979 and in the following years, I sensed a dark side. In the Oude Markt, I remember well the demonstrations: anti-nuclear and anti-racism, but also the counterdemonstrations that were pro-Flemish Nationalist and separatist. In the stacks of the university library, I especially remember witnessing the ongoing removal of the French language books to the new, French-language Université Catholique de Louvain. For me, it was a troubling encounter that still lingers in my mind today.

Within the expanded realm of urban "martyrdom" today, the phenomenon of the "Martyred Cities" of Flanders may seem distant. For myself, perhaps the recent images that come closest to 1914 in Leuven record the burning of the National Library in Sarajevo on August 25, 1992—the exact same day as in Leuven some 78 years earlier. In Sarajevo, one and a half million volumes were lost, 155,000 irreplaceable manuscripts and books, including the national archives. Today, when I think of Leuven, my thoughts also connect to Sarajevo and the meaning of that travesty and now, with even more immediacy, to the images from Mosul, from Aleppo, from Eastern Ghouta, or from Yemen. The Syrian refugee figures currently number more than 12 million, the entire present-day population of Belgium. Today, for most of the world's refugees, there is little hope to achieve the extraordinary level of rebuilding that was managed in Flanders in the 1920s and '30s. Still, one must hope that we can learn lessons from those experiences of a century ago that can be relevant for today and tomorrow, especially now that we understand that the world has not yet moved beyond such depravities—far from it. I think of the recent ISIS desecrations in Palmyra. We must ask ourselves about the meaning of the past—of the historical events that we commemorate. We might well question if now, after the passage of a century, if the commemorations of the Flemish martyred cites move ever closer to Guy Debord's *Société du Spectacle*, with the danger that the Belgian reconstruction becomes a matter of images.[13] Perhaps the most profound remembrance is to acknowledge that urbicide is alive and well.

I have found Paul Veyne's writing on history, truth, and tribalism to be instructive in my understanding of the realignment of propinquity. Perhaps the rebuilt "new Leuven" was Veyne's "palace of imagination," in the sense of his use of the term in the context of Greek mythology as a concept, "not built-in space .... [but] the only space available..."[14] One imagines that "truth" in the Leuven context was not the truth of Le Corbusier and Mies, but closer to the truth of Veyne, which is embedded in diversity—such that "every patchwork culture, with its diversity, opens the way to inventiveness." For Veyne, truth is tribal. The tribal engages propinquity. Perhaps it is Veyne's "tribal" that best accounts for the realignment of Leuven's propinquity, and from this we can gain understanding. Veyne's admonition in regard to Palmyra is nevertheless necessary today: "Yes, without a doubt, knowing, wanting to know, only one culture—one's own—is to be condemned to a life of suffocating sameness."[15] We can see the double edge, the dangers of the tribal then and now, but with diversity as a key to combating the dangers, and with propinquity as key to encouraging diversity.

13) Guy Debord, *The Society of the Spectacle*, trans. Donald Nicholson-Smith, New York: Zone Books (1995). For the political and commercial aspects of the World War I memorials, see Karen Shelby, *Belgium Museums of the Great War: Politics, Memory, and Commerce,* New York: Routledge (2018).

14) Paul Veyne, "The Final Foucault and His Ethics," in *Foucault and his Interlocutors,* ed. Arnold I. Davidson, Chicago: University of Chicago Press (1997), pp. 146-182.

15) Paul Veyne, *Palmyra: An Irreplaceable Treasure*, Chicago: The University of Chicago Press (2017), p. 85.

INDEX

A. T. Stewart mansion, 63
Abrams, Charles, 14, 171
acceleration, 12-20
Ackerson, Mark, 194
Adam's House in Paradise: Lower East Side, New York City (Park and Weiss), 63, 67
The Affluent Society (Galbraith), 12, 62
Africa, 19
Agent Orange, 16
agent-based mapping, 190
Aleksakova, Olga, 99
Aleppo (Syria), 200
Alger 1990. International Workshop on Housing Strategies and Urban Coherence, (Verschure and Loeckx), 102
Algiers (Algeria), 97-103
Algren, Nelson, 11, 13
Alvares Davila, Andres Julian, 5, 200
Ambrose, John, 72
American Century, 174
American Dream, 127
American Institute of Architects (AIA), 55-56, 60-61, 68, 128
American Renaissance, 76
American Society of Planners and Architects (ASPA), 58, 60
"American way of life," 12, 16, 30, 162, 174
Anthropocene, 11-13
Antwerp (Belgium), 139-141, 199
Aoki, Akihiro, 194
Apthorp Apartment Building (Manhattan), 63
Architects' Committee of the National Council of Soviet-American Friendship, 58, 61
Architects' Emergency Employment Committee, 55
Architectural Forum, 126-129,144-145
Architectural Guild of America (AGA), 56
Architectural Record, 144
Architecture Without Architects (Rudofsky), 171
architecture, 54-59
and research, 68-79, 112, 136,
and urbanism, 13-14, 17, 19, 21, 103, 118-122, 136, 139-145
pedagogy, 27, 32, 79, 110-117, 118, 136, 163-170
profession, 32-33, 57, 61, 123, 171
Armour Institute (Illinois Institute of Technology, Chicago), 57
Ashby, Ross, 135, 171
Auchincloss, Blake, 72
automobiles, 13, 30, 51, 130, 133-134, 140, 174
Avinguda Diagonal (Barcelona), 89-96

Bagnoli (Naples), 141
Baker, Charles, 190
Baldwin, James, 134
Bangkok (Thailand), 175
Baratloo, Moji, 157
Barcelona (Spain), 18, 89-95
Barr, Alfred H., Jr., 58
Baruch Houses (Manhattan), 37, 44
Bassett, James, 30
Battery Park City (Manhattan), 88, 104-109
Battisti, Eugenio, 26
Baudelaire, Charles, 188
Bauer, Catherine, 144-146
Beach 41st Street Houses (Queens), 146
Beck, Ulrich, 176
Bedford-Stuyvesant (Brooklyn), 46
Beer, David, 26
Beer, Stafford, 171
behavior, human, 32-35, 69-70, 74-75, 77, 135-136
Beirut (Lebanon), 20
Bekaert, Geert, 110-111, 114, 116
Belgium, 140, 192, 196, 200
Belknap, Ellen, 72
Bell, Fredric, 44
Benavides, Gonzalo, 120
Berlin (Germany), 50
Berman, Marshall, 17
Bernardi, Vera, 120
Between Edge and Fabric: Battery Park City (Strickland), 104
The birth of the Anthropocene (Davis), 11
Blakema, Rachel, 120
Bloomberg Administration (New York City), 162
Bolzoni, Giuseppe, 26
Bond, J. Max, Jr., 32
Bosnian War, 17
Bosporus houses (Istanbul), 105
Boudon, Philippe, 33
Boulding, Kenneth, 13
Braem, Renaat, 199
Brahmbhatt, Viren, 194
Breuer, Marcel, 57-58
Brock, Shelly, 120
Brooklyn College, 57

Brooklyn Heights (Brooklyn), 84
Brownsville (Brooklyn), 40, 80, 137
Brunzema, Meta, 92
Brussels (Belgium), 139-140, 194-196
Bryant Park (Manhattan), 187
built environment, 32-33, 68, 131, 170, 177, 187
informal vs. formal, 96, 159, 170, 180, 182-183
scale, 177
"unbuilding," 134
See also density
Buls, Charles, 196
Bunshaft, Gordon, 58
Bureau of Standards within the United States Department of Commerce, 75
Bush, George W., 174
Business Week, 123-124, 128

Cambodia, 21
Campbell, Tiko, 190
Canal Grande (Venice), 105
capitalism, 59, 62, 123
accumulation strategy, 16, 95, 175-176
globalization and, 159
See also consumer society
Caputo, Paolo, 26
Caracas (Venezuela), 139-141
Carl Schurz Park (Manhattan), 107
Carnahan, Steven, 30
Carrasco, Maria Isabel, 5, 66, 72, 102, 121, 187, 191
Cassel, Liana, 194
Central Brooklyn, 48-49, 88, 109, 116-117, 138
Central Harlem (Manhattan), 72
Central Park (Manhattan), 98, 105-106, 188
Central Park South, 66
Central Park West, 108
Centro Direzionale (Tange, Naples), 141
Cerdà, Illdefons, 89-90, 92
Charlotte Gardens (South Bronx), 163
Charlotte Street (South Bronx), 50
Chermayeff, Serge, 13, 14, 54, 57-58, 61-62, 113, 135, 176
Child Development Group of Mississippi, 24
China, 19, 169, 172
Chirathalattu, Bijou, 194
Cho, Minsuk, 120
Chrystie-Forsyth Street (Lower East Side), 64
Cité du 5 Juillet (Bab Ezzouar, Algiers), 97-103
Cimini, Alessandro, 5
cities, 11-18
and 18th century, 75
and 19th century, 32, 46, 63, 76, 84, 89, 104, 108, 123, 139-140, 150, 182, 195, 199
and 20th century, 11, 16, 19, 21, 35, 59, 108, 132, 139-140, 162, 170, 173, 191, 195-199
and 21st Century, 12, 15, 140, 157, 174, 183, 199
See also specific city
Citizens for a Local Democracy, 23
"City and Water" Organization (Antwerp), 141
The City is the Frontier (Abrams), 14, 171
La Ciudad y sus Lagos (Teodoro Gonzalez de Léon and Alberto Kalach, 1998), 154, 157
Clarke, Ronald V., 148
Clason Point Gardens (Bronx), 150
classicism, 76
climate change, 15-16, 172-177,184
climate science, 173, 178
Club of Rome, 14-15, 171, 174-175
Co-Op City (Bronx), 133
cognitive mapping, 186, 188
Cohn, Roy, 88
Cold War, 60, 129
Collegi d'Arquitectes de Catalunya, 89, 92
Columbia University, 19, 40, 133-134, 137
Earth Institute Urban Design Lab, 5, 14, 19, 172, 179, 186
School of Public Health, 148
School of Engineering, 168
Columbia Uinversity Graduate School of Architecture, Planning & Preservation (GSAPP), 5, 14-19, 32, 36-37, 40-48, 66, 72, 76, 86, 89, 92, 99, 110, 114, 117-120, 132, 148, 156, 163-166, 181
Advanced Architectural Design program (AAD), 166
Architecture and Urban Design program (MSAUD), 5, 166-168
Buell Center for the Study of American Architecture, 132
Division of Architecture, 168
Urban Design Research Group, 150, 172
Columbus Park (Manhattan), 64
Committee of the Arts, Sciences, and Professions, 58
Community and Privacy (Chermayeff and Alexander), 14, 113, 135
Community Design Centers, 27-28, 74-75
A Communications Theory of Urban Growth (Meier), 136
Comprehensive Community Mental Health Center Act (1963), 70

Conard, Michael, 148, 157
Congrès International d'Architecture Moderne (CIAM), 10, 54-62
CIAM, American, 55, 58
CIAM '59 in Otterlo (Newman), 113
CIAM 10, 136
CIAM 6 meeting of 1947 (Bridgewater), 55
CIAM Modernism, 54, 59
CIAM urbanism, 62
Congress of Industrial Organizations (CIO), 56
Constantine Plan (Algiers), 97
consumer society, 12-14, 22, 129-130, 176
"culture of consumption," 133-134, 159, 174
"city of consumption", 140
incompatibility with the city, 124
post-industrial production, 22, 125, 140
as space-consumptive, 139
suburbanization and, 128
and urbanism, 123-131, 140
Copenhagen Climate Change Conference (2009), 173
The Costs of Economic Growth (Mishan), 13, 134, 174
Coughlin, Father Charles Edward, 61
COVID-19 pandemic, 15, 187
Cowder, John, 190
critical thinking, 12, 15-18, 62, 69, 78, 110-117, 121, 136, 139, 165, 169, 174
Cronrath, David, 30
Cross Bronx Expressway (Bronx), 81, 133-134
Crossland, Earl, 30
Crotona Park (South Bronx), 46
Cupples, Andrew, 26
cyber age, 142
science, 135
theory, 135
technology, 16
philosophy, 16
Cybernetics (Weiner), 171
Cybernetics and Management (Beer), 171

Daley, Mayor Richard J., 28
Daley, Robert, 30
Dandenault, Audrey, 5, 26, 149
Davidoff, Paul, 24, 27, 136
Davis, Jeremy, 11
Day, Stephen, 86
de Carlo, Giancarlo, 14
de Jesus Ubri, Nelson, 5, 26, 190
de Llarena, Carlos Gómez, 141
de Meulder, Bruno, 196, 198
De Vita, Maurizio, 72
de Zurko, Edward, 135
Death and Life of Great American Cities (Jacobs), 39, 113, 135
DeBord, Guy, 133-134, 140, 201
defensible space, 148, 150
Defensible Space: Crime Prevention through Urban Design (Newman), 40, 148, 150
Defensible Space Evaluated: Research Topics in Public Housing (Plunz and Sheridan), 149
Delirious New York (Koolhaas), 138
density, 11, 20, 38-40, 42, 102, 116, 173, 181-182
de-densification, 145
and housing, 39-40, 49-53, 146, 163
public realm, 51, 96, 108, 134, 138, 144, 187
See also propinquity
Department of Housing and Urban Development (HUD), 23-24, 28, 31, 143-149
HOPE VI, 146, 149
Department of the Interior National Resources Committee, 130-131
Design + Urbanism LLC, 194
Design and Environment, 75
Design for a Brain (Ashby), 135, 171
Design Methods Group, 136
Design with Nature (McHarg), 172
design, 15, 31, 33-36, 55, 99, 115, 133, 140-141, 158-160, 176-178, 181, 199
academic studios, 17, 46, 79, 117, 163, 165, 166-170
criticism, 54, 69, 78, 116-117, 138, 167
culture, 140, 175, 177, 178
digital, 14, 19, 113, 136-137, 184-188, 190
pedagogy, 19, 57, 64
professions, 23-24, 27-28
research, 68-79
standards, 87
thinking, 20, 154, 171-172, 177
urbanism, 104, 141
See also behavior, human
See also Community Design Centers
Designers of Shelter in America (DSA), 57
Detriot (Michigan), 20, 122, 132, 139-140
Detroit Riots, 14, 135
Dia Art Foundation, 116
Disney, 140
Dresden (German), 50
Dumonovsky, Tamara, 148
Duong, Phu, 157

The Earth After Us: What Legacy Will Humans Leave in the Rocks? (Zalasiewicz), 11
Earth Day, 16
East 138th Street (Bronx), 117, 121
East New York (Brooklyn), 80
East River Drive (Manhattan), 106-107
East River Park (Manhattan), 106
East Tremont (Bronx), 133
East Village (Manhattan), 67, 81-82, 84
Eastern Ghouta (Syria), 200
Eberhard, John, 75
Echeverría, Iñaki, 154, 156
ECO-TEC New York International Forum: The Ecology of the Artificial, 116, 118
Ecole Polytechnique, 32
Ecole des Beaux Arts, 32
pedagogy, 78, 111, 135
ecology, 5, 15, 17, 66, 121, 156-158, 165, 172-176
Economic Opportunity Act of 1964, 70
Eigen, Edward, 113
El Bab Ezzouar (Algiers), 97-103
1199 Plaza (East Harlem), 107
The End of Nature (McKibben), 175
Engelke, Peter, 11-13, 16
Ensanche plan (Barcelona), 89-90, 92, 94-95
Environment and Behavior, 75
environment, 12-16, 31, 34, 70, 74-75, 103-106, 114-118, 135, 149-154, 157, 169, 174-177, 184-188
academic, 114, 167
cultural, 26, 104, 106, 160, 162, 165, 199
physical, 32-3, 68, 131, 135, 143, 170
social, 152
urban, 23, 157, 175
justice, 173
See also built environment
Environmental Design Research Association (EDRA), 74-75, 136
Esquire, 134
Estrada, Luis, 92
ethnicity and race, 14, 53
Euralille (Koolhaas), 141
Everline, Lewis, 30
The Evolution of Knowledge. Rethinking Science for the Anthropocene (Renn), 12
Explorations into Urban Structure (Webber), 136
The Explosion (Lefebvre), 14

Fagen, Jeffrey, 148
Federal Housing Act of 1949, 143
Federal Housing Administration (FHA), 125-129
"Better Housing" program, 125-126
Federation of Architects, Engineers, Chemists, and Technicians (FAECT), 56
Ferdinandopoli (Naples), 26
Ferioli, Rolando, 26
Fifth Avenue (Manhattan), 46, 63, 88, 105, 134
Five Points (Manhattan), 63-64
Flanders (Belgium), 192, 195, 199-200
Flemish Nationalism, 200
Flood, Paul, 26
Florida, 133
Floyd, John, 30
Flynn, John, 86
Folen, Peter, 30
Frampton, Kenneth, 137

Gaia, 118, 121
Galbraith, John Kenneth, 12, 62
Garden of Eden (Lower East Side), 66-67
gasoline, price of, 162
General Electric Committee on Planning, 129-130
General Electric Company, 123-131
General Motors, 131
The Generic City (Koolhaas), 138
gentrification, 46, 67, 82, 146
geography, 80, 90, 92, 106, 158-159
Giedion, Siegfried, 55, 59
Gilbert, Lawrence, 30
Gill, Eric, 111, 115
Gingerich, Jeffrey, 30
GIST, Inc., 120
Giudici, Patrizia, 26
Giuliani Administration (New York City), 141, 162, 164
Giurgola, Romaldo, 32
Glasberg, Eve, 184-188
Global North, 18
Global South, 18
globalization, 11-20, 76, 111, 138,141, 162, 164, 171-177, 179-180, 182-183, 199
and poverty, 22
and cities,11, 169, 166, 169, 199
and warming, 16, 172-174, 178
"glocalization" (Beck), 176
Glogau, Lawrence, 37
Goodman, Percival, 14
Gottmann, Jean, 171

Governor Alfred E. Smith Houses (Lower East Side), 134
Grand Concourse (Bronx), 133
Grand Place (Brussels), 140
Graybrook, Michael, 26
The Great Acceleration: An Environmental History of the Anthropocene Since 1945 (McNeil and Engelke), 11-13, 16
Great Depression, 55, 59, 81, 110-111, 123, 127, 144
green infrastructure, 98, 184
green space, 52, 63, 64, 67, 106, 158, 199
Greene, William, 30
Greenwich Village (Manhattan), 82
Groenerei (Brugges), 105
Gropius, Walter, 55, 58-59
gross domestic product (GDP), 173, 180
Guayaquil (Ecuador), 170
Guggenheim Museum Bilbao, 141
Gutman, Marta, 46, 48, 62, 72

Habib, Yosef, 120
Hamlin, Talbot, 76-77
Hancock Tower (Boston), 32
Hanoi (Vietnam), 20
Harlem River Houses (Manhattan), 64, 106
Harlem Urban Development Corporation, 72
Harlem (Manhattan), 17, 48-49, 83, 116
Harn, Richard, 30
Harris, Teri, 5
Harrison, Wallace K., 58
Hartman, Nicolai, 35
Hartung, Timothy, 26
Harvard University, 57, 74
Harvey, David, 15-16
Haskett, Paige, 5
Hays and Simpson, 128
Health Services Research, United States Public Health Service, 17, 75, 190
Hellemans, Émile, 196
Hicks, Leonard, 118, 120
High Line (Manhattan), 187
Hilberseimer, Ludwig, 57
Hitchcock, Henry-Russell, Jr, 58-59
Ho, Suenn, 86
Hollmeyer, Holly, 92
Hollywood blacklisting, 60
House of Committee on the Judiciary, 130
housing, 49-53, 60, 64, 81-82, 116, 126-128, 144-153, 163
  high-rise, 17, 36-44, 50, 81, 143-146, 151, 162
  low-rise, high density, 37-44, 51, 82, 100-102, 143, 146, 152
  Soviet-era, 18, 58, 61, 99, 102
  Zeilenbau pattern, 196, 199
  See also specific location
Housing and Urban Development Act (1968), 70
Housing Form and Public Policy in the United States (Plunz), 35, 44
Housing Manual for an Alternative Suburbia (Plunz and Regan), 30
Howe, George, 58
Hoyland, Earl, 30
Hurricane Katrina, 175

The Image of the City (Lynch), 188
income, 41, 46,49-50, 141, 145-146, 149, 161-162
  lower, 40-41, 57, 74, 83, 87-88, 106-107
  middle, 81-84, 87-88, 106-107, 132-133, 161
  upper, 63, 82, 84
industry, 26, 51, 60-61, 89, 105, 123, 133, 139, 140, 159-160, 162, 175, 181, 183
  building industry, 125, 177
  culture industry, 111-112, 117, 178
  fashion industry, 33, 117, 177-178
  post-industry, 81, 84, 106, 125, 127, 130-131, 132, 139-142, 157, 173, 179, 199
information technology, 68, 160, 165, 171, 184-188
infrastructure, 12, 19
  energy, 12, 68, 172-173, 181
  food, 183
  highway, 105, 107, 140-141
  rail, 105, 106, 139-140, 164, 182,
  sanitation, 181-182
  transit, 182-183, 184, 186
  water, 154-160, 172, 175, 183, 184
  See also automobiles
Institute for Applied Technology, 75
Institute for Architecture and Urban Studies, 40, 77, 137
Inter-Views: Trends of the Top Architecture and Urbanism Programs in Europe and North America (Wang and Ding), 167
Investigations into Group Form (Maki), 113
ISIS Islamic State, 200
Istanbul (Turkiye), 105
Italy, 5, 25-26, 78
Ito, Toyo, 141

Jackson Heights (Queens), 52-53, 163
Jackson, Earl, 194

Jacobs, Jane, 39, 82, 113
Jakmauh, Edward, 190
Johansen, John M., 58
John F Kennedy Airport (New York City), 164
Johnson, Philip, 58-60
Joint Center for Urban Studies at Harvard University and the Massachusetts Institute of Technology, 74
Josephson, Nancy, 86

Kahn, Louis, 58
Kalla, Ann, 72
Katholieke Universiteit Leuven (Belgium), 5, 54, 97, 102, 110, 191-192
  Post Graduate Center for Human Settlements, 97, 102
Kaufmann Jr., Edgar, 58
Kelleher, John, 30
Kells, James, 26
Kent State University, 21-22
Kenworthy, Bill, 194
Kharkiv (Ukraine), 20
Kilbridge, Chris, 120
Kim, Jun Sung, 92
Kinman, Ian, 120
Koch Jr., Carl, 58
Koch, Mayor Edward, 83-84
Koolhaas, Rem, 117, 138, 141
Kornier, Martine, 72
Kriebel, Michelle, 123
Kuhn, Ellen, 72

Lake Chalco (Mexico City), 158
Lake Xochimilco (Mexico City), 156
Lakes Project (Mexico City), 154-160
Lamar, Ignacio, 5
Lamine, Tahari Mohamed, 97, 102
Landsberg, Helmut E., 15
landscape, 167, 177
  architecture, 167, 171-172
  natural, 98, 144, 151, 160
  political, 13, 17
  social, 133
  urban, 89, 92, 156, 158, 171, 172, 17
Lang, Peter, 118, 120
Langer, Susanne, 171
Las Vegas (Nevada), 142
Lawrence Halprin and Associates, 39
Le Corbusier, 22, 33, 38, 137, 195, 199, 201
Lee, Gregory, 30
Lefebvre, Henri, 14, 18-19, 33
Leuven (Belgium), 191-201
Liebendorfer, Mark, 26, 30
Lincoln Center (Manhattan), 32, 83, 133-134
Lincoln Towers (Manhattan), 83
Lincoln West Apartments (Manhattan), 88
Lindsay Administration (New York City), 39, 81, 137
Litzinger, Wesley, 30
Instituto de Geografía, Universidad Nacional Autónoma de México (UNAM), 154, 158
Lomicka, Steven, 190
Long Island (New York), 133
Los Angeles (California), 134
Lower East Side (Manhattan), 17, 48-49, 63, 66-67, 82-83, 106, 134
Luce, Henry R., 127
Lynch, Kevin, 188

Maldonado, Tomás, 15
Malik, Rafiq A., 97, 102
Mantua (Philadelphia), 17, 36, 190
Manhattan Community Board, 15, 72
Mantua Community Planners, 190
Mantua Primer: Toward a Program for Environmental Change (Plunz), 190
Marcus Garvey Park Village (Brownsville, Brooklyn), 40, 137
Marcuse, Peter, 14
Marollen (Brussels), 196
Marseilles Folly Unite de Habitation (Le Corbusier), 38
Massachusetts Institute of Technology (MIT), 74
McBride, Leslie, 92
McCarthy era, 58, 60-61
McHarg, Ian, 172
McKibben, Bill, 15, 175
McKim, Charles Follen, 133
McLaughlin, Stephen, 30
McLuhan, Marshall, 62
McNeill, J. R., 11-13, 16
The Mechanical Bride (McLuhan), 62
Megalopolis (Gottman), 171
Mei, Jia, 166
Meier, Richard, 136-137
Menoff, Jylle, 72
Metabolism Movement (Japan), 113
metempsychosis, 198
Mexico City (Mexico), 19, 154-160

Mexico City Metropolitan Region (MCmr, Mexico City), 154-160
Mezquital Valley (Mexico), 158
Microsoft, 138, 142
Midtown (Manhattan), 46, 48, 81, 88
Mies van der Rohe, Ludwig, 22, 57
Miller, George, 26
Mishan, Ezra, 13, 134, 174
Mitchel Houses (Bronx), 36-44, 49
Model Cities Act (1966), 28, 70
Modern Housing (Bauer), 144
Modernism, 17, 21-22, 57, 60, 133, 135-137, 160, 195-196, 198-199
    Modern Movement, 33-34, 38, 110, 113, 115, 196, 199
    and urbanism, 61, 135, 160, 195-196
Moholy-Nagy, László, 57
Mont des Arts(Brussels), 194
Morales, Liza, 157
Morris, Robert, 112
Mortal City (ed. Lang), 118, 120
Moses, Robert, 39, 81, 105-107, 133-134
Mostar (Bosnia and Herzegovina), 17
Mostoller, Michael, 32
Mosul (Iraq), 20, 200
Mott Haven (Bronx), 86, 118, 120
Motzny, Amy, 186
Muir, Eden, 118, 120
Mulberry Bend, 64
Mumford, Lewis, 38-39, 143-144
Museum of Modern Art, 40, 46, 59
Department of Architecture, 59
International Style Exhibition, 59

Naming Names (Navasky), 60
narcissism, 164
National and University Library of Bosnia and Herzegovina (Sarajevo), 200
National Endowment for the Arts (NEA), 77
National Endowment for the Humanities (NEH), 46, 77
National Housing Act of 1934 (S-1246), 125
National Recovery Act of 1933, 56
Natural History (Pliny the Elder), 158
Navarro, Lucy, 5, 30, 66, 73, 92, 102, 157
Navasky, Victor, 60-61
Nazism, 60, 111-112
Neighborhood Development Program (NDP), 23-31, 67, 70, 135
    See also Urban Renewal (Title V)
Nelson, Ethan, 92
neoliberalism, 15-17, 22, 117
Neutra, Richard, 58, 129
New Bauhaus (Chicago), 57
New Brutalism, 107
New Deal, 19, 55, 61, 64, 123-124, 132
New Federalism, 28
New Monumentalism, 61
New Orleans (Louisiana), 173, 175
New Urbanism, 139, 146
"New York New York" Casino (Las Vegas), 142
New York City
    abandonment in, 49-50, 84, 86, 116, 132,
    and culture, 67, 77, 104, 133-134, 145
    effects of climate change on, 12, 175, 182
    gentrification in, 82-83, 87, 137-138
    income stratification in, 116, 122, 145, 146, 162
    waterfront, 18, 104-109
New York City Department of City Planning, 84
New York City Department of Housing Preservation and Development, 80, 86, 161
New York City Housing and Development Administration (HDA), 39-40
New York City Housing Authority (NYCHA), 36-44, 66, 143-153, 161
New York City Mayor's Committee on Slum Clearance, 39, 134
New York Landmarks Conservancy, 72
New York Ring, 17, 46-53
New York State Council on the Arts, 72
New York State Urban Development Corporation (UDC), 40, 83, 137
New York Times, 117
Newark Riots, 14
Newark (New Jersey), 14
Newman, Oscar, 40, 113, 148, 150
Neyman, Allen, 190
Niego, Suzanne, 92
Niemeyer, Oscar, 97-98
Nixon Administration, 28, 31, 67, 75, 136
Nolli, Giambattista, 188
North City Area-Wide Council (Philadelphia), 28
Notes on the Synthesis of Form (Alexander), 135
Nycum, William, 30

Ocasio, Daniel, 44
Ockman, Joan, 113
Oliver, Marisa, 92
Olmsted, Frederick Law, 105

Omnibus Housing Act of 1968 (S-3497), 23, 67, 190
Operational Philosophy (Rapoport), 171
Oppositions, 77
Origins of Functionalist Theory (de Zurko), 135
Oude Markt (Leuven), 191, 195, 200

Palm Sunday. An Autobiographical Collage (Vonnegut), 13
Palmyra (Syvia), 200-201
Palmyra: An Irreplaceable Treasure (Veyne), 201
Park Avenue, 108
Park Slope (Brooklyn), 46, 84
Park, Kyong, 66
pedagogy, 12, 74, 114, 140, 166-167
  See also architecture, pedagogy
  See also design, pedagogy
  See also Ecole des Beaux-Arts, pedagogy
Pei, I.M., 58
Pennsylvania State University
  Department of Architecture, 5, 17, 21-22, 26, 30, 36, 190
  Division of Man-Environment Relations, 75
Perret, Auguste, 195
Perspecta, 27, 77
Pew, Anna, 194
phenomenology, 163
Philosophy in a New Key (Langer), 172
Pierce, Mark, 30
Piketty, Thomas, 13
Pistilli, Robert, 190
Pitkin Avenue, Bronx, 121
Placa de les Glòries (Barcelona), 89
planning, 16, 20-23, 31, 52, 61, 83, 97-99, 123, 129-130, 137-140, 154, 158-160, 180, 184- 190, 196
  advocacy planning, 24, 27, 28, 31, 136
  master planning, 92, 154, 160, 198
  participatory planning, 23, 24, 28, 51, 67, 70, 149, 150, 160
  strategic planning, 22, 160, 163-165
  urban planning, 22, 151, 167, 192
Poblenou (Barcelona), 89-96
Politecnico di Milano, 26
The Politics of the Unpolitical (Read), 111-112
Poncavage, Daniel, 30
Post-History (Flusser), 179
post-Marxism, 22
Postmodernism, 17-18, 34, 111
Prince, David, 129
private vs. public sector, 13, 22, 51-52, 55, 64, 81, 144
  finance, 18, 82-83, 124, 137, 163, 164
  housing, 17, 19, 36-37, 49, 51, 60, 64, 80, 82, 84, 87, 143-153, 161, 199
  space, 41,44, 52, 72, 94-95, 99-102, 105, 107-108, 137, 156, 160, 168, 184-187, 194
  transportation, 53
  works, 61
Project Area Committees (PAC Groups), 23-24, 190
propinquity, 11, 20, 134-135, 138, 142, 191-201
Pruitt-Igoe, St. Louis, 36
Purple, Adam, 17, 64-67

Quaderns d'Arquitectura i Urbanisme, 89, 92
Quito (Ecuador), 175

Radiant City (Le Corbusier), 195, 199
Raman, Ashna, 5, 66
Rambla (Barcelona), 94
Rand, Ayn, 79
Rapoport, Anatol, 171
Read, Herbert, 111
Reading (Pennsylvania), 30
real estate markets, 67, 83, 87, 88, 105
"Red Ring" (Vienna), 48, 52-53
Reehl, William, 30
Re-envisioning Health in Kumasi: Spatial Strategies (Urban Design Lab), 179
Regan, Lawrence, 30
regionalism, 195-196
Reichskulturkammer, 112
Reinhardt, Ad, 33
Renn, Jürgen, 12
Rensselaer Polytechnic Institute, 5, 69
restoration ecology, 175
Resurgam: la reconstruction en Belgique après 1914 (Smets), 195
Revival After the Great War: Rebuild, Remember, Repair, Reform (Verpoest et al.), 191, 198
Reweaving the Urban Fabric: Approaches to Infill Housing (Norden), 72
Rhorty, Richard, 19
Rich, Nathaniel, 14
Richards, Kristen, 161-165
Rijksmuseum Kröller-Müller (Otterloo), 54
Riverside Park, 106
The Road Ahead (Bill Gates, 1996), 138

Rogers, Fred, Mr., 118, 121
Roma, Parigi, New York. Quale urbanistica per le metropoli? (Cecchini et. al.), 80
Rome (Italy), 172, 188
Roosevelt, Franklin, 130
Rosenbaum, Mark, 86
Ross, Andrew, 118
Roth, Emily, 92
Rothstein, Karla Maria, 120
Rudofsky, Bernard, 171
Rutgers University School of Criminal Justice, 148

Saarinen, Eero, 58
Saarinen, Eliel, 198
Sala, Chris, 5
San Francisco (California), 82
San Juan Hill (Manhattan), 133-134
San Leucio (Caserta, Italy), 26
San Leucio: Vitalità d'una Tradizion. Traditions in Transition (Plunz), 27
Sarajevo (Bosnia and Herzegovina), 17, 20, 200
Schan, Lawrence, 30
Schenectady (New York), 129-131
Schwarting, Jon Michael, 32
science, 13-15, 114, 164, 172-178
  behavioral science, 69, 70, 74, 77
  natural science, 172, 175, 177, 178
  political science, 177
  social science, 13, 115, 173
  See also climate science
  See also cyber-age, science
Section 235, National Housing Act of 1984, 86
Section 8, 149, 161
Seo, Hyeon, 120
Sert, Josep Lluís, 55, 57-58
Shaffer, Paul, 30
Shapiro, Meyer, 35
Shapiro, Stephanie, 120
Sheridan, Michael, 143, 148, 199
Siedlungen, Germany, 144
Silicon Alley, Manhattan, 138, 142
Sitte, Camillo, 196
16th Street railyards (Manhattan), 109
Skinner, Mary Jane, 120
Smalls, Gary, 190
Smets, Marcel, 192, 195
Smith, Albert, III, 44
Smith, Marcia, 86
Social Justice, 60
social media, 19, 184-188
socialism, 144
Société du Spectacle (DeBord), 201
Soho (Manhattan), 84
Sollohub, Darius, 86
Sondheim, Stephen, 134
South Bronx (Bronx), 17, 20, 42, 46-50, 80-81, 86, 109, 116-117, 118-122, 138, 149, 163
Southeast Asia, 21, 24
Soviet Union, 18, 99, 102
Sparling, A. Eugene, 72
Standard Oil, 131
Stanley, David, 30
Stavoy, James, 26
Steinschneider, Padriac, 37
Stern, Lord Nicholas, 172
Stern, Robert A.M., 32
Stolz, Gary, 194
Stonorov, Oscar, 58
Storefront for Art and Architecture, 63, 66, 116, 118, 120
Strickland, Lee, 190
Stübben, Josef, 196
Stubbins Jr., Hugh, 58
Stuyvesant Town (Manhattan), 134
suburbs, 19, 29-30, 51, 61, 83, 108-109, 123-138, 140-144, 150, 173
Sullivan, Mercer L., 148
Sutto, Maria Paola, 186
Swope, Gerard, 5, 123
Syracuse Community Action Program, 24
Syria, 200
Sysko, John, 26

Taft Houses (Manhattan), 36-44, 49
Tafuri, Manfredo, 12
Takahara, Katherine, 194
Tange, Kenzō, 141
Taylor, Melanie, 194
Team Ten (10), 22, 113, 136
  Team Ten (10) Primer, 113, 136
Technical America, 56-57
Teng, Paul, 157
Tenochtitlan (Mexico), 156-157
Teodari, Richard, 30
Time Inc., 127
Tolstoy, Leo, 59
tower-in-the-park, 17, 36-44, 49-53, 61, 64, 81-82, 133, 144, 152
Towers, Joel, 92

tribalism, 201
Tribeca (Manhattan), 84
Trump Tower (Manhattan), 87-88
Trump, Donald, 87-88
Tschumi, Bernard, 168
Tsukida, Toru, 120
Turner, John F. C., 171
Twitter, 184-188
typology, 79, 87, 109, 137, 145-146, 148, 151
 housing, 30, 36, 38, 48, 52, 81, 86-87, 94-96, 124, 126, 145, 162,-163
 urban fabric, 40, 42, 52-53, 72, 99-100, 144-145, 150

Uguccioni, Laura, 186
UNIDOS Community Organization, Mott Haven, 118, 120
The Uninhabitable Earth: Life After Warming (Wallace-Wells), 15
United Nations Center for Human Settlements, 97, 102
United States Department of Agriculture, Bureau of Home Economics, 126
United States Department of Justice, 40
Universidad Nacional Autónoma de México (UNAM), 158
Université Catholique de Louvain, 200
University of California at Berkeley, 20, 69
University of Michigan, 69
University of Science and Technology, Houari Boumediene (USTHB), 97
Upper East Side (Manhattan), 46, 82, 107
Upper West Side (Manhattan), 46, 81, 83-84, 88, 106, 108, 133-134
Urbach, Henry, 92
Urban Climate Change Crossroads forum (2008), 172
Urban Design Group (New York City), 142
urban development, 22, 24, 67, 70, 82, 84, 89, 96, 97, 131, 139, 153, 158, 164
 economic, 123, 176-177, 179-183, 184
 redevelopment, 24, 36-44, 50-53, 83-84, 87, 98-100, 104-106, 131, 146-152, 194
 formal vs. informal, 18-19, 63, 115, 159, 169-170, 180-183
 urban renewal, 17, 22, 132-138, 144
Urban Planning Today (Saunders), 143, 148
Urban Renewal (Title V), 23-24, 27, 31, 82
 See also Neighborhood Development Program
urban entropy, 20, 47-48, 62, 134
Urbanism as a Way of Life (Wirth), 90, 162, 195
urbicide, 17, 20, 201
Utopia (Thomas More, 1516), 140

Vacant City: Brussels Mont des Arts Reconsidered (De Meulder), 194
Vacant Lots (Willis and Genevro), 86
van der Woud, Auke, 54-55
Van Eyck, Aldo, 34, 115
van Loon plan (Leuven, 1649), 198
Venice (Italy), 105
Vergara, Camilo José, 116, 118, 120
Vermeulen, Paul, 97, 102
Veurne (Belgium), 191
Veyne, Paul, 201
Victory Garden, 67
Vidakovic, Maja, 194
Vietnam War, 16, 21-22, 24, 133
Ville Radieuse (Le Corbusier), 107
Villebrandt, Tanya, 194
Vonnegut, Kurt, 13

Wachsmann, Konrad, 58
Wallace-Wells, David, 11, 15
A Walk on the Wild Side (Algren), 11, 13
War and Peace (Tolstoy), 59
Warshauer, Isaac, 5, 44, 72, 193
Washington Square Park (Manhattan), 187
Waterside Plaza (Manhattan), 107
Watts Riots (1965), 14, 134
wealth, 13, 54, 61, 63
Webber, Melvin, 136, 138
Weiner, Norbert, 171
Weiss, Glen, 66
West End Avenue (Manhattan), 108
West Village Houses (Manhattan), 82
Westway (Manhattan), 109
White, Alfred Tredway, 64
Williamsburg Houses (Brooklyn), 64
Wilson, Charles Edward, 123-124, 130
Wirth, Louis, 90, 195
Works Progress Administration (WPA), 56
World Financial Center (Manhattan), 108
World War I, 19, 67, 192, 192-201
World War II, 16, 36, 50, 54-60, 67, 110-111, 123, 131

Yale University, 57, 77
Yemen, 200

Zalasiewicz, Jan, 11
Zanin, Michael, 30
Zavrou, Stella, 92
Zhuang, Ziyu, 166
Zócalo Plaza (Mexico City), 156
Zona Universitària (Barcelona), 90

RICHARD PLUNZ is a Professor Emeritus of Architecture, Planning and Preservation at Columbia University, where he has served as Chair of the Division of Architecture and Director of the post-professional Urban Design Program.

He was also an Earth Institute Professor and Founding Director of the Earth Institute's Urban Design Lab. He has been a frequent guest professor at the Katholieke Universiteit Leuven in Belgium.

He is known for a wide range of urban research, development and design projects both nationally and internationally, with a particular expertise in urban infrastructure and housing fabric.

He is the author of many articles, studies, and reports on urban development and ecology, including a revised edition of his pioneering study, *A History of Housing in New York City* (Columbia 1990) republished in 2016.

TITLE
NEW YORK_GLOBAL
Critical Writings and
Proposals 1970-2020

AUTHOR
Richard Plunz

EDITORIAL SUPPORT
Audrey Dandenault
Paige Haskett

PUBLISHED BY
Actar Publishers
New York, Barcelona
www.actar.com

GRAPHIC DESIGN
Ramon Prat Homs

DISTRIBUTION
Actar D, Inc.
New York, Barcelona

NEW YORK
440 Park Avenue South,
17th Floor
New York, NY 10016, USA
T +1 2129662207
salesnewyork@actar-d.com

BARCELONA
Roca i Batlle 2-4
08023 Barcelona, Spain
T +34 933 282 183
eurosales@actar-d.com

INDEXING
English ISBN:
978-1-638400-93-6
PCN: Library of Congress
Control Number: 2023931339

Printed in Europe, 2023